The
D-Day
Atlas

Charles Messenger
Preface by James Holland

The D-Day Atlas

Anatomy of the Normandy Campaign

With 178 illustrations, including 71 full-colour maps

Frontispiece: *US infantrymen pause under German unit signs during the advance on Cherbourg.*

Charles Messenger spent 19 years in the Royal Tank Regiment before pursuing a career as a military historian and defence analyst. He was the author of over 40 books, including *The Art of Blitzkrieg*, *The Commandos 1940–1946*, and *The Second World War in the West*.

James Holland is an author and broadcaster who specializes in the Second World War. He is the author of both fiction and non-fiction books on the subject, including *Normandy 44': D-Day and the Battle for France*. He is also the co-founder of the Chalke Valley History Festival and presents the podcast *We Have Ways of Making you Talk* with Al Murray.

First published in the United Kingdom in 2004 by Thames & Hudson Ltd, 181A High Holborn, London WC1V 7QX

First published in the United States of America in 2004 by Thames & Hudson Inc., 500 Fifth Avenue, New York, New York 10110

Paperback edition published in 2014
This hardback edition published in 2024

The D-Day Atlas © 2004, 2014 and 2024
Thames & Hudson Ltd, London
Preface © 2024 James Holland
Text © 2004 Charles Messenger
Maps © 2004 Cartographica Ltd, Derby

British Library Cataloguing-in-Publication Data
A catalogue record for this book is available from the British Library

ISBN   978-0-500-29764-3

Printed and bound in China by C & C Offset Printing Co. Ltd

Be the first to know about our new releases, exclusive content and author events by visiting
thamesandhudson.com
thamesandhudsonusa.com
thamesandhudson.com.au

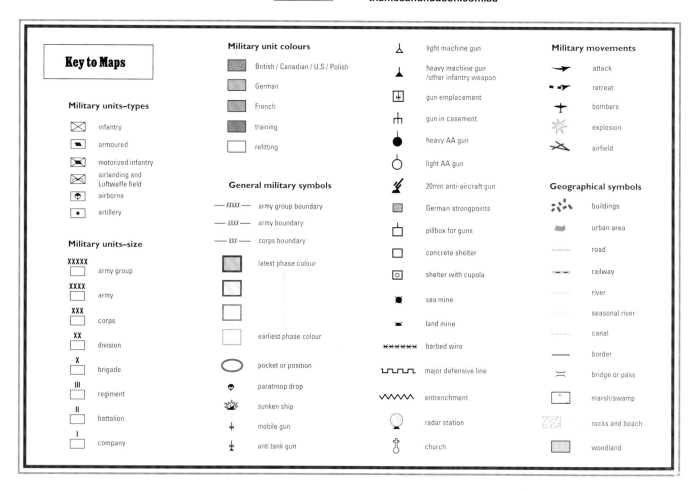

Key to Maps

Military units–types

⊠ infantry
▭ armoured
⊠ motorized infantry
⊠ airlanding and Luftwaffe field
airborne
• artillery

Military units–size

XXXXX ▢ army group
XXXX ▢ army
XXX ▢ corps
XX ▢ division
X ▢ brigade
III ▢ regiment
II ▢ battalion
I ▢ company

Military unit colours

British / Canadian / U.S / Polish
German
French
training
refitting

General military symbols

— XXXXX — army group boundary
— XXXX — army boundary
— XXX — corps boundary
latest phase colour
earliest phase colour
pocket or position
paratroop drop
sunken ship
mobile gun
anti tank gun

light machine gun
heavy machine gun /other infantry weapon
gun emplacement
gun in casement
heavy AA gun
light AA gun
20mm anti-aircraft gun
German strongpoints
pillbox for guns
concrete shelter
shelter with cupola
sea mine
land mine
barbed wire
major defensive line
entrenchment
radar station
church

Military movements

attack
retreat
bombers
explosion
airfield

Geographical symbols

buildings
urban area
road
railway
river
seasonal river
canal
border
bridge or pass
marsh/swamp
rocks and beach
woodland

Contents

Preface

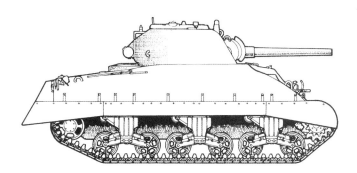

M4 Sherman, the main Allied tank in Normandy. It mounted a 75mm gun and a crew of five.

British soldiers training for D-Day.

DC-3 Dakota transports being prepared for the D-Day airborne assault.

Opposite: elements of the German defence – PzKpfw V Panther (above), infantry resting (below).

Flying over the Normandy coastline in the early hours of Tuesday, 6 June 1944, was Lieutenant-Colonel Francis 'Gabby' Gabreski, an American fighter commander in the US 56th Fighter Group. He'd taken off from southern England at 3.36 a.m., when it was still dark, but by the time he and his flight of P-47 Thunderbolts were nearing France the thin streaks of a cloudy dawn were casting a pale light across the sky. Gabreksi was a seasoned commander. He'd served on Hawaii at the time of Pearl Harbor back in December 1941, had flown with the RAF, and then joined the US 'Mighty' Eighth Air Force, which operated out of England. He was a leading American fighter ace and one of their most experienced fighter pilots, but he'd never witnessed anything like the scene that greeted his eyes that morning: a sea black with ships and landing craft, the mightiest invasion fleet yet known to man. 'It was,' noted Gabreski, 'one of the most spectacular sights that I have ever seen, a massive demonstration of power.'

So it was. Operation Overlord – launched on D-Day – was the largest amphibious invasion the world has ever known: nearly 133,000 men landed along eighty miles of coast; 22,000 were dropped or brought in by air; and nearly 7,000 vessels, including 1,213 warships and 4,127 landing craft, took part. Grabreski's Thunderbolt was one of a staggering 11,600 Allied aircraft that would fly that day. Collectively, these numbers are scarcely comprehensible today. It was a gargantuan enterprise and marked the start of the liberation of France and north-west Europe from the tyranny of Nazi Germany. The Normandy landings also involved a truly polyglot force – comprising primarily British, American and Canadian servicemen, but also those of many other nationalities: French, Dutch, Belgian, Polish, Norwegian, New Zealander, Australian, South African and others besides – and represents one of the most remarkable examples of international coalition, cooperation and collaboration ever witnessed. It rightly sits at the centre of our narrative of the Second World War, for the significance of the quest that was undertaken and for the astonishing demonstration of collective unity in pursuit of a common goal.

Maps were also a vital part of this mammoth enterprise and were produced in vast numbers ahead of the invasion:

very detailed surveys of the beaches where troops were to be landed or the drop zones into which paratroopers were to touch down. Aerial reconnaissance aircraft took millions of photographs beforehand, all of which were examined in minute detail. German defences, from minefields and wire entanglements to blockhouses, machine-gun posts and artillery positions, were all marked. Larger-scale maps offered details of terrain, the road network, rivers, canals, woods and forests.

While they were essential tools for those invading – or, indeed, defending – Normandy, anyone wishing to understand the events that surround the D-Day landings also needs maps, preferably ones of the highest quality possible. Colour helps, as it did back in 1944, as do detail and clarity. Fortunately, *The D-Day Atlas* offers these vital ingredients throughout, with each map beautifully produced and presented. Even better, those who prepared the original edition understood that, while D-Day really was just that, a single day, analysis of the invasion itself should be framed by wider events that occurred both before and after.

In fact, Overlord was part of a much more extended undertaking, not least the furious air battle that raged over north-west Europe in the run-up to 6 June 1944. An absolutely non-negotiable prerequisite for launching the invasion was to have control of the airspace over all of France and much of north-west Europe. This was because the Allied planners understood that the moment D-Day was launched the secret would be out, and a race would start in which each side would attempt to build up decisive strength in Normandy before the other. The Allies had the numbers, but bringing everything across the Channel by ship would take time. A vital part of the strategy was to slow down the German ability to reinforce. This could be done ahead of D-Day by blowing up bridges across key rivers such as the Seine and the Loire, attacking railways and marshalling yards, and destroying other parts of the German supply network.

This undertaking, however, required very accurate bombing, which in turn meant flying at low altitudes. Flying low made Allied bombers very vulnerable to enemy air attack, since height and speed were crucial advantages in air combat. Fortunately, after a heavy and concentrated air assault in the first part of 1944, by mid-April the skies were largely clear of the Luftwaffe, the German air force. A nine-week bombing campaign of German supply lines was begun, in which an incredible 197,000 tons of bombs were dropped on French targets alone. It was highly successful and paved the way for victory on land. This part of the pre-invasion plan is stunningly demonstrated in *The D-Day Atlas*.

So, too, is the plan for the naval campaign, Operation Neptune, which features such detailed information as the incredibly complex clearing of German minefields out at sea just before the landings. It's a reminder that D-Day was not just men leaping from landing craft but a tri-service operation in which air, sea and land forces were inextricably entwined.

D-Day itself was also just the start of what would become a 77-day campaign – a ferocious battle in which average daily casualties were higher than those of the Somme, Verdun and Passchendaele during the First World War. It was brutal. *The D-Day Atlas* again does not disappoint, for the Normandy campaign, as it played out, is captured with ever more stunning maps, guiding anyone wishing to learn about what came after the invasion and outlining a comprehensive progression from 6 June to the joining up of the bridgehead, the move south inland, the American capture of the Cotentin Peninsular, and the major operations and battles that followed.

An old, dog-eared copy of this excellent volume has been an ever-present fixture on my bookshelf for the past twenty years. I will cherish this handsome new edition equally, as should anyone wanting to get to grips with this defining battle of the Second World War.

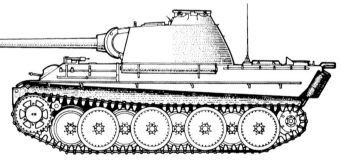

7

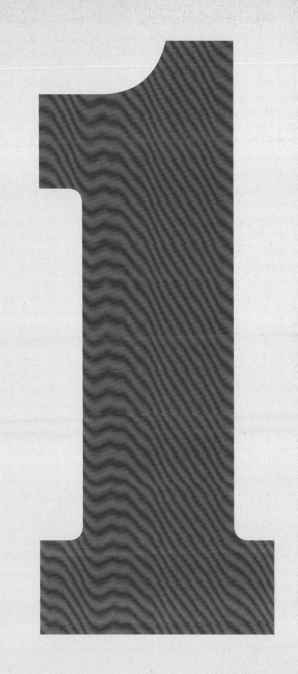

Planning and Preparation

On the morning of 4 June 1940, German troops entered the French port of Dunkirk. In the knowledge that during the previous week the Royal Navy had managed to rescue nearly 340,000 Allied troops from the trap that the Germans had set around the port, Prime Minister Winston Churchill made his famous speech of defiance: 'We shall fight on the beaches, we shall fight in the fields .... We shall never surrender.' The following day, the victorious German armies turned south to overrun the remainder of France. On 9 June, the French sought an armistice. Three days later, they signed an armistice with the Germans and then did the same with Italy, which had attacked the south of France on 20 June. The whole of Continental Western Europe was now under Hitler's thrall.

Few external commentators gave Britain much chance of holding out for long. The Army had left most of its heavy weapons in France and the RAF, whose strength was slender compared to that of the Luftwaffe, had also suffered during the Dunkirk evacuation. Only the Royal Navy remained relatively intact, but Luftwaffe attacks on shipping in the English Channel during July, the first phase of what was to become the Battle of Britain, forced the Admiralty to lay down that no warship larger than a destroyer would be allowed in these waters. Across the Channel, Hitler had, on 2 July, ordered preparations to be made for an invasion of Britain and the Army produced a plan just over two weeks later. Yet, as he stated in a triumphant speech in the Reichstag on 19 July, he

The final German plan called for a considerably narrower landing frontage than the original. Even so, it was wider than that used in the cross-Channel invasion four years later. The German invasion fleet aimed to hug the coast as long as possible before crossing the Channel at its nearest point. Once ashore, the main aim was to encircle London, rather than attempt to take the capital by storm.

British troops withdraw through the battered City of Dunkirk.

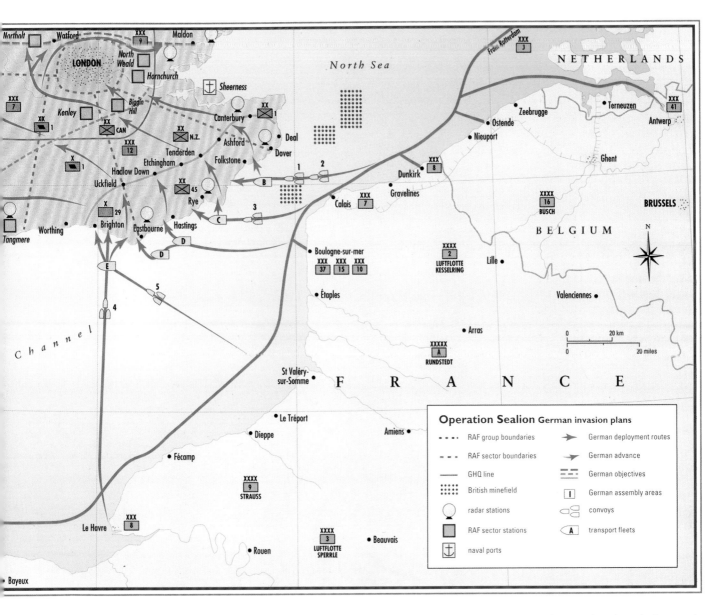

Operation Sealion German invasion plans

- - - - RAF group boundaries
- - - RAF sector boundaries
GHQ line
:::::: British minefield
radar stations
RAF sector stations
naval ports

German deployment routes
German advance
German objectives
German assembly areas
convoys
transport fleets

still hoped that Britain would make peace, a notion that was immediately rejected by Churchill.

Consequently, the German preparations for invasion continued. But there were serious differences between the Army and the Navy. The former regarded the operation as merely a river crossing, and wanted to land on as broad a front as possible so as to prevent the British being able to concentrate their reserves against the beachhead. The German Navy, conscious of the unpredictable nature of the Channel and the powerful threat presented by the Royal Navy, argued for a narrow front. Besides which, Germany possessed no amphibious capability for such a large undertaking. Instead, the authorities were forced to scour the inland waterways of Europe for barges, which then had to be converted so that they could be used as landing craft. In view of this, Hitler

accepted that the invasion could not take place before mid-September. But by then the window of opportunity would be narrow, since the waters in the Channel would be influenced by the vagaries of the autumn weather. He therefore had a mind to postpone Operation Sealion, as it was codenamed, until May 1941, but ordered preparations to continue for a September assault. To the fury of the German Navy, Hitler accepted the Army's plan for landings on a frontage of some 200 miles, although he did later compromise. He realised, however, as did both the Army and the Navy, that air supremacy over the Channel and the landing area was essential to the success of Sealion. The burden was thus shifted onto the shoulders of Hermann Goering's Luftwaffe. During August and the first half of September 1940, the German Air Force struggled in vain to sweep the RAF from the skies over

The initial German landings in Denmark and Norway took the defenders, who were ill equipped, by surprise. The use of airborne troops to seize Norwegian airfields was a critical factor in the German success. The Allied landings were poorly co-ordinated and, although they enjoyed naval superiority, they lacked the same in the air. Only at Narvik did the Allies enjoy a degree of success, but it proved too isolated for a force to be maintained there.

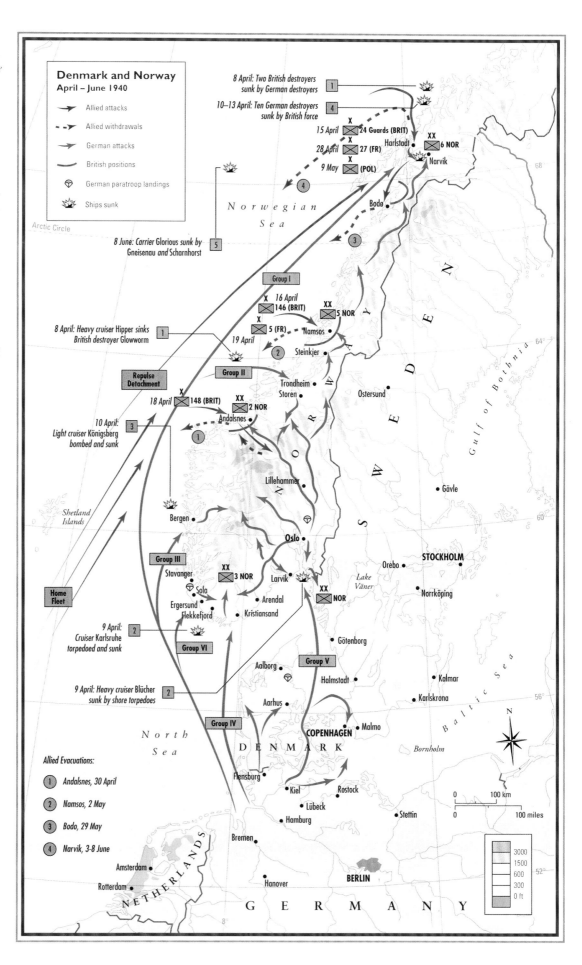

Denmark and Norway
April – June 1940

→ Allied attacks

--→ Allied withdrawals

→ German attacks

⌒ British positions

German paratroop landings

Ships sunk

8 April: Two British destroyers sunk by German destroyers

10–13 April: Ten German destroyers sunk by British force

15 April 24 Guards (BRIT)

28 April 27 (FR)

9 May (POL)

6 NOR

Harlstadt

Narvik

Bodo

Norwegian Sea

Arctic Circle

8 June: Carrier Glorious sunk by Gneisenau and Scharnhorst

Group I

16 April 146 (BRIT)

5 NOR

5 (FR)

Namsos

8 April: Heavy cruiser Hipper sinks British destroyer Glowworm

19 April

Steinkjer

Group II

Repulse Detachment

Trondheim

Storen

Ostersund

18 April 148 (BRIT)

2 NOR

Andalsnes

10 April: Light cruiser Königsberg bombed and sunk

Lillehammer

Gävle

Shetland Islands

Bergen

Group III

Stavanger

Sola

Oslo

STOCKHOLM

Orebo

Lake Väner

3 NOR

Larvik

NOR

Norrköping

Home Fleet

Ergersund

Flekkefjord

Arendal

Kristiansand

9 April: Cruiser Karlsruhe torpedoed and sunk

Group VI

Göteborg

Kalmar

Aalborg

Group V

Halmstadt

Karlskrona

9 April: Heavy cruiser Blücher sunk by shore torpedoes

Aarhus

North Sea

Group IV

DENMARK

COPENHAGEN

Malmo

Baltic Sea

Bornholm

Allied Evacuations:

① Andalsnes, 30 April

② Namsos, 2 May

③ Bodo, 29 May

④ Narvik, 3-8 June

Flensburg

Kiel

Rostock

Lübeck

Stettin

Hamburg

Bremen

NETHERLANDS

Amsterdam

Rotterdam

Hanover

BERLIN

GERMANY

0 100 km

0 100 miles

N

3000
1500
600
300
0 ft

southern England. The climax came on 15 September, when 58 German aircraft were shot down for the loss of 26 British. Two days later, Hitler postponed Sealion indefinitely and turned his eyes eastwards to the Soviet Union. Britain would now be subjected to a winter and spring of prolonged air bombardment, the Blitz, designed to wear down the morale of the British people.

Yet, if Britain seemed to be wholly on the defensive during the summer and autumn of 1940, underneath the surface the first stirrings of offensive action were being felt. As early as 3 June, Churchill had circulated a memorandum to his Chiefs of Staff calling for offensive action through the formation of raiding forces. This was the genesis of the Commandos, who mounted their first operation, an abortive raid on the French coast, on the night 24/25 June. Simultaneously, Churchill sought to fan the flames of resistance to the Nazis in Occupied Europe through the setting up of the Special Operations Executive.

He also looked to RAF Bomber Command to mount a sustained air offensive against Germany, but it would be some time before it possessed sufficient suitable aircraft to make such a campaign effective. Churchill also ordered his staff to draw up plans for more ambitious projects. These included operations against the Azores and Canaries in the event of a German threat to them and one to destroy the Finnish port of Petsamo, through which nickel and iron-ore, vital to Germany's war industry, passed. Finally, on 5 October 1940, Churchill ordered a plan to be prepared for major ground operations on the European mainland with a view to advancing to Germany's major industrial region in the west, the Ruhr. It was this directive which provided the starting point for the D-Day landings.

All these plans assumed a significant amphibious capability, something which Britain did not possess in 1940. Between the wars, little thought had been given to developing such a weapon, largely because memories of the carnage surrounding the Gallipoli landings in 1915 had convinced most that such operations were not practicable. Indeed, in 1930 there were precisely three landing craft in Britain. True, in May 1938 the Inter-Services Training and Development Centre (ISTDC) was established at Portsmouth to develop amphibious techniques and this did result in orders for a few more landing craft, but at the outbreak of war it was tem-

An early British landing craft. It was designated the Landing Craft Mechanized (LCM). Much of the construction of the amphibious fleet for D-Day was, however, carried out in the United States.

porarily all but disbanded, although it was resurrected at the end of 1939. The first British attempt at amphibious warfare was the landings in Norway in April 1940. These were initially unopposed by the Germans, but, not least because the Germans quickly achieved air supremacy, they could not be sustained and one after another of the landing forces had to be evacuated. Some of the precious stock of landing craft were lost, as well as others at Dunkirk. The net result was that in summer 1940 amphibious resources and expertise were still woefully lacking. This was borne out by the fiasco at Dakar in September 1940.

This was de Gaulle's attempt to establish a Free French foothold in French North-West Africa with considerable

British Commandos carry out a practice landing in Scotland. For much of the early part of the war they were one of the few means the British had of directly attacking the Germans in occupied western Europe. They also helped to develop amphibious warfare. The US Rangers were later modelled on the Commandos.

The interception of the three French cruisers on 19-20 September alerted the French in Dakar. The defences were much stronger than the planners of Operation Menace realized and they did inflict embarrassing damage on Force M when it attempted to carry out a landing during 23-24 September. The lessons learnt from this fiasco were taken to heart for subsequent Allied amphibious landings.

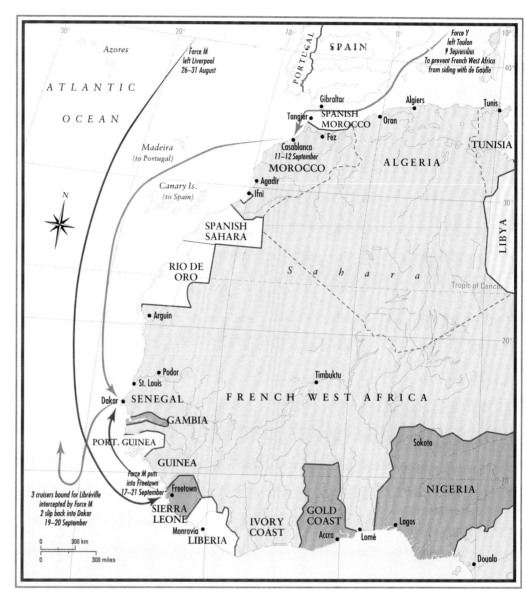

The Dakar Operation
August – September 1940

→ Allied force
→ French movements
British possessions
French possessions
Spanish possessions
Portuguese possessions
Italian possessions
Independant state

British naval and some military support. Intelligence on the Vichy French military strength at the port and the will to resist was poor. The landing troops, both British Royal Marines and Free French, had no training for the operation, which had been hastily mounted, and liaison between the British commanders and de Gaulle was poor. When the force appeared off Dakar, it was surprised by the intensity of the fire from the shore. Air attacks mounted from the carrier *Ark Royal* were also repulsed and, after the battleship HMS *Resolution* had been torpedoed by a Vichy French submarine, the force made an ignominious withdrawal. Dakar reinforced the need to build up an effective amphibious capability and, to this end, a Combined Training Centre was opened at Inverary in Scotland in January 1941 to teach and develop landing techniques. Admiral Sir Roger Keyes, who had

planned and executed the famous Zeebrugge Raid of St George's Day 1918, was appointed Director of Combined Operations. The first fruits of these efforts came in March 1941 with a highly successful Commando raid on the Lofoten Islands off northern Norway.

In spite of the planning and efforts by the British to develop the tools needed for re-entering the Continent of Europe, Churchill realized from the outset that, while Britain could defend itself, it lacked the resources to defeat Hitler and Mussolini on its own. Only the United States of America

(Right) Most operations were carried out by very small groups and were designed to test the Germans defences and, if possible, seize prisoners. Those in Norway played their part in tying down German troops. A further series of reconnaissance operations to check beach obstacles was carried out by the Commandos in mid-May 1944.

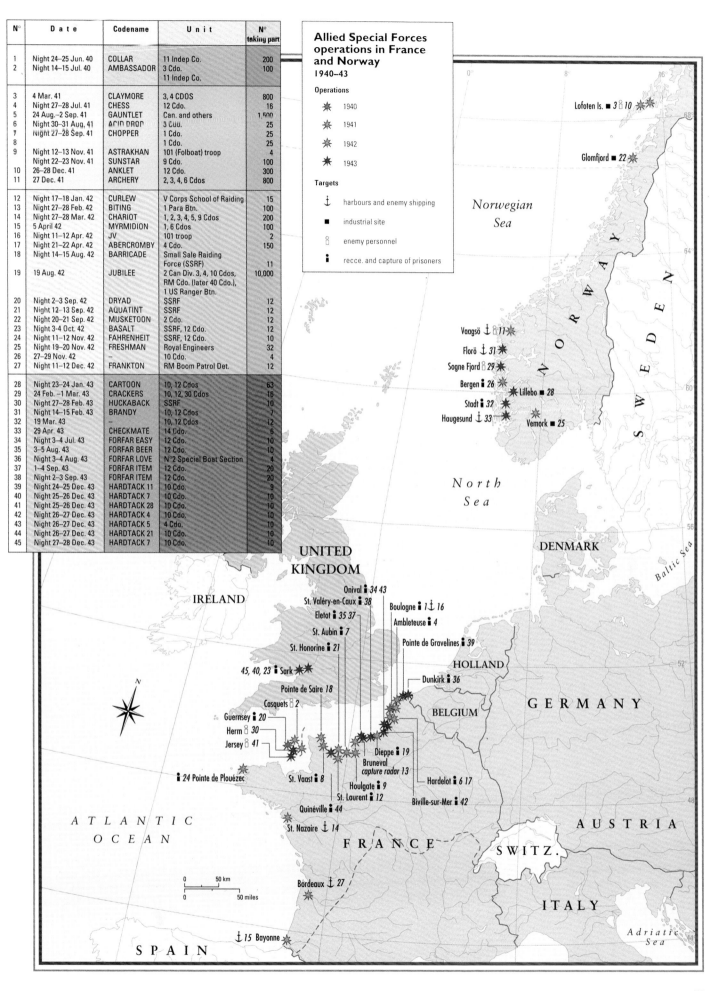

N°	Date	Codename	Unit	N° taking part
1	Night 24–25 Jun. 40	COLLAR	11 Indep Co.	200
2	Night 14–15 Jul. 40	AMBASSADOR	3 Cdo.	100
			11 Indep Co.	
3	4 Mar. 41	CLAYMORE	3, 4 CDOS	800
4	Night 27–28 Jul. 41	CHESS	12 Cdo.	16
5	24 Aug.–2 Sep. 41	GAUNTLET	Can. and others	1,500
6	Night 30–31 Aug, 41	ACID DROP	3 Cdo.	25
7	Night 27–28 Sep. 41	CHOPPER	1 Cdo.	25
8			1 Cdo.	25
9	Night 12–13 Nov. 41	ASTRAKHAN	101 (Folboat) troop	4
	Night 22–23 Nov. 41	SUNSTAR	9 Cdo.	100
10	26–28 Dec. 41	ANKLET	12 Cdo.	300
11	27 Dec. 41	ARCHERY	2, 3, 4, 6 Cdos	800
12	Night 17–18 Jan. 42	CURLEW	V Corps School of Raiding	15
13	Night 27–28 Feb. 42	BITING	1 Para Btn.	100
14	Night 27–28 Mar. 42	CHARIOT	1, 2, 3, 4, 5, 9 Cdos	200
15	5 April 42	MYRMIDION	1, 6 Cdos	100
16	Night 11–12 Apr. 42	JV	101 troop	2
17	Night 21–22 Apr. 42	ABERCROMBY	4 Cdo.	150
18	Night 14–15 Aug. 42	BARRICADE	Small Sale Raiding Force (SSRF)	11
19	19 Aug. 42	JUBILEE	2 Can Div. 3, 4, 10 Cdos, RM Cdo. (later 40 Cdo.), 1 US Ranger Btn.	10,000
20	Night 2–3 Sep. 42	DRYAD	SSRF	12
21	Night 12–13 Sep. 42	AQUATINT	SSRF	12
22	Night 20–21 Sep. 42	MUSKETOON	2 Cdo.	12
23	Night 3-4 Oct. 42	BASALT	SSRF, 12 Cdo.	12
24	Night 11–12 Nov. 42	FAHRENHEIT	SSRF, 12 Cdo.	10
25	Night 19–20 Nov. 42	FRESHMAN	Royal Engineers	32
26	27–29 Nov. 42	–	10 Cdo.	4
27	Night 11–12 Dec. 42	FRANKTON	RM Boom Patrol Det.	12
28	Night 23–24 Jan. 43	CARTOON	10, 12 Cdos	63
29	24 Feb. –1 Mar. 43	CRACKERS	10, 12, 30 Cdos	16
30	Night 27–28 Feb. 43	HUCKABACK	SSRF	10
31	Night 14–15 Feb. 43	BRANDY	10, 12 Cdos	7
32	19 Mar. 43	–	10, 12 Cdos	12
33	29 Apr. 43	CHECKMATE	14 Cdo.	6
34	Night 3–4 Jul. 43	FORFAR EASY	12 Cdo.	10
35	3–5 Aug. 43	FORFAR BEER	12 Cdo.	10
36	Night 3–4 Aug. 43	FORFAR LOVE	N°2 Special Boat Section	4
37	1–4 Sep. 43	FORFAR ITEM	12 Cdo.	20
38	Night 2–3 Sep. 43	FORFAR ITEM	12 Cdo.	20
39	Night 24–25 Dec. 43	HARDTACK 11	10 Cdo.	9
40	Night 25–26 Dec. 43	HARDTACK 7	10 Cdo.	10
41	Night 25–26 Dec. 43	HARDTACK 28	10 Cdo.	10
42	Night 26–27 Dec. 43	HARDTACK 4	10 Cdo.	10
43	Night 26–27 Dec. 43	HARDTACK 5	4 Cdo.	10
44	Night 26–27 Dec. 43	HARDTACK 21	10 Cdo.	10
45	Night 27–28 Dec. 43	HARDTACK 7	10 Cdo.	10

Allied Special Forces operations in France and Norway 1940–43

Operations
✹ 1940
✹ 1941
✹ 1942
✹ 1943

Targets
⚓ harbours and enemy shipping
■ industrial site
⚑ enemy personnel
⚑ recce. and capture of prisoners

could provide these and so Churchill embarked on a campaign to persuade President Franklin D. Roosevelt to bring his country into the war on the British side. It was to be a difficult struggle. While Roosevelt had every sympathy with the British cause, he was very conscious that the majority of his countrymen continued to support the isolationism that had kept America out of the League of Nations. They had no wish to become embroiled in another European war. Even so, Roosevelt did what he could to help the British. In August 1940, he supplied fifty elderly destroyers to the Royal Navy in exchange for the lease of British naval bases in the Caribbean. He also sent a team of military observers across to Britain and, in preparation for what he saw as America's eventual inevitable entry into the war, set up a programme for increased shipbuilding and implemented limited conscription. Roosevelt's position became more secure after the November 1940 presidential election and one of the first steps of his second presidency was to introduce his Lend-Lease Bill to Congress. This would enable the

President Franklin D. Roosevelt and Prime Minister Winston Churchill meet on board the battleship HMS Prince of Wales *in Placentia Bay, Newfoundland, in August 1941. While Churchill failed to persuade the President to enter the war, the Atlantic Charter that they drew up provided a vision for a new post-war world and was the blueprint for the United Nations.*

USA to supply Britain and China, embroiled in a desperate struggle against the Japanese, with war matériel, which could be repaid in kind after the war. This became law in early March 1941. Simultaneously, he agreed to joint talks between the British and US military staffs.

Even though the USA's foreign policy was strictly isolationist, the US military still needed strategic scenarios on which to base planning and armed forces structure. Prior to the outbreak of World War 2 these were very hypothetical and considered war against single countries. These included Germany and Japan, but also even Canada and Britain. As war clouds gathered in Europe during summer 1939, there was a rethink and a new series of plans was drawn up. These were based on the premise of the probability of war against more than one enemy and in more than one theatre. While the earlier plans had single colour names (Red, Orange, Blue, etc), the new set came out under the title of Rainbow. Rainbow-1 and -2 were concerned with defence of the US and its trade, as well as protecting democratic powers, notably the Philippines, in the Pacific. Rainbow-3 covered the Western Pacific and was aimed at Japan, while Rainbow-4 dealt with the South America option. Rainbow-5, however, not only acted as a blanket cover for the first four, but also provided for the sending of forces to Europe or Africa to help the British and French defeat Germany and Italy. It was with this background that the US staff entered what were called the ABC (America, Britain, Canada) talks. They were held in Canada and at the end of March 1941 firm agreement was reached. Priority, once America entered the war, would be the defeat of Germany and Italy and the main US military effort would be in the European theatre. A strategic defence would be conducted against Japan, with the US Navy giving priority to the Pacific. The talks provided a firm basis for planning, even though the agreements made were not binding on either country.

Potential US operations in both Europe and the Pacific would inevitably contain an amphibious element, but the US

(Right) Many of these plans reflected Churchill's rstless determination to strike back at the Germans. In particular, he favoured a landing in Norway, although his military staff were very much against this because of the difficulties of supporting a force at such a range from Britain. The Americans were dedicated to Round-Up from the outset, but were eventually persuaded to postpone it in favour of invading French North-West Africa.

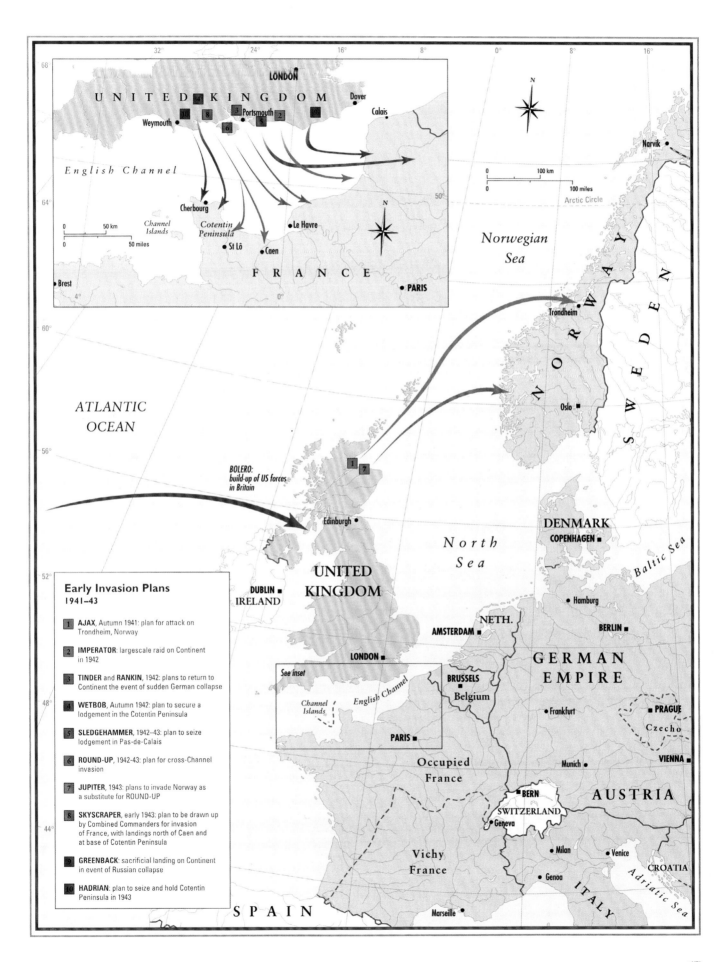

Early Invasion Plans
1941–43

1 **AJAX**, Autumn 1941: plan for attack on Trondheim, Norway

2 **IMPERATOR**: largescale raid on Continent in 1942

3 **TINDER** and **RANKIN**, 1942: plans to return to Continent the event of sudden German collapse

4 **WETBOB**, Autumn 1942: plan to secure a lodgement in the Cotentin Peninsula

5 **SLEDGEHAMMER**, 1942–43: plan to seize lodgement in Pas-de-Calais

6 **ROUND-UP**, 1942-43: plan for cross-Channel invasion

7 **JUPITER**, 1943: plans to invade Norway as a substitute for ROUND-UP

8 **SKYSCRAPER**, early 1943: plan to be drawn up by Combined Commanders for invasion of France, with landings north of Caen and at base of Cotentin Peninsula

9 **GREENBACK**: sacrificial landing on Continent in event of Russian collapse

10 **HADRIAN**: plan to seize and hold Cotentin Peninsula in 1943

capability in this field was limited, although considerably ahead of that of the British in 1939. This was thanks to the US Marine Corps, which worked hard during the 1920s and 1930s to develop amphibious doctrine for what became the Fleet Marine Force, whose primary role was establishing forward bases in the Pacific in the event of war against Japan. They even developed an amphibious armoured vehicle, the Landing Vehicle Tracked (LVT), which became a crucial element of the successful island-hopping operations in the Pacific. Where the Marine Corps was frustrated, however, was in the lack of suitable amphibious shipping. Furthermore, it was not until 1940 that the US Army began to display any interest in amphibious warfare.

On 22 June 1941, The Germans invaded the Soviet Union, putting a very different complexion on the war. For Britain it meant a significant reduction in pressure, but as the Germans drove deeper into Russia, clamour grew within Britain and from Moscow for the immediate opening of a Second Front to draw off German divisions. This was beyond the British capability since there was still only suffi-

HMS Campbeltown wedged into the lock gates at St Nazaire moments before exploding, vapourizing the large group of German soldiers inspecting the wreck.

cient shipping to carry 6,000 men at one time. Even so, Churchill did order his military staff to draw up plans for a large-scale raid on northern France, mentioning specifically the Cherbourg peninsula, but the concept was rejected as impracticable. Meanwhile, Roosevelt was slowly extending his assistance to the British. In April he extended the zone in the western Atlantic in which US warships would protect their own merchant vessels almost to Iceland, simultaneously deploying troops to Greenland. In July 1941, US troops

also relieved the British garrison in Iceland. Then, in August 1941 came the historic meeting between Roosevelt and Churchill off Newfoundland. Nothing concrete came out of it, however. The British Chiefs of Staff were disappointed that their American opposite numbers appeared to have a very defensive view of the western hemisphere and had little clear-cut strategy for the defeat of Germany. The Americans, on the other hand, thought that the British focus on the Mediterranean was an irrelevancy and the likely effect on Germany of strategic bombing over-emphasized. They also criticized the British lack of focus on planning a major campaign in Europe.

British dreams of the USA finally entering the war were at last realized in December 1941. As a result of the Japanese air attack on the US Pacific Fleet base at Pearl Harbor, Hawaii on the 7th, Roosevelt declared war against Japan. He hesitated to declare war on Germany, but Hitler solved the problem by declaring war on the USA. Churchill immediately set sail in the battleship HMS *Duke of York* to meet Roosevelt in Washington DC in what was to be the first of many Allied strategic conferences. Even though American interests were more directly threatened by Japan, Roosevelt did agree to uphold the decisions made at the ABC talks earlier in the year. The priority would remain on first defeating Germany. Strategy would be directed by Churchill and Roosevelt through the Combined Chiefs of Staff (CCS), which comprised the US Chiefs of Staff and the British Military Mission to the USA. As for the way ahead, the Washington Conference had four major plans to consider. Sledgehammer was a major operation somewhere in Western Europe to be mounted in 1942 to relieve pressure on the Russians. Round-Up, the preferred US option, was a cross-Channel invasion in 1943. The British, on the other hand, pushed for Gymnast, which was an invasion of French North-West Africa. At the time, the British forces in Libya had just mounted a successful counter-offensive and Gymnast was seen as a way of threatening the rear of the Axis forces and securing the whole of North Africa. The one plan on which both sides agreed was Bolero, a build-up of US forces in Britain. Indeed, the first US troops arrived before the end of January 1942.

The focus of the debate which would occupy the Allies for much of 1942 was Round-Up versus Gymnast. The

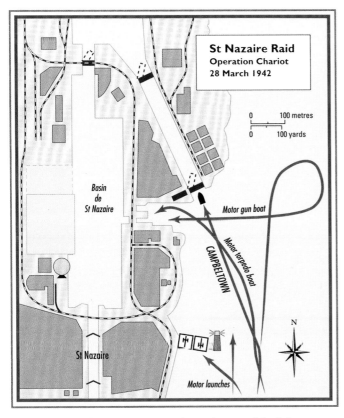

This was one of the most spectacular and successful of the cross-Channel raids. The Commandos provided demolition teams and were responsible for neutralizing the dock defences. Motor launches were used instead of landing craft and HMS Campbeltown, packed with explosives, was to literally ram the lock gates. She was disguised as a German torpedo boat. Casualties were heavy, however, with over 350 killed or captured.

British were lukewarm over the former, believing that there would not be enough amphibious shipping to ensure success. This itself was measured in terms of the Landing Ship Tank (LST), which was ocean-going and with draught sufficiently shallow to be capable of delivering tanks direct to the landing beach. The British view was that at least fifty LSTs would be needed for Round-Up, but, because the development of an effective type had been slow, they doubted whether sufficient would be available in time. Both sides blew hot and cold over Gymnast, the British especially so after Rommel mounted a successful counter-offensive in Libya in January 1942. But Sledgehammer, too, caused much heart-searching. While the Russians had succeeded in rebuffing the Germans in front of Moscow in December 1941 and had mounted limited counter-offensives, there were grave doubts whether they could stand up to an inevitable renewed German offensive in spring 1942. The British planners therefore began to examine in detail how Sledgehammer could be

mounted. Admiral Lord Louis Mountbatten, who was now Chief of Combined Operations, favoured the Cherbourg peninsula, but this was rejected because the distance from Britain meant that insufficient air cover could be provided. On the other hand, he rejected a raid on the Pas-de-Calais on the grounds that re-embarkation would be very difficult in the light of the expected German reaction. The US view was summed up by General George C. Marshall, Chairman of the Joint Chiefs of Staff, namely that Sledgehammer should only be mounted if the situation on the Eastern Front became desperate, or if there was a fatal weakening of the German forces in the West. One good thing, however, did come out of these discussions. This was the realization that it was essential that the ports on Britain's south coast, which had been allowed to decay since summer 1940, were made fully functional once more and, indeed, improved, since it was from them that any major cross-Channel assault would be mounted.

In the meantime, during winter 1941-2 two large-scale and successful Commando raids had been carried out. The first, on 27 December 1941 was against the Norwegian port of Vaagso. It was followed, on the night of 27/28 March 1942, by an operation to deny the Germans the use of the dry dock at the French Atlantic port of St Nazaire. This was done by ramming an elderly destroyer filled with explosives against the dock gates. There were also, as there had been in 1941, a series of small-scale Commando raids on the French Atlantic coast with the object of testing the German defences. All these helped to develop amphibious techniques. At the same time, because British shipyards were filled to capacity building other types of ship, increasing orders for amphibious shipping were placed with the Americans. Thus, during 1942 the Allied amphibious capability began to grow.

In April 1942, the Japanese onrush in the South-West Pacific began to threaten Australia. The Americans felt forced to divert two divisions earmarked for Bolero and were forced to admit that they would have less than three divisions in Britain by mid-September. This was another nail in the coffin for Sledgehammer and the British Chiefs of Staff decided that a major cross-Channel raid should be mounted instead, although planning for Sledgehammer would continue. But Roosevelt, conscious of both the sacrifices that the

Russians were making and that if US troops were not in action in Europe soon, US public opinion might well start to agitate for priority to be switched to the Pacific, was still keen that Sledgehammer should go ahead in some form. Pressure, too, came from the Russians themselves, with foreign minister Vyacheslav Molotov flying to London and then Washington to plead the Russian case. While the British would make no immediate commitment, Roosevelt did reassure Molotov that a Second Front would be opened before the end of 1942, although he was careful not to say where.

The British became more and more convinced that Sledgehammer was merely a sacrificial operation which would gain little. In this context, Churchill had been pressuring Roosevelt to reconsider Gymnast as an alternative. General George Marshall remained totally opposed to this and even proposed a Pacific option to the President, which, of course, ran totally counter to the Germany First agreement. Indeed, Roosevelt rejected it, likening the proposal to 'taking up your dishes and going away', and by mid-July was coming round to Gymnast. Simultaneously, the British Joint Planning Staff were telling the Chiefs of Staff that it would not be possible to mount Round-Up within twelve

The Dieppe Raid was essentially a frontal assault against a well defended position, with insufficient fire support (naval) to deal with the numerous coastal batteries. The only successes were by No.4 Commando in silencing the Hess Battery and No.3 Commando, which successfully distracted the Goebbels Battery. Valuable lessons were learnt for the D-Day landings, but at a high cost.

months of Gymnast. Roosevelt now sent Marshall to London to resolve the dilemma. Supported by General Dwight D. Eisenhower, the recently appointed Commanding General European Theatre of Operations (ETOUSA), Marshall proposed gaining a lodgement in the Cotentin peninsula in autumn 1942 and holding it until Round Up was mounted. The British pointed out the difficulties with the weather at that time of year. They were supported by the US Navy representatives in Britain and on this Sledgehammer foundered. It was, in Eisenhower's eyes, 'the blackest day in history'.

Throughout this debate, however, the British, had been preparing a major cross-Channel raid. It was Mountbatten's HQ which decided on the port of Dieppe as a target, believing it to be lightly defended. The original plan, approved by the British Chiefs of Staff in May 1942, envisaged a frontal assault by 2nd Canadian Division, with airborne forces being used to neutralize the coastal batteries on the flanks. The assault would be preceded by an attack by RAF Bomber Command and there would be extensive fighter support, which it was hoped would draw the Luftwaffe into the air and inflict heavy casualties upon it. General Bernard Montgomery, then in charge of South-East Army, was in overall charge. He held two rehearsals in June and decided that the raid should go ahead on 4 July or the first fine day after that. Unfortunately, there was a spell of bad weather in early July, which forced a postponement. Montgomery

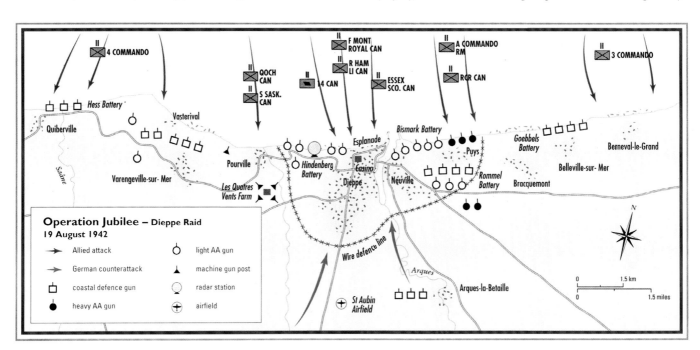

Germans inspect the beach at Dieppe after the disastrous raid in August 1942. Many of the tanks could not get off the beach because the shingle jammed their tracks. It was as a result of this that the British developed specialized armoured vehicles to facilitate the landing of tanks and enable them to get off the beach.

believed that it should be cancelled, fearing that the raid had been compromised, but Mountbatten insisted that it go ahead. It was rescheduled for August, but changes were now made. The preliminary air bombardment was cancelled through fears of inflicting French civilian casualties and the airborne element was also withdrawn because of weather uncertainties. In its place, Commandos were detailed to deal with the coastal batteries. Another problem was that the Navy maintained its policy of no warship larger than a destroyer being allowed in the Channel, which severely limited the fire support for the landings.

After a 24-hour postponement because of the weather, the raiding force sailed from four South Coast ports on the evening of 18 August. They arrived off Dieppe before dawn and the raid began. It was a disaster, with only the Commandos on the flanks enjoying any success. The Germans had been expecting something and were ready. The Canadians were subjected to heavy fire as they approached the beaches and the 4.7-inch guns of the supporting destroyers proved ineffective. Many of those who got ashore were shot down before they could get off the beach. A battalion of hastily converted Churchill tanks found the shingle too much for their tracks to cope with and were all knocked out. The landing force commander,

who was on board one of the destroyers, had little idea of what was happening and sent in follow-up waves, which also suffered. In the skies above, the battle did not go as the British expected. They lost 106 aircraft, while the Luftwaffe had only forty-eight shot down. General Roberts, the Force Commander, realized at 9am that withdrawal was the only answer, but it took another four hours to complete. Some four thousand men, mainly Canadians, were left behind dead or prisoners of war.

For the Germans, Dieppe was a major propaganda coup. Many Canadians regarded it, and still do today, as a needless slaughter. Indeed, it remains one of the major controversies of World War 2. Yet valuable lessons for subsequent amphibious assaults were learnt. First, security had to be very much tighter. Naval gunfire support needed to be very much heavier. Air supremacy had to be established before the landings took place. The landing force commander needed a dedicated command ship with good communications to the shore, the air, and the naval element. Armoured Fighting Vehicles (AFV) had to be developed which could get ashore and cope with the inevitable obstacles that would be found on the landing beach and beyond. Finally, to land at a defended port was to court failure. When the cross-Channel invasion did come, it would have to be over open beaches,

U.S. troops land in North Africa as part of the Allied Operation Torch.

but without the facilities of a port how was the force ashore to be supplied and reinforced so that it could push inlan

Dieppe did give an indication of what might have happened if Sledgehammer had taken place, but, in any event, it was now history. On 30 July 1942 the Allies confirmed that Gymnast, now renamed Torch, would take place on 7 October. The original plan was for US-only landings at Oran and Casablanca, but, on British insistence, landings were also to take place at Algiers with British participation. This would put the Allies considerably closer to Tunis, which was the final objective. Since this meant assembling more shipping, Torch was postponed until the end of October. Because the operation was largely American, Eisenhower was put in charge, which was personal consolation for the cancellation of Sledgehammer. There were, however, serious implications for Round-Up. While the landings at Casablanca were to be mounted from the USA, the forces for the other two landings would sail from Britain. This meant drawing on the Bolero forces and would put a brake on the build-up for Round-Up. Furthermore, a significant proportion of the US Eighth Air Force in Britain, which was just beginning to join the RAF in the air offensive against Germany, was also sidetracked to Torch. Furthermore, Stalin would have to be told that there would be no Second Front in Europe in 1942. To this end, Churchill and Roosevelt's personal representative, Averell Harriman,

flew to Moscow in mid-August. Stalin grudgingly accepted Churchill's explanation that 'it was as well to strike at the belly as the snout' of a crocodile.

The Torch landings themselves duly took place on 8 November 1942, just as Bernard Montgomery, who had taken charge of the British Eighth Army in Egypt in August, was beginning to pursue Rommel into Libya after his decisive breakthrough attack at El Alamein. The Vichy French put up little more than token resistance and sought an armistice after three days. The lessons of Dakar and Dieppe had been learnt in terms of command and control at Oran and Algiers in that the landing force commander for each did have a dedicated command ship. At Casablanca, however, General George S. Patton did not, which he found frustrating, especially since he was not able to get ashore until long after he wanted to. Poor navigation and confusion on the landing beaches pointed to inexperience, and the loading of the ships left much to be desired, since many of the items that the force required as soon as it landed were not immediately accessible.

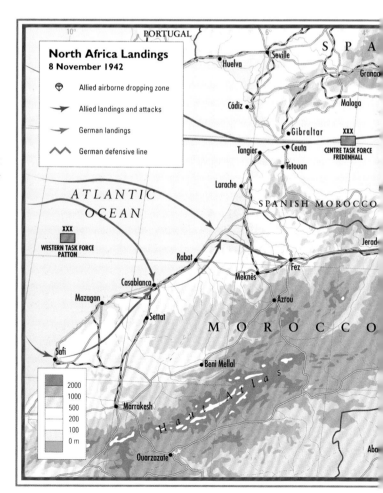

With Morocco and Algeria secured, the Allies quickly moved into Tunisia. The initial landings had taken the Axis powers by surprise, but they reacted quickly and were soon flying troops into Tunisia. As the Allies advanced into the country, a series of engagements took place. Even so, the Allies managed to reach 20 miles from Tunis before they were finally halted. German counter-attacks and an adverse air situation forced the Allies to halt and, by the end of 1942, stalemate ensued.

It was in this climate that Roosevelt and Churchill met once more, this time at Casablanca, Morocco in mid January 1943. Prior to the Conference, Churchill's own view had been that Tunisia could be secured in January 1943. The Allies would then go on to capture Sardinia, to neutralize Italy by the end of March, and then begin preparing for Round-Up, which could be mounted in August or September 1943. His Chiefs of Staff did not agree, however. They argued that it would simply take the pressure off the Germans while Round-Up was being prepared and that there was not the shipping available, especially to make good the

shortfall in Bolero brought about by Torch. Rather, they said, it would be better to concentrate on the Mediterranean during 1943 and knock Italy out of the war. To this Churchill agreed. In Washington, however, the general feeling was that Round-Up must be the priority for 1943. The US Army planners were, however, pessimistic. They feared that logistics might mean that it could not be mounted before mid-1944 and were concerned over the heavy casualties suffered at Dieppe. Hence, unlike the British, the Americans arrived at Casablanca with no clear-cut strategy on the way ahead. This was to be to their grave disadvantage.

The Casablanca Conference itself did reach a number of significant decisions. The better-prepared British team got

Torch represented the first major Anglo-US operation in the European theatre. The landings took the Axis by surprise and the only significant, albeit brief, opposition was at Algiers. It was also the first time that the Allies used airborne forces on a large scale, primarily to secure airfields. Unfortunately, once they advanced into Tunisia, they found themselves with very long lines of communication. This and the semi-mountainous terrain meant that the campaign lasted very much longer than planned.

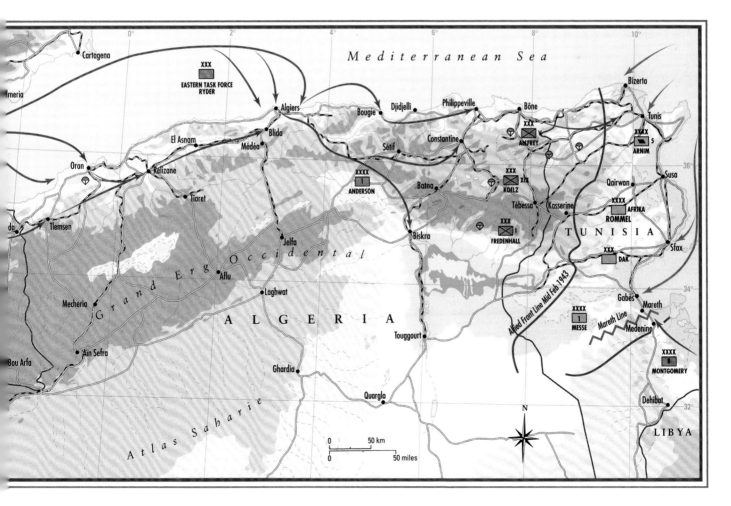

General George S. Patton commanded the 7th Army during the invasion of Sicily.

before his appointment was confirmed by the Combined Chiefs of Staff and he could gather a planning team, but this did give him time to study the work that had been done by another British body which had been considering the problem for some time.

The Combined Commanders committee had been established on a part-time basis before the end of 1941 to consid-

its way over priority for the Mediterranean in 1943, with Sicily being the next objective after North Africa had been cleared of the Axis presence. The Americans, however, were not prepared to agree to further operations in the Mediterranean after Sicily. Bolero was to continue, with a target of 384,000 US troops in Britain by 1 August 1943 and well over 900,000 by the end of the year. While a full-scale cross-Channel invasion was out of the question in 1943, it was agreed that a combined planning staff for it should be set up in Britain under a British officer. On the other hand, more limited operations might be feasible, including, if a favourable situation developed, establishing a lodgement. These, however, were mere contingencies to which the British agreed to placate the Americans. In the wider context, both sides agreed that winning the Battle of the Atlantic was a priority because of the U-boat threat to the supply lines from North America. Finally, the USAAF and RAF were to mount a combined bomber offensive, code-named Pointblank. The aim was to pave the way for invasion by fatally weakening the German war industry and the morale of the people.

The Tunisian campaign continued, with Montgomery forcing Rommel back across the border with Libya and entering the country himself. Thereafter it was a question of gradually squeezing the Axis forces from the south and from the west. Not, however, until early May did they finally surrender. In the midst of this, on 12 March 1943, Lieutenant-General Frederick Morgan was appointed Chief of Staff to the Supreme Allied Commander (COSSAC) and tasked with producing a coherent plan for Round Up in line with the decision made at Casablanca. It would be a month

Apart from the airborne element, which was widely scattered, the initial landings went well. The Americans then cleared the western half of the island, while the British advanced up the east coast. While the Italian will to fight was fading, the German forces on Sicily conducted a skilful withdrawal and managed to escape across the Strait of Messina.

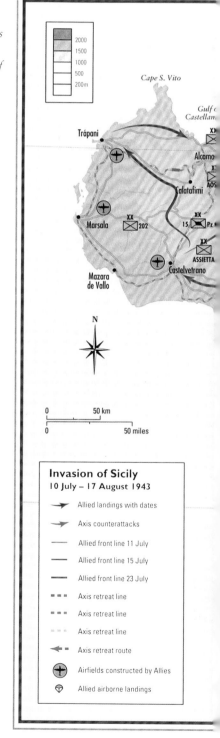

Invasion of Sicily
10 July – 17 August 1943

- ⟶ Allied landings with dates
- ⟶ Axis counterattacks
- — Allied front line 11 July
- — Allied front line 15 July
- — Allied front line 23 July
- ∎∎∎ Axis retreat line
- ∎∎∎ Axis retreat line
- ∎∎∎ Axis retreat line
- ⟵∎ Axis retreat route
- ✛ Airfields constructed by Allies
- ⊕ Allied airborne landings

er the problems of a cross-Channel invasion. It consisted of a senior sailor, a soldier, and an airman and produced a number of papers for the British Chiefs of Staff. One of the final tasks of the Combined Commanders was to consider possible landing areas. They considered these in terms of air cover, enemy airfields, the German naval threat, enemy fixed defences, the ability of the Germans to use flooding as a defensive weapon and to deploy reserves, the presence of ports, and landing beaches. Their conclusions were that fighter cover was needed over the beaches and that airfields must be captured early so as to maintain air support once the force advanced inland. The rate of build-up of the force must be at least equal to the deployment of German reserves, and the beaches themselves needed to be sheltered

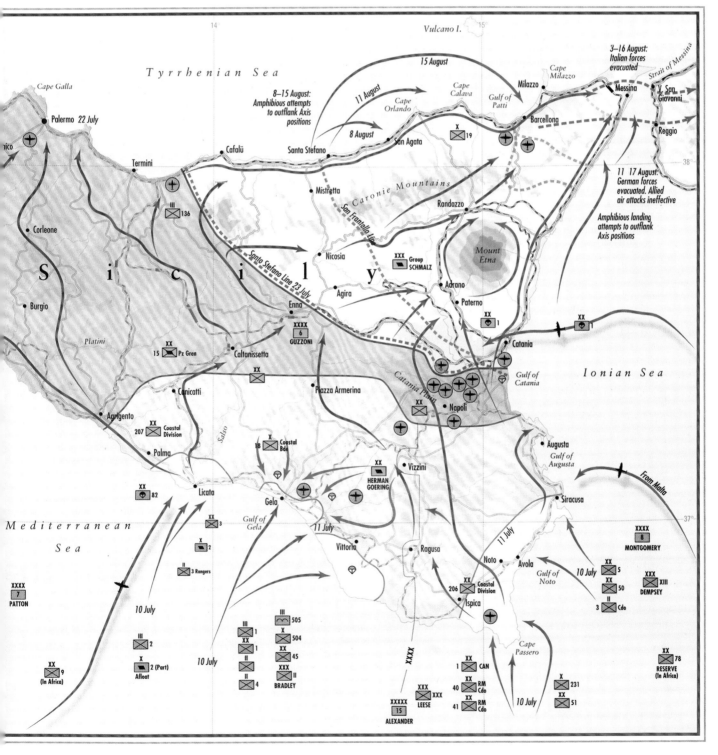

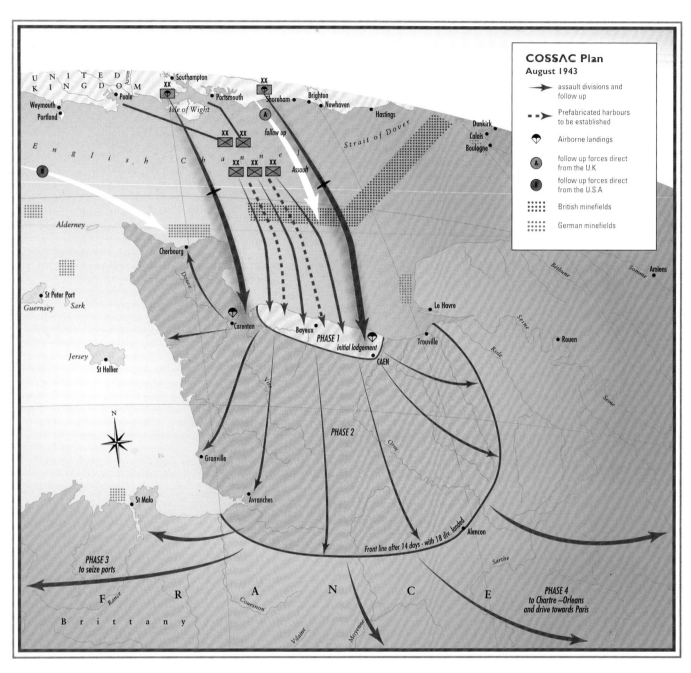

The initial assault would be made by US First Army, with one US, one British, and one Canadian divisions. One airborne division was to be used on each flank, with that in the east tasked with capturing Caen. On D+7 the Canadian First Army would be formed, with responsibility for the eastern half of the lodgement, while HQ 21st Army Group took over command from US First Army.

from the weather. They stressed the need to capture a sizeable port early. They dismissed the Dutch coast as being beyond adequate fighter cover and also because the country was too prone to inundation. Belgian beaches were too exposed and of limited capacity. The Combined Commanders also did not consider the Pas-de-Calais as suitable, even though it was closest to the English coast and thus maximum air cover could be provided. The defences were too strong, most beaches were exposed and all were dominated by cliffs. The sector could, however, be used for a feint attack. The coast around the mouth of the River Seine suffered much the same problems. In addition, the beaches were too small. Moving to Normandy, the coast north of Caen was much more promising. The Seine provided a natural flank for the landing forces, the beaches were of reasonable size and sheltered, and there were good airfields in the Caen area. The defences were also weaker than to the east. The only major drawback was the lack of a suitable port. The Cotentin peninsula, on the other hand, did have the port of Cherbourg, but the beaches were more limited and the base of the peninsula could cause a bottleneck, which would make a break-out difficult. But the Commanders did conclude that if the Caen sector was selected, there would have to be a subsidiary operation against the eastern side of the Cotentin peninsula so as to secure Cherbourg. In this lay the foundations of the eventual Overlord plan. As for Brittany and the Bay of Biscay, these were beyond the range of fighter cover and only suitable for subsidiary operations to capture further ports once the main assault had been mounted.

This appreciation provided COSSAC with a most useful basis for his planning. He was also aware that the British GHQ Home Forces had for a long time been gathering intelligence in support of Round-Up planning. It came from several sources. Continuous photographic air reconnaissance missions were being flown; there was information obtained from radio intercepts, including Ultra material from decryptions of Enigma traffic. Further information was provided by the various Resistance movements. Commando raids also brought back valuable intelligence on the German defences. There had even been a drive to collect people's holiday postcards and photographs of coastal areas. A further source of intelligence was pigeons. Since the spring of 1941, they had been dropped by parachute over Occupied Europe. Each had a questionnaire, which the finder was invited to complete. In all, over 16,500 pigeons were despatched and nearly 2,000 did return to their lofts.

COSSAC arranged his staff so that each of the planning branches – Navy, Army, Air, Administrative – had two principal staff officers, one British and one American. The only exception was Intelligence, which had just a Briton in charge. To gain a better understanding of the planning of amphibious operations, he sent one of his senior officers to monitor the planning of Husky, as the invasion of Sicily was codenamed. In May there was another Allied conference, Trident, which was held in Washington DC. This confirmed

that Round-Up, while not possible in 1943, would be mounted by 1 May 1944. It was envisaged that nine divisions, including two airborne, would be available for the actual assault, with twenty earmarked as follow-up divisions. Four US and three British divisions would be sent back to Britain from the Mediterranean after 1 November. With regard to future operations in this theatre, Trident confirmed that there should be subsequent assaults to Husky, with the aim of knocking Italy out of the war. The Americans opted for Sardinia, while the British wanted to invade the Italian mainland, but no decision was made.

It was clearly helpful that COSSAC knew the forces that would be at his disposal, but the critical factor was the amount of amphibious shipping which would be available. The production of landing craft, in particular, in the USA was low throughout 1943, and there were the demands from the Pacific to be met. It did not appear that there would be anything like enough to transport the seven assault divisions across the Channel. Consequently, the COSSAC planners decided that the initial assault could be undertaken by only three divisions. He accepted the Combined Commanders' conclusion that the Caen sector was the only suitable area for the assault and intended to use the airborne divisions to secure the flanks of the beachhead. Once ashore, the invasion force would advance into the Cotentin peninsula to secure Cherbourg, and then move south and west into Brittany and across the Seine. Simultaneously, COSSAC had to develop two further plans. The first, Cockade, was a series of deception operations designed to keep the German forces pinned down in the West. It had three elements. Starkey was aimed at an early reduction in strength of the Luftwaffe in northern France and the Low Countries through a feint assault on the Pas De Calais. This was mounted on 8 September 1943, with British forces carrying out an embarkation exercise on the Kent coast. However, the Germans failed to react and so it was a failure. Wadham was aimed at Brittany and was an American responsibility. It consisted of air attacks on U-boat bases, air reconnaissance, the mobilization of certain divisions in the USA, and the leakage of false information. The final element, Tindall, was designed to tie down German forces in Norway through air reconnaissance and the display of dummy aircraft and gliders on Scottish airfields. The other area that COSSAC

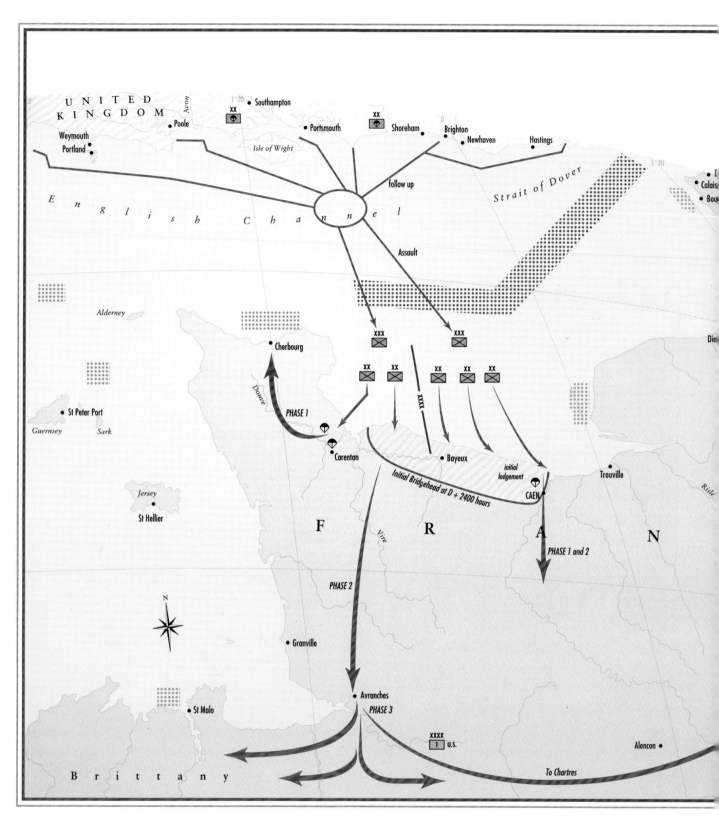

Apart from extending to initial assault westwards and increasing the force to five divisions, with separate sectors for the American and British/Canadian formations, the main difference from the COSSAC plan was the decision that the Americans carry out the break-out from the west rather than the British and Canadians across the Seine. Instead, they would shield the break-out and draw the maximum German forces away from the Americans.

had to consider was what to do in the event of a weakening of the German defences in the West. He drew up plans under the codename Rankin to deal with three eventualities. Rankin A was based on the premise that the Germans thinned out their coastal defences, but did not abandon any

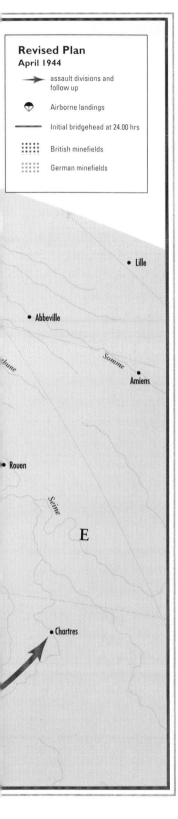

Revised Plan
April 1944

→ assault divisions and follow up

🌀 Airborne landings

— Initial bridgehead at 24.00 hrs

⋮⋮⋮⋮ British minefields

⋮⋮⋮⋮ German minefields

Lille

Abbeville

Somme

Amiens

Rouen

Seine

E

Chartres

territory. Rankin B dealt with evacuation of a portion or portions of the defences, while Rankin C was in response to a sudden German collapse and did forecast what eventually came to pass, namely the occupation of Berlin by the Allies and the division of Germany into zones of occupation.

COSSAC's plan for the cross-Channel invasion was presented at the Allied conference held at Quebec (Quadrant) in August 1943. The Sicily landings had taken place on 10 July. The coast defences were comparatively weak and what counter-attacks there were against the beachheads were hesitant. Only the airborne element did not go well. Poor navigation and high winds resulted in scattered drops mainly in the wrong place. Apart from this, in the view of the COSSAC staff there was little relevant to Overlord, which Round-Up had now been renamed. The Americans now had a change of heart over the next objective and agreed that, with Italy near to collapse, landings should take place on the mainland. This meant, however, that landing craft due to be returned to Britain and others which were to be redeployed to Burma would now be retained in the Mediterranean. These measures were approved at Quadrant, as was the COSSAC Overlord plan. It was recog-

nized, however, that the size of the German forces in France was a very significant factor in mounting Overlord and that the initial assault force should, if possible, be increased by 25 per cent. This, however, was dependent on more amphibious shipping becoming available than was forecast. Quadrant also took on an American proposal for landings in the south of France. These were seen both as a diversion and an adjunct to Overlord. But if the German strength grew so strong as to put Overlord in doubt, a new plan, Imperator, was to be drawn up for an invasion of Norway. This reflected a near obsession on the part of the British prime minister, who had throughout the past three years constantly prodded his staff to consider an attack on this country.

COSSAC was now instructed to proceed with the detailed planning and preparation for Overlord. Ground forces, in the shape of the British 21st Army Group and US 1st Army Group, were already being allocated to him, although the

Eisenhower and Montgomery attend a U.S. exercise in early 1944. Both men made a great effort to be seen by their troops.

latter was as yet a paper organization. Two commanders had been appointed. The Overlord air commander was to be Sir Trafford Leigh-Mallory, whose Allied Expeditionary Air Force (AEAF) of fighters and day bombers of the US Ninth Air Force and British 2nd Tactical Air Force, together with transport aircraft, was already in being. The naval commander was to have been the Commander-in-Chief Portsmouth, Admiral Sir Charles Little, but Churchill objected to this on the grounds that he lacked the necessary capacity to deal with such a major undertaking. Instead, he proposed Sir Bertram Ramsay, the man who had masterminded the evacuation from Dunkirk, and had then been the deputy naval commander for Torch and in charge of the naval forces supporting the British landings on Sicily. He had also served as a member of the Combined Commanders. This was accepted by the Combined Chiefs of Staff, although Ramsay himself would not return to Britain until December 1943. A land commander had yet to be chosen, as had the Supreme Commander, although the US media had concluded that Marshall was the front-runner. This left COSSAC himself in an awkward position, since he had no executive powers. His charter therefore had to be hastily amended by the Combined Chiefs of Staff.

The Italian landings duly went ahead. The British made virtually unopposed landings in the toe of Italy on 3 September. In Lisbon, Portugal, on the same day, an Italian representative signed an armistice agreement with the Allies. It was agreed that this would be kept secret until the second landing. This took place at Salerno on 8 September in the face of fierce and unexpected German opposition. There was also a serious flaw in the planning in that the beachhead was too wide for the available amphibious lift, making it difficult to defend. Even so, the Germans did eventually withdraw, enabling the Allies to break out. But hopes that Rome might be quickly secured were soon dashed. The Germans reacted quickly, pouring in reinforcements through northern Italy and taking advantage of the hilly and mountainous terrain. The autumn rains slowed the Allied progress still further and by the end of the year they were held up by the formidable Gustav Line in the mountains south of Rome. This was to have a bearing on Overlord.

Allied relations in the Mediterranean became strained in autumn 1943. In the immediate aftermath of the Italian surrender, Churchill gave orders for the Dodecanese islands in the Aegean to be occupied. It was part of his desire to bring Turkey into the war on the Allied side and develop a campaign in the Balkans. The problem was that the British garrisons on the islands lacked air support and the Americans were not prepared to divert any from Italy. The German forces in Greece took advantage of this and overran the garrison on Cos at the beginning of October. Churchill ignored advice to withdraw the remaining garrisons and they, too, were forced to surrender. It was another salutary lesson that air-power rather than sea power was often the decisive factor.

Battle-hardened US and British divisions were sent back from Italy to Britain in line with the decision made at Trident. The question over who would be the overall commander for Overlord was also finally resolved. It had been agreed that it should be an American, while his subordinate single-service commanders were to be British. Roosevelt wanted to appoint Marshall, as much as anything to reward him for his outstanding service as Chairman of the Joint Chiefs of Staff. Marshall himself was more than willing. But others close to the President advised him that Marshall was more valuable where he was and, indeed, would be very difficult to replace. The only other option was Eisenhower, who now had over a year's experience as a coalition commander and certainly had the diplomatic skills to bind the Allies together, even if he had no combat experience a lower level. As for the ground commander, Montgomery was the obvious choice. In spite of his bumptious character, which did at times irritate Americans, he had clarity of mind and drive, and had proved himself the most successful British general of the war so far. Thus, at the end of 1943, both handed over their commands, with Eisenhower being replaced by General Sir Henry Wilson.

At the beginning of January, Montgomery arrived back in Britain, while Eisenhower flew back to the States for a short break. But they left a skeleton in the Italian cupboard. As early as October 1943, with the Allied advance slowing, thought began to be given to making an outflanking attack from the sea. By the end of November this had crystallized into a landing at Anzio, just over thirty miles south of Rome, once the Allied forces had reached a point forty miles to the south of the Italian capital. Going back to the basic measure of amphibious shipping, the LST, there were 105 in theatre at the time. Fifty-six of these should have been sent back to Britain for Overlord by mid-December. But, in view of the stalemate on the Gustav Line, General Mark Clark, who had originated the Anzio plan and was commanding the US Fifth Army, now proposed that it be mounted as soon as possible. Churchill and Roosevelt agreed that the LSTs could be retained. The Anzio landings duly went ahead on 22 January 1944. They achieved initial surprise, but instead of exploiting this and advancing inland, the landing force concentrated on consolidating the beachhead. The Germans soon reacted and the Allies found themselves fighting desperately to retain their foothold. As for the main force, it continued to butt its head in vain against the Gustav Line. The upshot was that the majority of the LSTs earmarked for Overlord had to be retained to support the Anzio beachhead. This would influence the timing of Overlord.

Eisenhower had already seen a copy of the COSSAC plan for Overlord at the end of October 1943, well before he was given overall command of it, and commented that there was insufficient punch in the initial attack. Montgomery had his first sight of it when he was shown a copy by Churchill during a stopover at Marrakesh on his way back to Britain. He agreed with Eisenhower's view and also stated that the landing front was too narrow and would inevitably lead to congestion on the beaches as follow-up forces were landed. He wanted each corps to have its dedicated group of beaches so that its follow-up divisions could land on them, and stressed that the British and American beaches must be kept separate. On 3 January he convened the first of many meetings at St Paul's School, London. The COSSAC staff presented their plan, which Montgomery immediately tore to shreds. Four days later, he produced his own plan. The landing frontage was greatly extended and now stretched from the east coast of the Cotentin peninsula to the west bank of the River Orne. Five divisions would now make the initial assault, two from the US First Army in the west and three from the British Second Army in the east. The task of the Americans would be to seize Cherbourg and then advance south and west into Brittany and east towards Paris, while the British provided a shield for them. It was, in many ways, remarkably similar to the Combined Commanders' appreciation of February 1943.

But COSSAC had been constrained by likely amphibious shipping availability and doubts remained whether there would be sufficient to support a five-division landing.

Eisenhower arrived in Britain on 12 January. Two days later General Morgan held his last weekly staff meeting, and on 17 January Eisenhower took over, the headquarters now becoming Supreme Headquarters, Allied Expeditionary Force (SHAEF). He had brought his own chief of staff, Walter Bedell Smith, and so Morgan stepped

into the background, although he remained on the SHAEF staff. At the same time, a Deputy Supreme Allied Commander was appointed, the British airman Arthur Tedder, with whom Eisenhower had worked closely in the Mediterranean. On 21 January, Eisenhower held his first conference and approved Montgomery's plan. He was, however, very conscious of the shipping problem. In order to ensure that there was enough for the revised Overlord, he asked the Combined Chiefs of Staff if the invasion could be postponed until June. They eventually agreed, albeit grudgingly, stipulating that D-Day must now be 31 May or a few days either side. There was also the question of the simultaneous landings in the south of France, codenamed Anvil. The British, who had never really been in favour of them, pointed out that this operation merely served to aggravate the shipping problems and pressed for its cancellation. The Americans were resistant to this and the debate continued.

In spite of this, the detailed planning of Overlord could now get underway. There was, however, another debate over how the airborne forces should be used. Eisenhower wanted two airborne divisions in the initial phase, with a third as an immediate follow-up. The British were concerned over the lack of transport aircraft, but were won round when they were assured that these would become available. General Marshall saw them as a spearhead, however. He wanted to use all four airborne divisions in Britain and drop them well inland so as to act as a blocking force against the German mobile reserves moving to counter the landings. Eisenhower resisted this on the grounds that lightly armed paratroops would be no match for tanks. Consequently, the two US airborne divisions would be used to help secure Utah Beach, while the British Division secured the left flank.

Detailed beach reconnaissance was carried out by specialist teams. There was particular concern over the types of obstacle that the Germans were placing on them. Beaches also had to be found in Britain which were similar to those that would be used in Normandy so that the assaulting troops could train on them. The US assault divisions were the 1st Infantry Division, veterans of Tunisia and Sicily, and the unblooded 4th Infantry Division, which arrived in Britain in January 1944. The British contribution was much the same in terms of experience. The 50th (Northumbrian) Division had fought in North Africa from 1941 onwards,

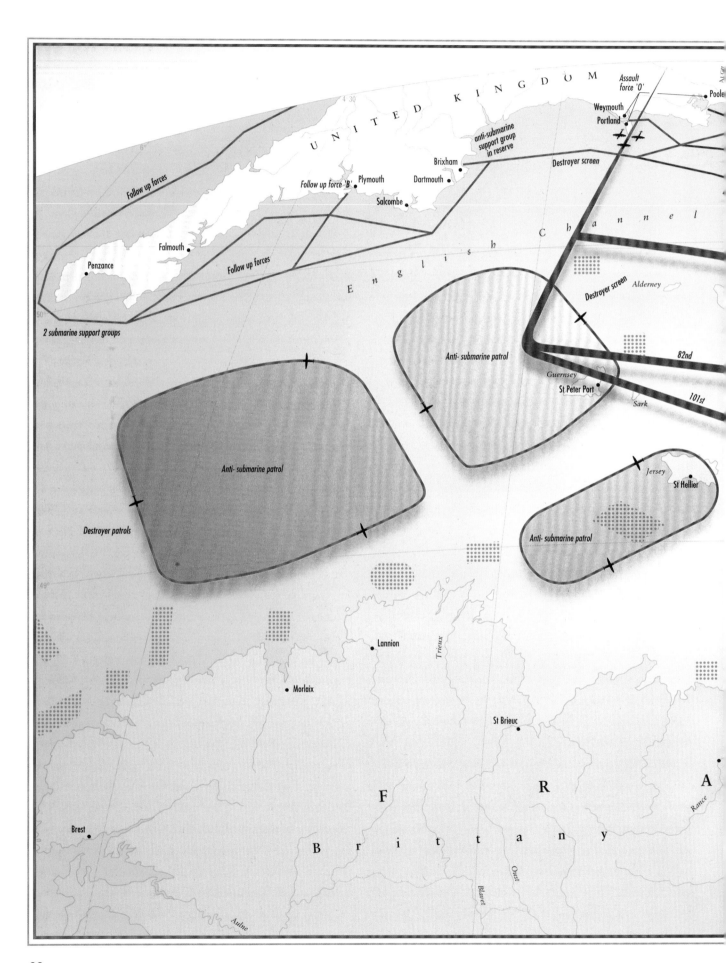

UNITED KINGDOM

Assault force 'O'

Poole

Weymouth

Portland

anti-submarine
support group
in reserve

Brixham

Destroyer screen

Plymouth

Dartmouth

Follow up forces

Follow up force 'B'

Salcombe

English Channel

Falmouth

Destroyer screen

Alderney

Penzance

Follow up forces

50°

2 submarine support groups

Anti- submarine patrol

82nd

Guernsey

St Peter Port

Sark

101st

Anti- submarine patrol

Jersey

St Hellier

Anti- submarine patrol

Destroyer patrols

Anti- submarine patrol

49°

Lannion

Trieux

Morlaix

St Brieuc

F   R   A

Rance

Brest

B   r   i   t   t   a   n   y

Oust

Blavet

Aulne

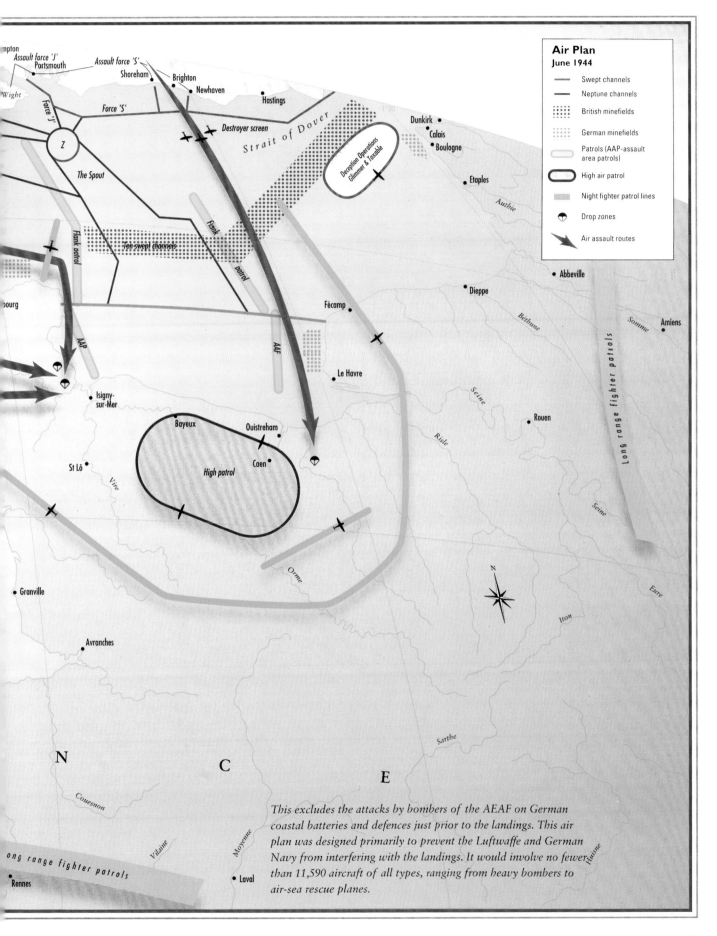

Air Plan
June 1944

Swept channels

Neptune channels

British minefields

German minefields

Patrols (AAP-assault area patrols)

High air patrol

Night fighter patrol lines

Drop zones

Air assault routes

mpton
Assault force 'J'
Portsmouth
Assault force 'S'
Shoreham
Brighton
Newhaven
Wight
Force 'J'
Force 'S'
Hastings
The Spout
Destroyer screen
Strait of Dover
Dunkirk
Calais
Boulogne
Deception Operations
Glimmer & Taxable
Etaples
Flank
patrol
Authie
Flank patrol
Ten swept channels
Abbeville
bourg
Dieppe
Amiens
Fécamp
Somme
AAP
AAF
Béthune
Le Havre
Seine
Rouen
Isigny-
sur-Mer
Risle
Long range fighter patrols
Bayeux
Ouistreham
St Lô
Caen
High patrol
Vire
Seine
Orne
Iton
Granville
Eure
N
Avranches
Sarthe
N
C
E
Couesnon
Mayenne
Vilaine
Maine
ong range fighter patrols
Laval
Rennes

This excludes the attacks by bombers of the AEAF on German
coastal batteries and defences just prior to the landings. This air
plan was designed primarily to prevent the Luftwaffe and German
Navy from interfering with the landings. It would involve no fewer
than 11,590 aircraft of all types, ranging from heavy bombers to
air-sea rescue planes.

U.S. troops embark in landing craft for one of the early D-Day rehearsals. Later they would progress to cross-decking from transport vessels to landing craft.

while the 3rd Infantry Division had not seen combat since France in 1940. The 3rd Canadian Division had been in Britain since arriving from Canada in July 1941. Of the airborne divisions, the US 82nd had served in North Africa and Sicily, but the 101st was without combat experience, as was the British 6th Airborne Division. Those divisions which had not seen recent combat did, however, have some veterans posted in. Now, while the ground forces intensified their training, other elements of the Overlord plan were already being put into effect.

The Allies knew full well that the Germans were expecting them to launch a cross-Channel assault at some time and that the options of where it would strike were limited. It was also impossible to hide the growing activity in ports along the English South Coast as the shipping required for Overlord was gathered. What the Allies could do, however, was to deceive the Germans. Under the codename of Bodyguard an elaborate deception plan had been drawn up. It had two aims. The first was to present threats elsewhere to dissuade the Germans from bringing in reinforcements from other theatres of war. The other was to make the Germans believe that the main assault would be in the Pas-

de-Calais. There were three essential elements to Bodyguard. Fortitude North aimed to tie down the sizeable German forces in Norway through presenting the threat of a diversionary attack, which would be followed by an assault on the Pas-de-Calais in July 1944. One of the key elements was the establishment of a fictional British Fourth Army in Scotland, with its own radio communications. Fortitude South was implemented somewhat later and concentrated on the Pas-de-Calais. It was based on the mythical 1st US Army Group (FUSAG) based in south-east England. The flamboyant General George S. Patton, who was already regarded as one of the most thrusting Allied commanders, was placed in charge in the hope that the Germans would be sure that he would be involved in any major assault. Once the Normandy landings had taken place, Fortitude South would be maintained to convince the Germans that they were a diversion and that the main landing was still to come. Finally, there was Zeppelin, which aimed to tie down German troops in the Balkans. To aid the deception, much use was made of German agents, whom the British had captured and turned. Under what was called the Double Cross system, they transmitted false information back to Germany.

In the event, while the Germans did not reinforce from Norway or the Balkans, they only really believed Fortitude South.

The other part of Overlord which was initiated early was the air campaign. The first task of the AEAF was to fatally weaken the Luftwaffe in France and the Low Countries. On 20 February 1944, the Allied air forces began a systematic assault on the Luftwaffe. The heavy bombers of the Eighth Air Force in Britain and the Fifteenth Air Force in Italy launched massive attacks on German aircraft factories in southern Germany, while the AEAF concentrated on airfields. Big Week, as it became known, struck a crippling blow from which the Luftwaffe never really recovered. However, what the Allied air forces should do next was the subject of a fierce debate. Eisenhower supported a plan conceived by a British scientist, Solly Zuckerman. Based on experience in Italy, he proposed a campaign against communications, with the idea of destroying road and railway communications leading into Normandy so that the Germans could not deploy their reserves. For this to be effective, Eisenhower needed the services of the Eighth Air Force and

RAF Bomber Command, which were not part of the AEAF or under his command. They were still pursuing the Pointblank strategy agreed at Casablanca and had very different ideas on how to proceed. The American view, as postulated by General Carl Spaatz, commanding the US Strategic Air Forces (USSAF), was that oil should be the prime target in that this would totally cripple the German war effort. Indeed, he began to concentrate on this target immediately on the conclusion of Big Week. Air Chief Marshal Sir Arthur ('Bomber') Harris, who was in charge of RAF Bomber Command, was convinced that morale held the key. If that of the German people could be broken by a continuation of the 'round the clock bombing' to which they were being subjected, there would be no need for an invasion. The Bomber Barons also resented the prospect of being

The Allied High Command for D-Day – Standing (left to right) General Omar Bradley (First U.S.Army), Admiral Sir Bertram Ramsay (Naval Commander), Air Chief Marshal Sir Trafford Leigh-Mallory (Air Commander), General Walter Bedell Smith (Chief-of-Staff). Sitting (left to right) Air Chief Marshal Sir Arthur Tedder (Deputy Supreme Commander), General Dwight Eisenhower (Supreme Allied Commander), General Sir Bernard Montgomery (21st Army Group).

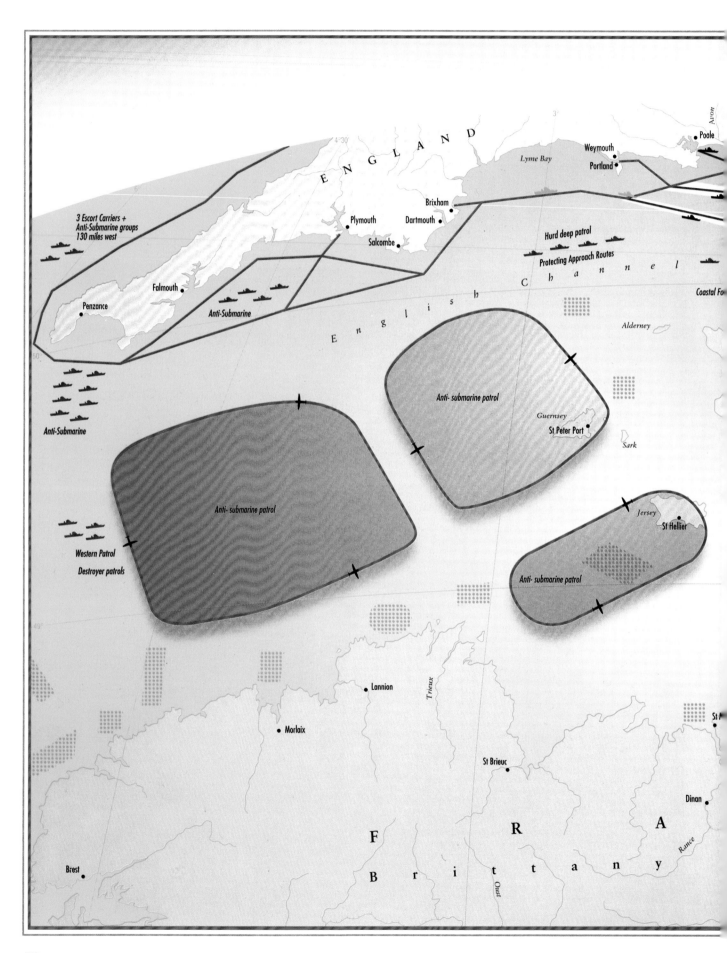

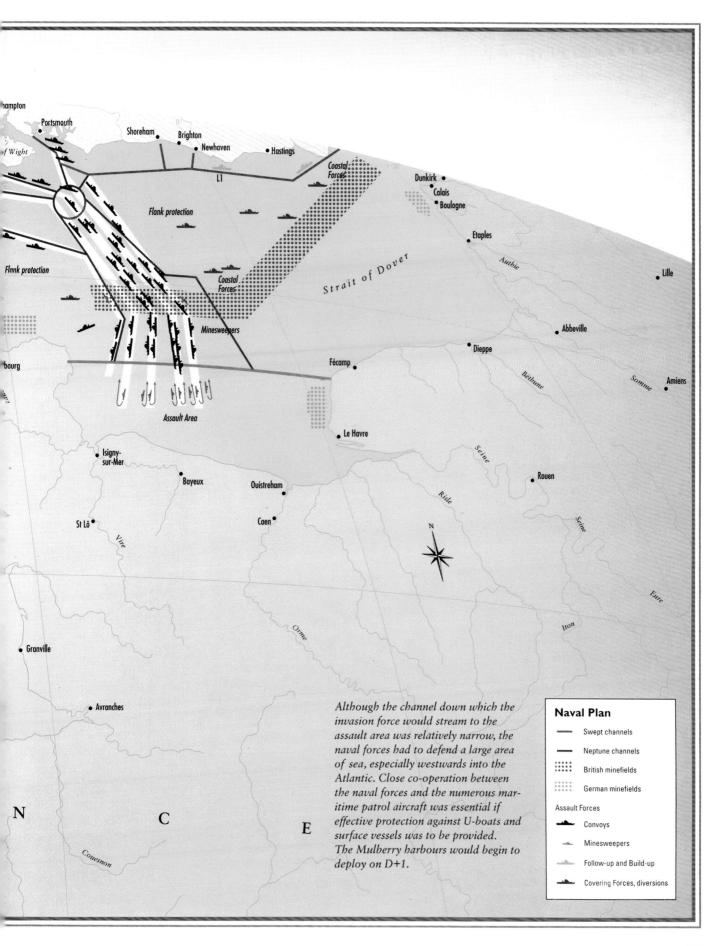

hampton

Portsmouth

Shoreham

Brighton

Newhaven

Hastings

of Wight

Coastal Forces

L1

Flank protection

Dunkirk

Calais

Boulogne

Etaples

Flank protection

Coastal Forces

Aubie

Lille

Strait of Dover

Minesweepers

Abbeville

bourg

Fécamp

Dieppe

Béthune

Somme

Amiens

Assault Area

Le Havre

Isigny-sur-Mer

Seine

Bayeux

Ouistreham

Rouen

St Lô

Caen

Risle

Seine

Vire

N

Eure

Granville

Orme

Iton

Avranches

N   C   E

Couesnon

Although the channel down which the invasion force would stream to the assault area was relatively narrow, the naval forces had to defend a large area of sea, especially westwards into the Atlantic. Close co-operation between the naval forces and the numerous maritime patrol aircraft was essential if effective protection against U-boats and surface vessels was to be provided. The Mulberry harbours would begin to deploy on D+1.

Naval Plan

— Swept channels

— Neptune channels

British minefields

German minefields

Assault Forces

Convoys

Minesweepers

Follow-up and Build-up

Covering Forces, diversions

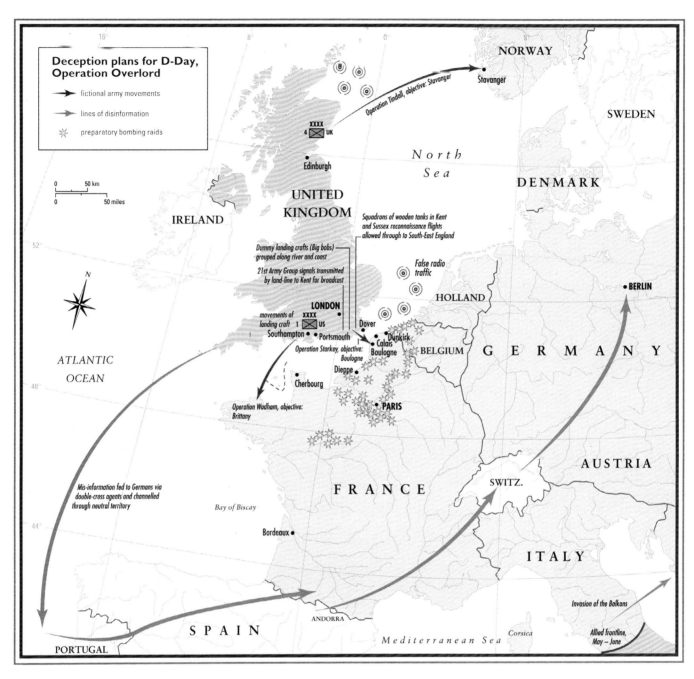

Deception plans for D-Day, Operation Overlord

→ fictional army movements

→ lines of disinformation

✳ preparatory bombing raids

Operation Tindall, objective: Stavanger

Squadrons of wooden tanks in Kent and Sussex reconnaissance flights allowed through to South-East England

Dummy landing crafts (Big bobs) grouped along river and coast

21st Army Group signals transmitted by land-line to Kent for broadcast

False radio traffic

movements of landing craft

Operation Starkey, objective: Boulogne

Operation Wadham, objective: Brittany

Mis-information fed to Germans via double-cross agents and channelled through neutral territory

Invasion of the Balkans

Allied frontline, May – June

Operation Bodyguard was multi-faceted and very elaborate. The key elements were the dummy US 1st Army Group and British Fourth Army. The part played by the preparatory air campaign, which dropped the major part of its bomb tonnage on areas outside Normandy, should also not be ignored. The double-cross agents, whom the British had turned, were also very valuable.

put under the control of Leigh-Mallory.

Eisenhower believed that campaigns against oil and morale would take too long to achieve a significant effect and his Deputy, Tedder, supported him. The command problem was overcome by Tedder personally conducting the Air Plan, but Spaatz and Harris were still resistant to the Transportation plan. Eisenhower became so frustrated

that he threatened to resign. The crunch came at a meeting held on 25 March. Eisenhower stuck to his guns and won the day. The strategic air forces were placed under his control from 14 April and the Transportation plan was put into effect. In support of Fortitude, for every bomb that was dropped in the Normandy area, and this included attacks on coastal batteries and airfields, two were dropped outside it.

While the air debate continued, the question of obtaining sufficient amphibious lift for Overlord remained a problem. The stalemate at Anzio continued and Anvil remained in being. Eisenhower realized that Anvil could not be mounted simultaneously with Overlord and that it should be postponed. This was especially since Wilson, whose forces were still unable to break through the Gustav Line in Italy, warned that a break-out from Anzio was unlikely before mid-May and he wanted to keep his LSTs. Eventually, the Combined Chiefs of Staff agreed to the postponement of Anvil and that LSTs be sent back to Britain from the Mediterranean. They would, however, be replaced by new LSTs from the United States, where production had significantly increased during the winter. This would enable Wilson to capture Rome by the time D-Day took place. Even so, some of the LSTs did not return to Britain until just three weeks before the Normandy landings.

Another race against time involved technology. The post-Dieppe decision that the landings would have to be on open beaches led to the need to develop some form of artificial port to enable reinforcements, supplies, and heavy equipment to be landed.

Work began in Britain in 1943 to develop such a floating harbour. The concept for what eventually became known as the Mulberries was agreed at the Quebec Conference. Two were to be constructed. Mulberry A would support the US beaches and have a capacity of unloading 5,000 tons per day while Mulberry B, with a 7,000-ton capacity, would operate in the British sector. In essence, they consisted of breakwaters, with piers within them. Construction did not begin until December 1943. Massive amounts of concrete and steel were required, as well as a very large work force. The operation involved firms all over Britain. The various elements were then towed to South Coast ports, where they were sunk to conceal them from German air reconnaissance. Getting them positioned in time was one of Admiral Ramsay's greatest concerns, but it was done. Another means of keeping the Allies supplied once they were ashore was to be the laying of an oil pipeline in the English Channel. Development work on PLUTO (PipeLine Under The Ocean) had been initiated by the British Combined Operations in 1942. A pumping station was established on the Isle of Wight and trawlers towing huge drums of the flexible piping would then lay it

Constructing one of the many massive concrete caissons which provided the foundations for the Mulberry harbours.

German soldiers preparing beach obstacles run for cover as low-flying Allied photograph reconnaissance aircraft passes over. The obstacles shown were designed to impale landing craft and would be hidden at high tide. Some had explosive devices attached.

between here and Cherbourg, once that port had been captured.

The spectre of the beached and knocked-out Churchill tanks at Dieppe prompted the development of specialized types of armoured vehicle. At the forefront of these was the Duplex Drive (DD) swimming tank. This came in the form of a kit consisting of a collapsible canvas screen to give the tank buoyancy and a propeller system, which was driven off the tank's gearbox. It enabled the vehicle to swim at four knots and all the tanks in the initial assault would use this means of getting onto the beaches rather than being landed directly from landing craft. The British also developed other types – flail tanks for clearing mines, bridge-laying tanks, flamethrower tanks, tanks mounting a spigot mortar for attacking concrete blockhouses, and others which would lay track over boggy ground. Known affectionately as the Funnies, they were concentrated in the British 79th Armoured Division.

To give the troops fire support as they were closing into the beaches, the Landing Craft Support (LCS) had been developed. A few, but by no means enough, were used at Dieppe. There were Landing Craft Guns (LCG) each armed with two 4.7-inch guns and LCT (R), which fired salvoes of 5-inch rockets, and, to provide protection against air attack, the Landing Craft Flak (LCF). These would escort the landing waves into the shore, while the warships remained offshore. Each of the five main landing beaches had its own dedicated naval task force, which included a command ship. The warships involved ranged from battleships down to gunboats. Minesweepers, too, played a vital part. First, they had to sweep the approaches to the beaches and then the lanes in which the naval bombardment forces would operate. It was important, too, to protect the flanks of landings, especially against the U-boat threat. To this end, they were covered by anti-submarine vessels and aircraft. All in all, just under 6,500 vessels of all types would be involved.

As April 1944 progressed, operations orders, some running into hundreds of pages, were issued. Nothing could be left to chance and every detail had to be covered. But, for security reasons, the assaulting forces were not informed of their precise objectives. Indeed, security was a constant worry and there were a number of breaches. One scare, which proved to be mere coincidence, was the appearance of many of the Overlord codewords as answers to a *Daily Telegraph* crossword puzzle. There were briefcases with secret documents left unattended, and individuals in the know who let slip indiscreet remarks in public. The biggest scare of all came on the night 27/28 April, when German E-boats got among the amphibious shipping carrying elements of the US 4th Infantry Division during a landing exercise at Slapton Sands on the South Devon coast. Three LSTs were sunk and other vessels damaged, and some 640 soldiers and sailors lost their lives. Ten of them were officers who were cleared to highest security level, Bigot, and there were fears, until their bodies were found, that some might have been captured. As it was, a veil of secrecy was drawn over the incident and it was not until well after the war that the next-of-kin of those who perished learned what had happened. The three torpedoed LSTs represented the only reserve available for Overlord and replacements had to be hurriedly sent from the Mediterranean, such was still the pressure on amphibious shipping.

Another security aspect concerned what to tell the Governments-in-Exile in Britain, in particular de Gaulle and his Free French. His HQ was notoriously insecure and there were fears that the cat would be out of the bag if he was told too early. It was therefore decided to tell de Gaulle only on the very eve of launching Overlord.

Towards the end of April, Montgomery and Ramsay moved to their HQ for Overlord at Southwick House, Portsmouth, while Eisenhower remained at SHAEF, which was located, since March, at Bushey Park close to the Thames on the western outskirts of London. During 3–8 May Ramsay conducted Exercise Fabius, the final invasion exercise, with all five naval task forces being involved. A week later, on 15 May, Eisenhower held a final conference at St Paul's School, London. Both King George VI and Churchill were present and each commander presented his final plan. Montgomery, in particular, spoke with great confidence. He spoke of getting well inland on the first day and would then 'crack about and force the battle to swing our way'. Churchill, who had been pessimistic over the chances of success, and he was by no means alone, was filled with a sense of optimism. Indeed, he wanted to set sail with the invasion force and watch the naval bombardment. It was only by enlisting the help of the King that he was eventually persuaded against this. The only key item not revealed at the conference was the actual date for D-Day, for Eisenhower had still to decide on this and would not do so for another week.

In the meantime, there were a number of further scares. On the night 17/18 May a beach reconnaissance team was captured by the Germans. Luckily, it was in the Pas-de-Calais and so helped further Fortitude South. There were difficulties in bringing the Mulberry parts back to the surface because of pumping equipment inadequacies. A US naval officer mentioned the place and rough date of the invasion and was promptly sent Stateside. Twelve copies of a SHAEF advance communiqué announcing the invasion blew out of a window in the War Office. Eleven were quickly located and the twelfth was handed over to a sentry on Horse Guards Parade by a civilian who was apparently wearing thick glasses. These incidents, and others like them, were wearing on the nerves of those at the very top of the Overlord tree.

As for D-Day itself, it had to fit in with a number of requirements, all weather-related. The air forces wanted a moonlit night so that they could be confident of landing the paratroops and gliders in the right place. The navies wanted to cross the Channel under cover of darkness and to open the bombardment in daylight so that target identification would be easier. The armies wanted to land at low tide and have a full day to consolidate the beachheads. There were just two periods in June in which these conditions were present, one beginning on the 4th and the other later in the month. Eisenhower opted for the night 4/5 June for the mounting of Overlord so as to give himself the maximum possible leeway and informed his subordinate commanders on 23 May that D-Day itself, when the Allies set foot on French soil, would be 5 June.

Now began the move of the ground assault forces to their ports of embarkation. The roads of southern England were clogged with military convoys, all travelling to carefully planned march schedules. The troops moved into staging camps, which were sealed from the outside world. Here they went about their final preparations and briefings in which they were finally told their objectives. In the skies above, the final phase of the preliminary air campaign began. On 31 May, the assembly of the naval task forces started and vessels began to be loaded. That night, ten sonic underwater buoys were laid at the entrances to the lanes which the naval task forces would use to cross the Channel. This was to guide the minesweepers. The BBC

Sherman tanks being loaded on board an LST. They were reversed into the ship so that they would arrive on the beach with their thicker frontal armour to the fore.

began to send coded messages to alert the French Resistance. All seemed to be going generally to plan, but one crucial factor remained a concern.

From 29 May onwards, Eisenhower ordered his chief meteorologist, Group Captain J. M. Stagg, to hold a daily weather briefing for himself and his senior commanders. At the time, there was a hot spell over England, but there were growing doubts that it would hold up. Stagg himself had daily conferences with three agencies, the Admiralty in London, the British Central Forecasting Office at Dunstable in Bedfordshire, and the USAAF weather centre at Teddington on the Thames west of London. From 1 June they were anxiously watching a ridge of high pressure over the Atlantic, which they hoped would reach the British Isles. Signs grew that it was beginning to slip south. Dunstable was gloomy, while Widewing put a more optimistic gloss on its forecasts. The Admiralty took a middle position, but on 3 June began to support the Dunstable view that a depression was about to arrive over the English Channel. Stagg also took the Dunstable view and at 4.15am on 4 June passed this

to Eisenhower, who had established himself at Portsmouth two days earlier. At the time, though, the weather was still bright and clear and the assault troops were embarking. At 9.30pm that evening Stagg gave out another forecast. This time he was certain that 5 June would be stormy, with a low cloud base, the very worst conditions. Eisenhower decided to sleep on it, but did go so far as to warn the US Navy carrying the troops to Utah and Omaha, since they had the furthest to go. Eisenhower and his subordinates had another session with Stagg at 4.30am the following morning. By this time the weather was beginning to deteriorate. Stagg said that sea conditions were slightly better, but the cloud base would remain low. Eisenhower turned to his subordinates. Montgomery was all for continuing, Tedder and Leigh-Mallory argued for a postponement, while Ramsay would not commit himself. Eisenhower, conscious that he had only one chance to launch Overlord, decided on a 24-hour postponement and the message was sent out. The US naval task forces and other vessels already at sea returned to port. The only vessels which could not were two British midget submarines deployed off the British landing beaches to act as navigational beacons. They were forced to continue to remain submerged in a sea that grew ever more unruly.

The question that now haunted Eisenhower and, indeed, everyone else involved, was would the weather improve. If it did not, he could not keep the troops cooped up in their ships until the next favourable day, which was 19 June, and to disembark them would have a serious effect on morale. There was also the fear that a delay might compromise the whole operation. On the evening of 4 June, Eisenhower and his commanders met Stagg again at Southwick House. He reported that there would be a 36-hour break in the weather. The rain would stop, the winds would moderate, but cloud would still be present. Montgomery was again for proceeding, Leigh-Mallory and Tedder thought that air operations would be hampered, and Ramsay told Eisenhower that he must tell the US naval task forces one way or the other within the next half hour. If they sailed again and were recalled, it would take them 48 hours to turn round, which would take the invasion outside the window for the right conditions. The ultimate decision rested with Eisenhower. At 9.45 pm he said: 'I am quite positive that the order must be given.' D-Day was on for 6 June and the ships began to sail.

US Paratroopers prepare to board their aircraft on the evening of 5 June.

The assault divisions moved into their concentration areas close to the South Coast in the weeks before D-Day. Apart from the US 29th Division, which was the follow-up division for Omaha, the remainder were deployed from west to east in accordance with the position of their beaches. This avoided the danger of congestion and confusion caused by the various naval forces having to cross one another's paths. Reinforcing formations would move into these concentration areas once they had been vacated by the assault divisions.

Concentration of Allied forces in the United Kingdom

First line of troops

Second line of troops

Third line or reserves

Areas of restricted access

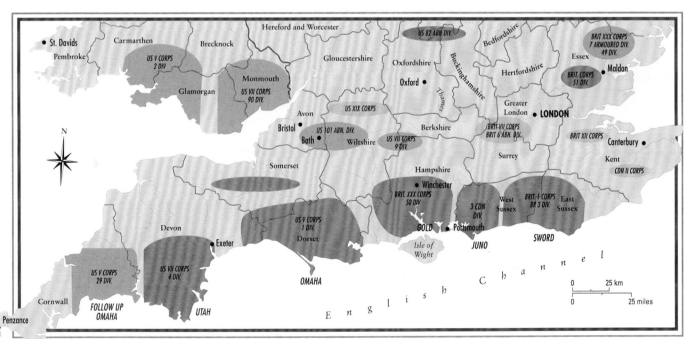

2

Fortress Europe

When, in autumn 1940, Hitler decided to abandon the idea of invading Britain and turn on Stalin's Russia, he went over to the defensive in the West. France itself had been split into two as a result of the June 1940 Armistice. The northern half came under German military government. The south was allowed a degree of autonomy under the government of Marshal Philippe Pétain, although the coastal regions remained under Italian (the Mediterranean coast) or German control. The Luftwaffe presence in France remained strong so as to pursue its bombing campaign against Britain, while the Kriegsmarine now deployed to France, notably a significant part of its U-boat arm, which took advantage of the French Atlantic ports. In contrast, the bulk of the ground

A cross-section of a typical gun emplacement on the Atlantic Wall, which gives an indication of the large amount of concrete used. The gun in this case is a 50mm coastal gun.

forces which had taken part in the victorious summer 1940 campaign were redeployed to prepare for the attack on Russia. The rump that remained was formed into Army Group D under the elderly Field Marshal Erwin von Witzleben, who was also made Commander-in-Chief West. His divisions were generally low grade and were seen as little more than a police force.

Along the coasts work gradually began to emplace coastal batteries. These had initially been deployed to protect Axis shipping in the English Channel during what was to have been Operation Sealion and to bombard the English coast. Fixed concrete emplacements began to be

constructed in September 1940, but priority was given to Norway, reflecting Hitler's desire to secure his northern flank for the invasion of Russia. The cross-Channel Commando raids showed how vulnerable the French coast was and the St-Nazaire operation, in particular, concerned Hitler. Priority was therefore given to the protection of ports and to the construction of concrete pens to protect the U-boats from air attack.

Not until 1942 did the creation of what became known as the Atlantic Wall begin in earnest. Many of the ports were personally designated Festungen, or fortresses, by Hitler in the belief that if and when invasion came it would have to be close to a port. He amplified his vision in a directive issued in August 1942, which called for the establishment of a network of concrete strongpoints. These would each be manned by up to seventy men armed with machine guns and anti-tank weapons. In all, there were to be 15,000 of these strongpoints, although Fritz Todt, in charge of the Reich labour organization, doubted whether he could complete more than 6,000 by spring 1943. As 1943 wore on further problems arose. Todt had to

(Right) This map shows the position before Hitler's Directive No. 51 of 3 November 1943 took effect. Prior to this, the biggest weakness that von Rundstedt was suffering was a shortage of mobile formations, with only 21st Panzer Division permanently assigned to him. Many of his other divisions were also low grade.

German machine gun post on the Atlantic Wall.

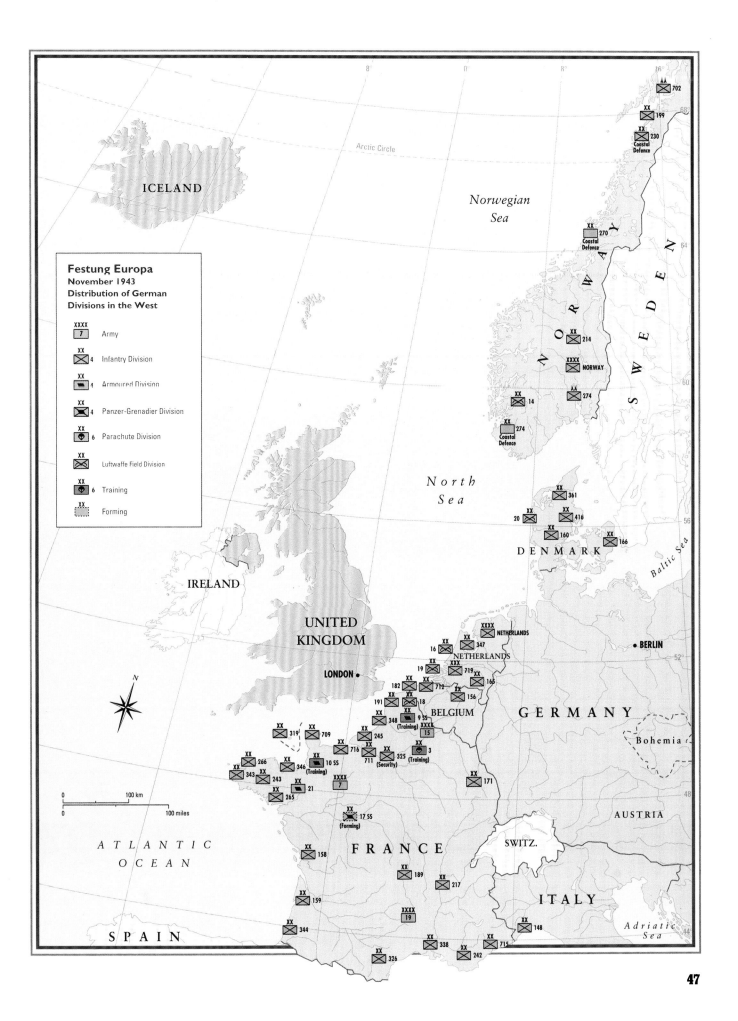

Festung Europa
November 1943
Distribution of German
Divisions in the West

XXXX 7	Army
XX 4	Infantry Division
XX 4	Armoured Division
XX 4	Panzer-Grenadier Division
XX 6	Parachute Division
XX	Luftwaffe Field Division
XX 6	Training
XX	Forming

ICELAND

Norwegian Sea

Arctic Circle

NORWAY

SWEDEN

702
199
230 Coastal Defence
270 Coastal Defence
214
NORWAY
14
274
274 Coastal Defence

North Sea

361
20
416
160
166

DENMARK

Baltic Sea

IRELAND

UNITED KINGDOM

LONDON

• BERLIN

GERMANY

NETHERLANDS
347
16
NETHERLANDS
19
719
712 165
182
156
191 18
348
9 SS (Training)
BELGIUM
15
319 709
245
3 (Training)
716
266 346 711 (Security) 325
10 SS (Training)
343 243 21
7
265
171

Bohemia

17 SS (Forming)

AUSTRIA

SWITZ.

158

FRANCE

189
217

ITALY

159
19
148

Adriatic Sea

SPAIN

344
338
715
242
326

0   100 km
0   100 miles

N

ATLANTIC OCEAN

A sentry guarding a 105mm coastal gun. The armament used in the Atlantic Wall ranged from 25mm anti-tank weapons to massive 305mm guns.

of command, however, was by no means clear-cut. Von Rundstedt may have been the theatre commander, but he was actually only responsible for coast defence and the Navy and Luftwaffe were only answerable to him in this respect. Internal security came under the military governors of France and Belgium and Luftwaffe General Christiansen in the Netherlands and they answered directly to Hitler's supreme headquarters, the Oberkommando der Wehrmacht (OKW). There was also a separate chain of command for the SS police. Consequently, in many ways von Rundstedt had his hands tied.

Von Rundstedt's forces became more stretched in November 1942. In response to the French scuttling their fleet at Toulon, Hitler ordered the military occupation of Vichy France. But what concerned von Rundstedt most was a lack of mobile reserves. He became convinced that the only way to defeat an amphibious assault was on the beaches themselves. Reserves which could be quickly deployed were essential. During the last half of 1942 and in 1943 he did receive Panzer and Panzer Grenadier divisions, but these were either newly formed or mere skeletons from the Eastern Front. The former needed training, while the latter, once they had been brought back up to strength, were redeployed to other theatres of war. Indeed, by autumn 1943 von Rundstedt was left with just three Panzer Grenadier divisions as a mobile reserve, one of which was entirely untrained.

divert some of the labour working on the Atlantic Wall to repair bomb damage in Germany and the decision to begin fortifying the Mediterranean coast after the Allied invasion of Sicily further dissipated the effort.

In March 1942, von Witzleben fell sick and was replaced by Gerd von Rundstedt, the doyen of the Prussian officer corps. By this time, his forces had been increased from a low of eighteen divisions during the winter 1940–41 to twenty-five, which were organized in three armies. First Army covered the coastal region of south-west France, while the north-west, from the River Loire to Caen, came under Seventh Army. Finally, Fifteenth Army was responsible for the coast from Caen to the Belgian port of Zeebrugge. The Dutch coast, which also came under von Rundstedt, was the responsibility of the military commander in the Netherlands, a Luftwaffe general. The chain

The most significant improvement since November 1943, apart from strengthening the physical defences of the Atlantic Wall, was the dramatic increase in the number of panzer divisions. Hitler's decision to place four of them under direct control as OKW reserve would prove a costly error. The Static divisions were designated such, because they had very limited transport and were not capable of quick redeployment.

Festung Europa, German Defences in the West
June 1944

⬭	Armoured Reserves: in OKW Reserve
– – –	Army boundaries
•••••	Army Group boundaries
——	Rear boundary of the OB West

XX ⊠	Field Infantry Division
XX ◼	Panzer Division
XX ◉	Parachute Division
XX ▲	Static Division
XX ◣	Refitting
XX ⊠	Training
XX ⊠	Luftwaffe Infantry Division

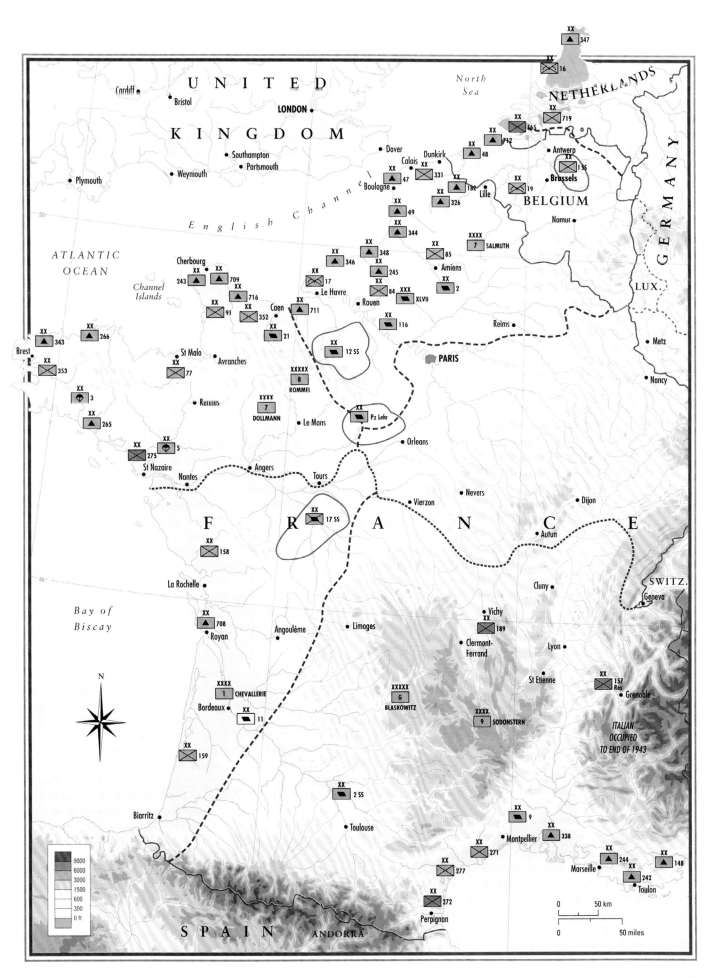

Von Runstedt's growing concern, set against the backdrop of a now inevitable Allied invasion of Western Europe, prompted him to present a survey on the defences in his theatre to Hitler. He pointed out that he had some 1,600 miles of coast to defend and there was no way in which a solid barrier could be created. As it was, he could provide little more than a screen of troops to cover the Atlantic coast, that is if he was to develop any form of effective defence on the more vulnerable Channel coast. While the Atlantic Wall was "indispensable and valuable for battle as well as propaganda", an invasion could only be defeated through the use of "a mobile and armoured reserve", which he did not have. Von Rundstedt's report had the desired effect. On 3 November 1943, less than a week after he submitted it, Hitler issued Directive No 51.

Sowing 'dragon's teeth'. These concrete obstacles were used to prevent tanks from getting off the beach.

It accepted that everywhere German forces were now on the defensive: "The danger in the East remains, but a greater danger now appears in the West; an Anglo-Saxon landing!" To this end, the West would be reinforced, especially with mobile forces, anti-tank weapons, and artillery. Two days later, he ordered Field Marshal Erwin Rommel to carry out an inspection tour of the defences.

In British and, to a lesser degree, American eyes, Rommel was an outstanding general who had demonstrated a flair in North Africa, which had earned him the name 'the Desert Fox'. He had latterly been given command of Army Group B, with responsibility for the defence of northern Italy. However, Albert von Kesselring, the German theatre commander had decided that he would defend the whole of Italy and not just the north and so Rommel found himself with a headquarters, but with no role to play. Now he went racing round the coasts of France and the Low Countries, while von Rundstedt wondered whether he had been sent to replace him as commander-in-chief. His own view of Rommel reflected that of many other senior German officers, namely that he had won his spurs in a mere sideshow and had not experienced the 'real war' on the Eastern Front. Von Rundstedt respected Rommel's bravery and considered him a good operational commander, but not fitted for the higher levels of command. Indeed, he called Rommel 'Field Marshal Cub'. But the Desert Fox had experienced the growing matériel power of the Anglo-US alliance at first hand and had developed a healthy respect for it.

Von Rundstedt did not actually meet Rommel until 19 December 1943, at the conclusion of Rommel's tour of inspection. Von Rundstedt stressed his lack of a decent reserve and Rommel appears to have agreed that the situation appeared grim. Eight days later, Rommel presented his report to C-in-C West. He believed that the most likely landings areas were the Pas-de-Calais and the area between Boulogne and the River Somme. He foresaw the Allies enjoying air superiority, which meant that it would be difficult to deploy the reserves if they were too far inland. Furthermore, the Atlantic Wall, as it stood, would not stand up to the might of the Allied air and sea bombardment and, once the Allies had secured beachheads, it would be very difficult to drive them back into the sea.

They must therefore be defeated on the beaches, which was in line with von Rundstedt's thinking. Rommel appeared to be reasonably satisfied with the Pas-de-Calais sector and wanted to concentrate on strengthening the Boulogne-Somme coast, especially through laying extensive minefields and beach obstacles. He also wanted to deploy two of the reserve divisions in this sector. Rommel's report was generally accepted by Hitler and he was placed in charge of the coast from the Netherlands to the mouth of the River Loire, but under von Rundstedt's overall command. He now set in train a high-pressure programme to strengthen the defences, which soon began to show results.

By March 1944 von Rundstedt had eight Panzer and two Panzer Grenadier divisions under his command. These were formed into Panzer Group West under the command of Geyr von Schweppenburg. At the same time, OKW was looking again at the likely Allied landing areas. They concluded that Normandy was also a possibility and that there could be feints, both on the Atlantic and Mediterranean coasts. Von Schweppenburg saw this estimate as a strong reason for keeping the armour concentrated so that it could strike in any direction. Rommel, however, was still insistent that it be deployed close to the coasts, which, of course, meant dissipating it. Von Rundstedt tried to calm the troubled waters with a compromise. He allocated three divisions to Army Group B and the same number to Army Group G, which covered the Atlantic coast south of the Loire and the Mediterranean. The remaining four would be retained by Panzer Group West. This did not really satisfy either and at the end of April Hitler decided that Panzer Group West was not to be deployed without his permission. Thus, von Rundstedt had lost all control of his mobile divisions. This would have a significant bearing on what actually happened on D-Day.

On 8 May 1944, von Rundstedt made another appreciation of the situation. He was well aware of the growing intensity of the Allied air campaign and intelligence reports suggested that the invasion might well take place during the first half of May and that it could fall anywhere between the Scheldt and the tip of Brittany. He noted that the main Allied concentrations were in the Southampton-Portsmouth area and that their preparations were complete, which was still far from the case. He believed, however, that the most likely landing area would be along the Boulogne-Normandy coast. Once the danger period passed with no move from the enemy, von Rundstedt breathed a sigh of relief.

A growing distraction for von Rundstedt was the French Resistance, which was gathering strength. It had always been a major target for SOE, but, as in the other countries of Occupied Europe, it took time to create an effective network. One of the main problems was the number of Resistance organisations involved. Indeed, no fewer than six SOE sections were involved with France, ranging from F Section, perhaps the best known, which worked with the independents, RF Section, responsible for the Gaullists, who also had their own co-ordinating section in de Gaulle's headquarters in Britain, and the small EU/P Section, which handled Polish agents. There were also Socialist Resistance movements and, after Hitler's invasion of Russia, a Communist organization. However, it was F Section which took the lead as far as the British were concerned. Its first task was to establish Resistance networks, or 'circuits'. SOE agents usually operated in teams of three – an organizer, a radio operator and a courier. Many of the last-named were women, since they tended to attract less suspicion. In the early years, SOE found that it was easier to operate in Vichy France, rather than in the German-occupied north. Even so, the south had its dangers, notably from the paramilitary police force, the Milice. While F Section concentrated on those groups with no significant political affiliations, it also made efforts to co-ordinate with other networks, with varying success. One of the important aspects of SOE's job was to arrange for supplies of weapons, explosives and ammunition to be delivered to the Resistance. These were usually dropped by parachute.

Initially, the Resistance concentrated on making life difficult for the Germans through sabotage of French industry working for them, ambushes of vehicles and assassinations. It also published underground newspapers. But only a very small percentage of the French people were involved. Most understandably tried to get on with their lives as best they could. While some of Right Wing persuasion actively collaborated with the occupiers and were responsible for the betrayal of Resistance members, the majority had little option but to offer passive collaboration, especially when German troops were billeted in their homes. Yet, the fact that most people attempted to lead a normal life acted as a vital camouflage, without which the Resistance would have found it very much more difficult to operate.

In 1942, the Germans instituted compulsory labour service in Germany for young Frenchmen. To avoid this, many fled to the forested and hilly hinterland of southern France. This came to the attention of the SOE and its US counterpart, the Office of Strategic Services (OSS), and arms supplies were arranged for the Maquis, as these groups were known, from the Corsican brushwood which had traditionally hidden resisters. It was clear, however, that much closer co-operation was needed for the Resistance to become truly effective. De Gaulle had sent his own emissary, Jean Moulin, to France at the beginning of 1942 to effect this, but it took him nearly eighteen months to form the Conseil National de la Resistance (CNR). This had representatives of all the main Resistance groups and was directed by de Gaulle from London. Shortly afterwards, Moulin was betrayed by a fellow agent under torture by the Gestapo and was executed.

The establishment of the CNR was, however, timely. The COSSAC plan for the invasion of France envisaged a preliminary phase designed to wear the Germans down. Besides air and sea action, propaganda, political and economic pressure, and sabotage were to be employed. The French Resistance had a valuable part to play in this and in autumn 1943 COSSAC began to take over SOE and OSS operations. The emphasis was on sending back information on German deployments, but the pattern of sabotage and ambushes continued, as did assassinations. Indeed, von Rundstedt himself noted that by the end of 1943 there was a serious problem with communications between northern and southern France, because of ambushes, and that at times HQ Army Group G at Toulouse was virtually cut off. In the north of the country, especially near the coastal areas, life for the Resistance was much more difficult. The coasts themselves were barred to civilians without special permits and there was also a preponderance of German troops. Furthermore, the Gestapo was steadily penetrating many of the networks and arresting key personnel. So seri-

ous did this become that on 18 February 1944 the RAF mounted a daring and very skilful low-level Mosquito raid on the prison at Amiens, which held a number of Resistance members, enabling a number of them to escape.

February 1944 also saw the formation by de Gaulle of the Force Françaises d'Intérieur (FFI) under General Marie Pierre Koenig, hero of the Free French stand against Rommel at Bir Hacheim in June 1942. This embraced all the Resistance movements, although some Communist groups remained outside it. Initially, it consisted of just 30,000 men, including the Maquis, but was to rise to over 200,000 by D-Day. The FFI was to play a significant part in the Transportation Plan, but the Allies did not want it to strike early, but to wait until D-Day, when it could really hinder the deployment of the German mobile reserves. SOE and OSS agents briefed them on their targets, many of which were railway cuttings. To co-ordinate the efforts of the FFI and ensure that their operations tied in with the main campaign plan Jedburgh teams were formed. Each consisted of an American, a Briton, and a Frenchman, with a radio. They were to parachute into France from D-Day onwards and work with local Resistance units. Under the codename Cooney, the French Special Air Service (SAS) in Britain was to drop similar three-man teams into Brittany to operate with FFI elements, their initial object the destruction of railway lines into Normandy to prevent the deployment of reserves. There were also two-man intelligence-gathering teams known as Sussex. They were recruited from members of the French Army in North Africa and trained by MI6 and began to deploy in February 1944. Unlike the Jedburgh and Cooney teams, they did not wear uniform.

By the beginning of June 1944 all was ready as far as the French Resistance was concerned. All they needed to know was when D-Day would happen. On the evening of 1 June the BBC transmitted a series of coded messages, which told the Resistance that D-Day was imminent. On the German side, the picture was somewhat different. Von Rundstedt informed Hitler on 30 May that he did not think that invasion was likely in the very immediate future. OKW was not so sure and, on 2 June, asked von Rundstedt why he had not increased the alert state. He replied that this would only affect the French railways, whose rolling stock would be commandeered for moving reinforcements and matériel. This would merely aggravate discontent among the French. The storm that blew up in the Channel further convinced von Rundstedt that the threat was low, but German weather forecasting was unable to look far into the Atlantic and so did not detect the break in the weather which would allow D-Day to take place on 6 June. Consequently, C-in-C West allowed Rommel to depart on a short leave to Germany on 5 June, during which the Desert Fox intended to call on Hitler to demand further reinforcements. Von Rundstedt himself planned a four day inspection trip of part of the Cotentin peninsula. He would set out on 6 June.

Rommel left General Friedrich Dollmann in charge of Army Group B. He commanded the German Seventh Army, which was responsible for Normandy and Brittany.

would actually land. The 716th Division covered that north of Caen and had a frontage of 21 miles, far too wide, especially for a formation which consisted in general of older soldiers from Rhineland and Westphalia and most of whom had not experienced combat. General Wilhelm Richter, the commander, had constructed a series of strongpoints, but they were too far apart from one another and he lacked the troops to provide any depth to the defence. Facing Omaha Beach was the 352nd Division.

This had only been formed in November 1943, but most of its men had seen combat. It was not deployed to the coast until March 1944, however, and found itself working desperately to improve the defences along some 35 miles of coast. Finally, there was the 709th Division, which was very similar in character to the 716th and covered the coast from Utah up to Cherbourg. The one mobile division

A 155mm coastal defence gun in its massively built concrete emplacement. When firing out to sea these guns came under the command of Admiral Kranke but when engaging targets on the beaches they came under Army Command. This complication proved a serious weakness in German defensive operations.

In terms of the quality of its troops, it was significantly worse off than its eastern neighbour, Hans von Salmuth's Fifteenth Army, which covered the coast from east of Caen to Zeebrugge, since the High Command still believed that the Pas-de-Calais or the Boulogne-Somme sector were the most likely landing areas. Many of Dollmann's troops were either Ostruppen, Russians who had enlisted in the German Army to fight Communism, or Volksdeutsche, ethnic Germans from the enlarged Reich, and their fighting power was inferior to that of the ordinary German soldier. The only quality formation he had was the II Parachute Corps, which was Army Reserve. Three divisions held the portion of the coast on which the Allies

available was 21st Panzer Division. This was scattered on both sides of the River Orne, with its artillery on the coast, not a particularly satisfactory position. Its commander, General Edgar Feuchtinger, was a Nazi favourite, but an inefficient soldier, whom Rommel had been unable to sack because of his powerful political connections. Dollmann, like his masters, did not think that the invasion was about to be mounted and decided to hold a map exercise for many of his subordinate commanders at Rennes, which lies at the base of the Brittany peninsula. It was to begin on 6 June and most commanders travelled there the day before. As for Feuchtinger, he decided to spend the night 5/6 June with his mistress in Paris.

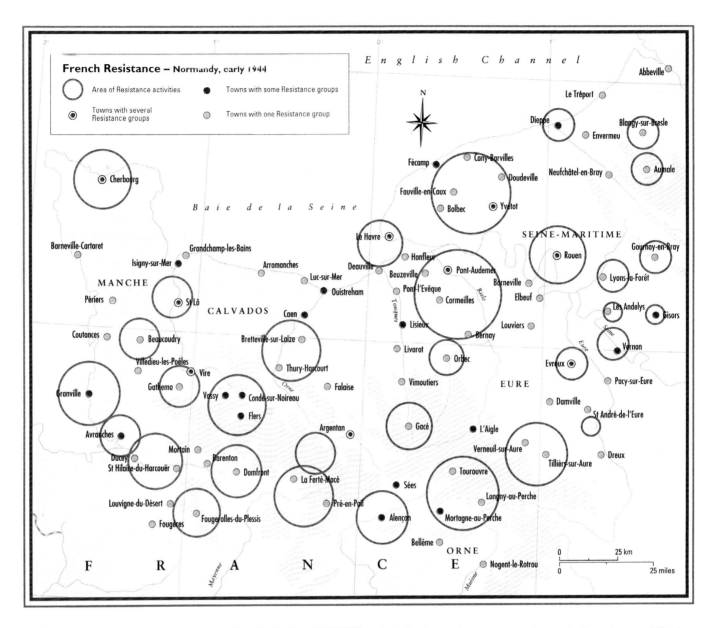

French Resistance – Normandy, early 1944

○ Area of Resistance activities   ● Towns with some Resistance groups

◉ Towns with several Resistance groups   ○ Towns with one Resistance group

E n g l i s h   C h a n n e l

Abbeville

Le Tréport

Dieppe   Blangy-sur-Bresle

Envermeu

Cherbourg   Fécamp   Cany-Barvilles   Neufchâtel-en-Bray   Aumale

Doudeville

Fauville-en-Caux   Yvetot

B a i e   d e   l a   S e i n e   Bolbec

SEINE-MARITIME

Le Havre   Gournay-en-Bray

Barneville-Cartaret   Grandchamp-les-Bains   Honfleur   Rouen

Isigny-sur-Mer   Arromanches   Deauville   Pont-Audemer   Lyons-la-Forêt

MANCHE   Luc-sur-Mer   Beuzeville   Barneville   Elbeuf   Les Andelys

Périers   St Lô   Ouistreham   Pont-l'Évêque   Gisors

CALVADOS   Caen   Cormeilles   Louviers   Vernon

Coutances   Beaucoudry   Bretteville-sur-Laize   Lisieux   Bernay

Villedieu-les-Poêles   Thury-Harcourt   Livarot   Orbec   Evreux   Pacy-sur-Eure

Granville   Vire   Falaise   Vimoutiers   **EURE**   Damville

Gathemo   Vassy   Condé-sur-Noireau   Gacé   St André-de-l'Eure

Avranches   Flers   L'Aigle   Verneuil-sur-Aure   Dreux

Ducey   Mortain   Argentan   Tilliers-sur-Aure

St Hilaire-du-Harcouër   Barenton   Tourouvre

Domfront   La Ferté-Macé   Longny-au-Perche

Louvigne-du-Dèsert   Sées   Mortagne-au-Perche

Fougères   Fougerolles-du-Plessis   Pré-en-Pail   Alençon

Bellême   **ORNE**

F   R   A   N   C   E   Nogent-le-Rotrou

0   25 km

0   25 miles

The Resistance in the Normandy area had much more difficulty in operating than that in the hinterland of central and southern France. Apart from the larger presence of German troops, there was very restricted access to the coastal areas. During the months before D-Day, the Resistance was more concerned with intelligence gathering and preparing to play its part in the attacks on road and rail communications leading into Normandy.

The results of a French Resistance sabotage attack.
The Resistance proved an increasing irritation for the Germans but it needed to be held in check in the weeks before D-Day so that its operations against communications could be tied into the overall allied plan.

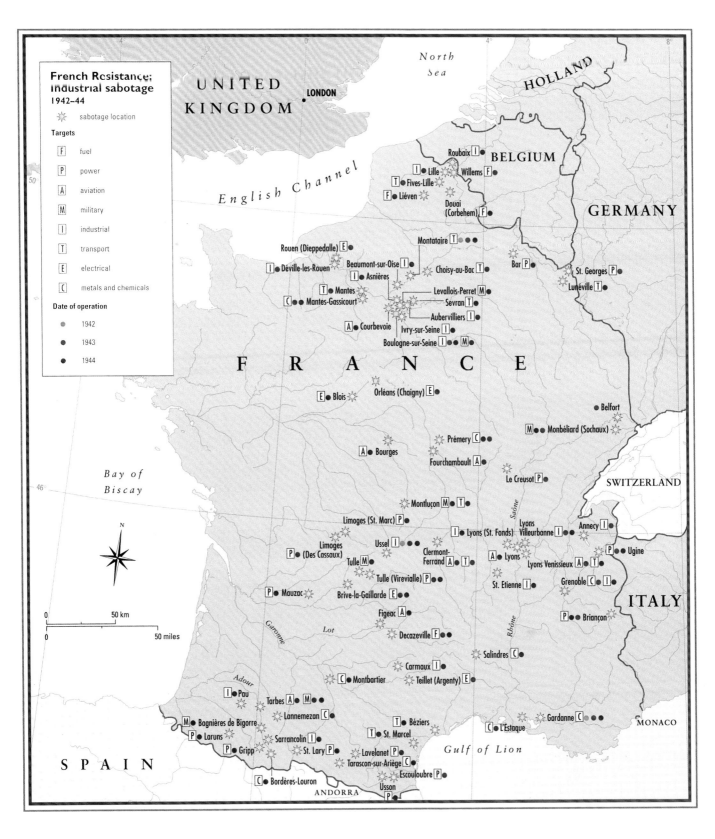

French Resistance; industrial sabotage 1942–44

❄ sabotage location

Targets

F	fuel
P	power
A	aviation
M	military
I	industrial
T	transport
E	electrical
C	metals and chemicals

Date of operation

● 1942
● 1943
● 1944

One of the major activities of the Resistance was the sabotage of French industry being used by the Germans to assist their war effort. From small beginnings in 1942, it intensified in 1943, once the Resistance began to become better organized. Much of it was very subtle and went unnoticed by the Germans. The Resistance also began to make direct attacks on German troops and communications, although these often resulted in dire reprisals against the local population.

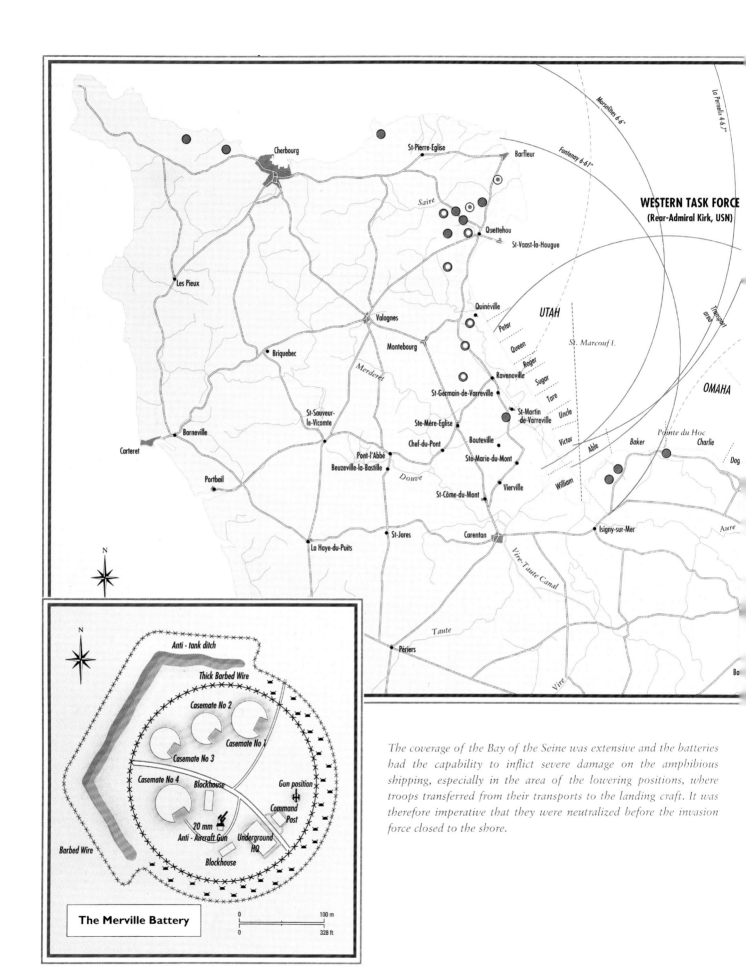

WESTERN TASK FORCE
(Rear-Admiral Kirk, USN)

Cherbourg

St-Pierre-Eglise

Barfleur

Saire

Quettehou

St-Vaast-la-Hougue

Les Pieux

Valognes

Quinéville

UTAH

Peter

Montebourg

Queen

St. Marcouf I.

Merderet

Briquebec

Roger

Ravenoville

Sugar

St-Germain-de-Varreville

Tare

St-Sauveur-
le-Vicomte

OMAHA

Ste-Mère-Eglise

St-Martin
de-Varreville

Uncle

Pointe du Hoc

Barneville

Chef-du-Pont

Bouteville

Victor

Able

Baker

Charlie

Carteret

Pont-l'Abbé

Ste-Marie-du-Mont

William

Beuzeville-la-Bastille

Dog

Portbail

Douve

St-Côme-du-Mont

Vierville

Isigny-sur-Mer

Aure

St-Jores

Carentan

La Haye-du-Puits

Vire-Taute Canal

Taute

Périers

Vire

Ba

The coverage of the Bay of the Seine was extensive and the batteries had the capability to inflict severe damage on the amphibious shipping, especially in the area of the lowering positions, where troops transferred from their transports to the landing craft. It was therefore imperative that they were neutralized before the invasion force closed to the shore.

Anti - tank ditch

Thick Barbed Wire

Casemate No 2

Casemate No 1

Casemate No 3

Casemate No 4

Blockhouse

Gun position

Command
Post

20 mm

Anti - Aircraft Gun

Underground
HQ

Barbed Wire

Blockhouse

The Merville Battery

100 m

0

328 ft

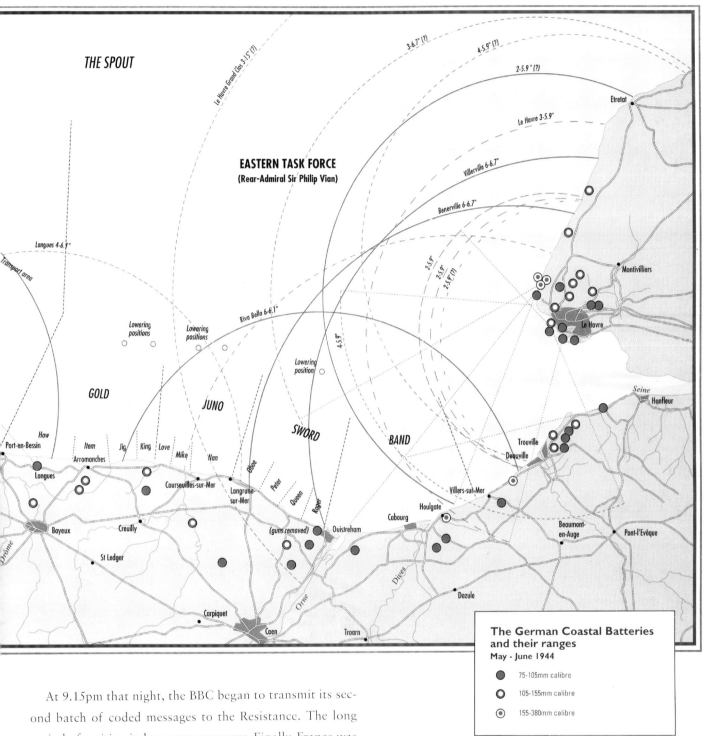

THE SPOUT

EASTERN TASK FORCE
(Rear-Admiral Sir Philip Vian)

Le Havre Grand Clos 3-15" (?)

3-6.7" (?)

4-5.9" (?)

2-5.9" (?)

Etretat

Le Havre 3-5.9"

Villerville 6-6.7"

Montivilliers

Benerville 6-6.7"

Langues 4-6.1"

Transport area

2-5.9"
2-5.9"
2-5.9" (?)

Le Havre

Riva Bella 6-6.1"

Lowering positions

Lowering positions

4-5.9"

Lowering positions

Seine

Honfleur

GOLD

Lowering position

JUNO

SWORD

BAND

Trouville

Deauville

How

Port-en-Bessin

Item

Arromanches

Jig | King | Love

Mike

Nan

Orne

Peter

Queen

Roger

Villers-sur-Mer

Houlgate

Cabourg

Longues

Courseuilles-sur-Mer

Langrune-sur-Mer

Ouistreham

Beaumont-en-Auge

Pont-l'Évêque

Creully

Bayeux

(guns removed)

St Ledger

Dives

Dozule

Drôme

Carpiquet

Orne

Caen

Troarn

**The German Coastal Batteries
and their ranges**
May - June 1944

● 75-105mm calibre
◎ 105-155mm calibre
◉ 155-380mm calibre

At 9.15pm that night, the BBC began to transmit its second batch of coded messages to the Resistance. The long period of waiting in hope was now over. Finally, France was about to be liberated and there was work to be done to help the Allies ashore. The German military intelligence, the Abwehr, noted that the broadcast went on considerably longer than the usual five to ten minutes and became suspicious. They alerted von Rundstedt's headquarters and he ordered a heightened state of alertness. He also warned that there might well be an increased level of sabotage. Sentries and gun crews on the coast stared out to sea through the gloom of the cloudy night, but all seemed quiet. Then came the sound of aircraft engines, but this was nothing different to what had happened over many past nights. At 1.30am von Rundstedt's headquarters received reports of parachute landings on the east side of the Cotentin peninsula. The state of alert was raised still further. But was it a mere raid or the beginning of the invasion?

D-Day

he first D-Day actions by the Allies were a series of airborne deception operations mounted by the RAF. Almost as soon as dusk had fallen on 5 June, Lancaster bombers of 617 Squadron, the Dambusters, were overflying the Strait of Dover in a precise elliptical course, dropping strips of aluminium foil known as Window. Below them sixteen small ships towed balloons fitted with reflectors. The idea was to present to the German coastal radars a picture of a convoy crossing towards the Pas-de-Calais. Stirlings of 218 Squadron were carrying out a similar exercise off Boulogne, while other Stirlings and Halifaxes dropped dummy parachutes and various devices to represent rifle fire in order to simulate airborne landings well to the south of the drop zones of the two US airborne divisions. These had a vital task, blocking the approaches to Utah beach.

A week before D-Day many of the Drop Zones (DZ) for the two US airborne divisions had to be changed because air reconnaissance had revealed that the Germans had placed obstacles on the original selections. Trafford Leigh-Mallory, the overall Allied air commander, was also very concerned

Apart from the landings on Juno and Sword, which were conducted by one corps, each of the other major landing beaches was the responsibility of a single corps. Utah and Omaha were under the overall direction of Bradley's US First Army, while the remainder came under Dempsey's Second British Army. Unlike the original COSSAC plan, this meant that there would be no major organizational changes once the Allies advanced inland.

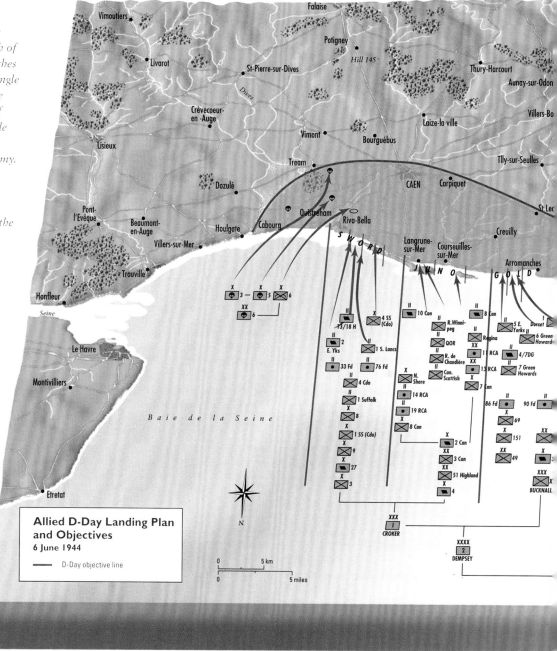

Allied D-Day Landing Plan and Objectives
6 June 1944

—— D-Day objective line

that adverse weather conditions might precipitate a disaster. A further problem was that there were insufficient aircraft to transport the two divisions in one lift, something which applied to the British 6th Airborne Division as well. The 82nd and 101st Airborne Divisions were preceded by pathfinder groups whose task was to drop thirty minutes before the main landings to mark the DZs with beacons. The aircraft would not fly direct to the DZs, but would execute a dog-leg over the Cotentin peninsula so that the approach would be from the south-east in order to assist surprise. This created problems

for the navigators. High winds did not help, and neither did the fact that many of the marking beacons did not function. Pilots also dropped the paratroops at far too great a height, partly because of the anti-aircraft fire from the ground. In consequence, the landings were very scattered. Apart from the 709th Division on the coast, there were two other German formations in the area. Opposing the airborne drops in the north was the 91st Airlanding Division, a recently raised formation, which had been deployed to the Cotentin peninsula just two weeks earlier. It was responsible for the defence of

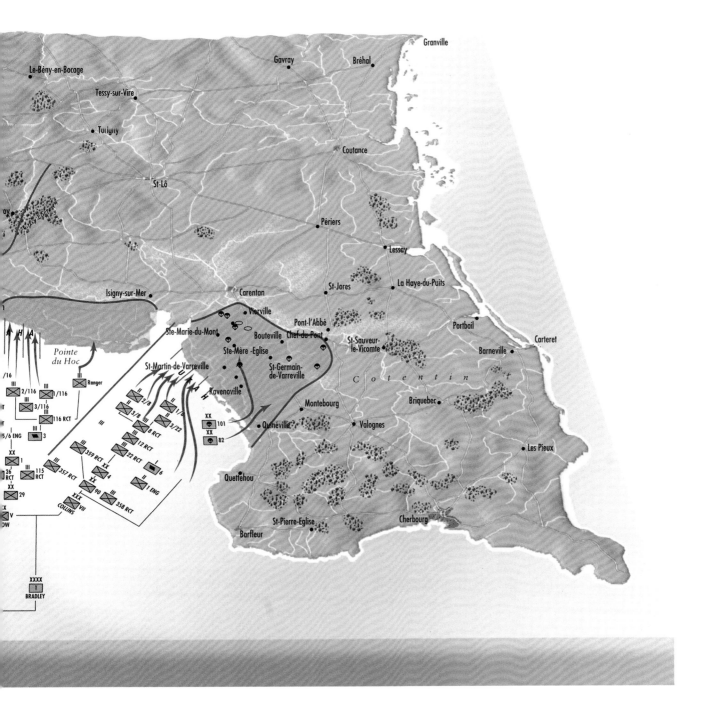

the southern part of the peninsula, from the west coast to the River Merderet. It had, however, carried out some training in anti-airborne operations. In the south, and based at Carentan was Colonel Freiherr Friedrich-August von der Heydte's 6th Parachute Regiment. This was part of 2nd Parachute Division, which was refitting in the Cologne area of Germany prior to moving to France.

The first to land, at 1.30am on 6 June, was Major-General Maxwell Taylor's 101st Airborne Division, the Screaming Eagles. Its task was to drop two miles behind Utah beach and secure the causeways leading to it. The landings were very scattered, with some sticks being dropped as much as ten miles from their DZ. It naturally took time for small groups of men to orientate themselves in the darkness. To help them identify one another, each man had been issued with a small metal object, which when pressed made a noise like a cricket. Inevitably, some of these fell into German hands and were used to trap the US paratroops. The 502nd Parachute Regiment was more fortunate than the other regiments in that it was able to gather sufficient men together to quickly secure St-Martin-de-Varreville and then move to the coast, where they discovered an unmanned coastal battery whose guns had been removed. After this, they established themselves astride the causeway at Audouville-la-Hubert. One small group attacked the village of Le Mézières, in which men of the neighbouring St-Martin coastal battery were billeted. Entering one house after another, they killed or captured some 150 German soldiers. Other elements established road-blocks around Foucarville. One battalion of the Regiment dropped in the 82nd Airborne Division's sector near St-Mère-Église. The battalion commander managed to gather some 250 men together and began to move eastwards towards Utah.

General Taylor himself dropped with the 501st Regiment whose DZ was just west of St-Marie-du-Mont. Luckily, the regimental commander landed roughly in the right place. His key objective was the lock on the Douve River at La Barquette, since it was feared that the Germans might use it to flood the surrounding area. The 501st's other objectives were to blow bridges on the road running from St-Côme-du-Mont south to Carentan, capturing the former village if possible, and destroy the railway bridge over the Douve to its west. Colonel Howard R. Johnson, the regimental commander, collected some 150 men and secured the lock at La

Barquette against minimum opposition. But, when other parts of the regiment tried to advance to the Douve bridges they faced increasing resistance from von der Heydte's German paratroops. The American paratroopers did not know at the time that German engineers had demolished the bridges. The commander of the third regiment of the Screaming Eagles, the 506th, which Eisenhower had visited just before they boarded their planes, had the worst time. The drop was scattered, but within two hours of landing Colonel Robert F. Sink was able to gather ninety men of his own HQ and fifty from his 1st Battalion and establish himself at Culoville. He was principally tasked with securing the southern exits from Utah Beach. His 3rd Battalion, which would drop with the 506th south of Vierville, was to capture bridges over the Douve at Le Port. The 2nd Battalion, or at least the 200 men who could be collected, were advancing towards the exits at Hodienville and Pouppeville well before dawn, but soon ran into German machine guns, which brought them to a halt. Sink had no communication with the Battalion and so decided to send the fifty men of the 1st Battalion that he had with him to tackle the Pouppeville beach exit. They, too, were considerably slowed by German opposition. Sink, however, had little contact with this group once it set out and also little with Divisional HQ, which Maxwell Taylor had established at Hiesville. Worse, Sink's HQ was in the midst of a German artillery battalion and he was continually faced with attempts to infiltrate his position. His poor communications with Maxwell Taylor caused the latter to send the divisional reserve, the 3rd Battalion of the 501st to Pouppeville, which it reached at 8am.

Major-General Matthew Ridgway's 82nd Airborne Division suffered much the same confusion. His DZs were to the west of those of 101st Airborne and his overall task was to clear from the River Merderet east to the coast and to establish a bridgehead on the west bank of the river. A major problem was that this sector was close to the assembly area of the 91st Airlanding Division. Initially, matters went well. The 505th Regiment's DZ was just west of St-Mère-Église. It

(Right) Although its drop was just as scattered as that of the 82nd Airborne Division, 101st Airborne had a slightly easier task in that it was closer to Utah beach and so could expect to link up earlier with the troops landing here. It was able to distract German troops defending Utah and also secured routes inland for the US VII Corps.

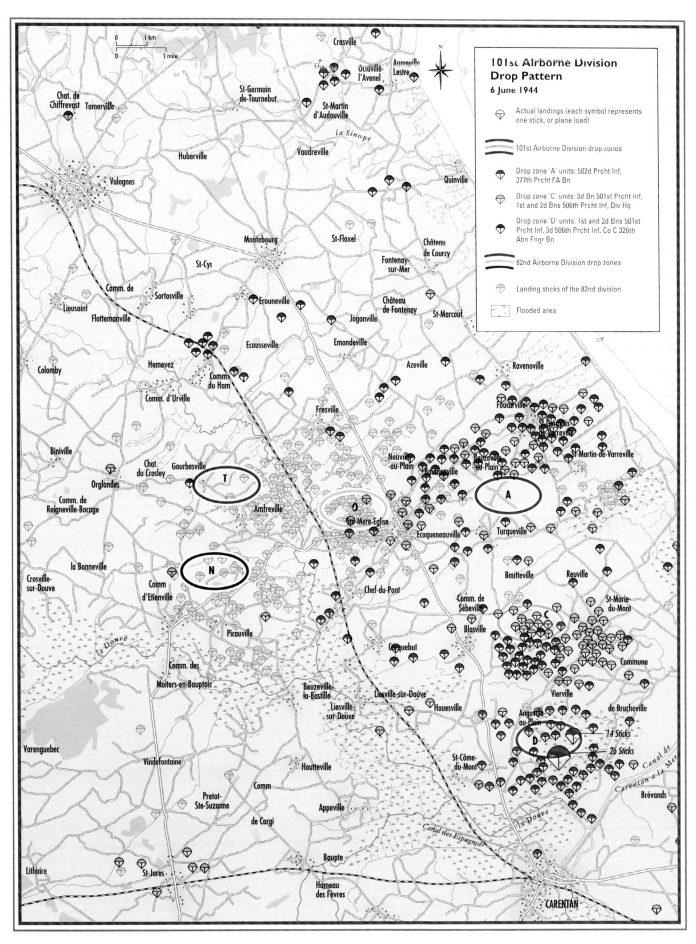

101st Airborne Division Drop Pattern
6 June 1944

Actual landings (each symbol represents one stick, or plane load)

101st Airborne Division drop zones

Drop zone 'A' units: 502d Prcht Inf, 377th Prcht FA Bn

Drop zone 'C' units: 3d Bn 501st Prcht Inf, 1st and 2d Bns 506th Prcht Inf, Div Hq

Drop zone 'D' units: 1st and 2d Bns 501st Prcht Inf, 3d 506th Prcht Inf, Co C 326th Ahn Engr Bn

82nd Airborne Division drop zones

Landing sticks of the 82nd division

Flooded area

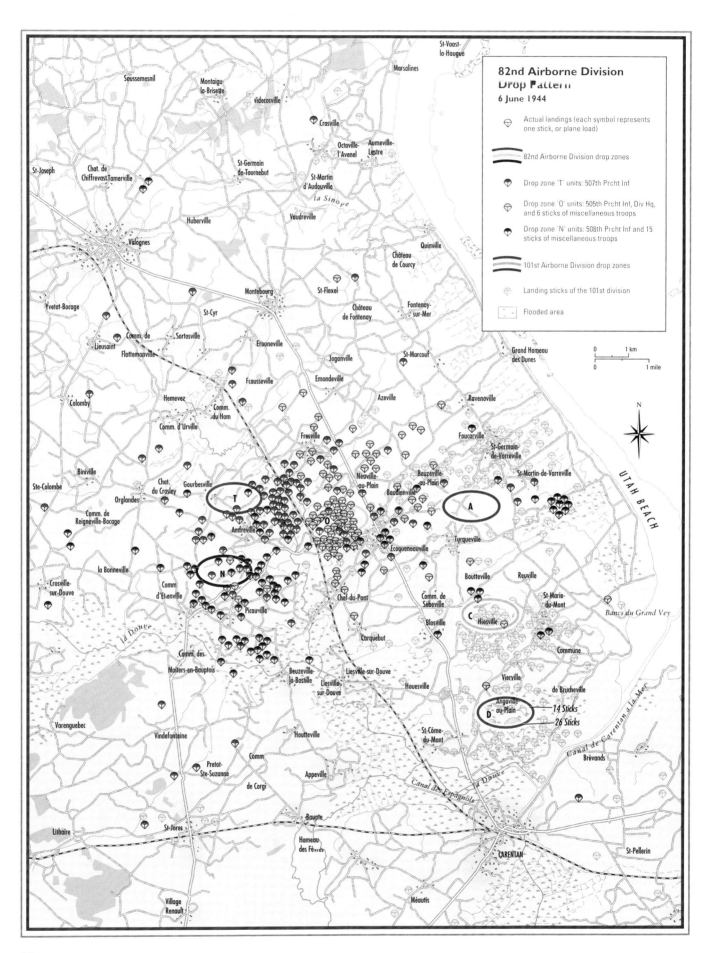

**82nd Airborne Division
Drop Pattern**
6 June 1944

Actual landings (each symbol represents one stick, or plane load)

82nd Airborne Division drop zones

Drop zone 'T' units: 507th Prcht Inf

Drop zone 'O' units: 505th Prcht Inf, Div Hq, and 6 sticks of miscellaneous troops

Drop zone 'N' units: 508th Prcht Inf and 15 sticks of miscellaneous troops

101st Airborne Division drop zones

Landing sticks of the 101st division

Flooded area

0   1 km
0   1 mile

was to seize the town, secure crossings over the Merderet in the La Fiere and Chef-du-Pont area and establish a defensive line. The pathfinders had managed to clearly mark the DZ and, although the 505th's planes were scattered, they were able to turn back and drop the paratroops in a fairly concentrated pattern, although a few did actually land in the town itself. Furthermore, there were no Germans in the vicinity. The Regiment's 3rd Battalion was to capture St-Mère-Église and moved swiftly. It entered the town and used just knives, bayonets, and grenades to secure it well before dawn, killing ten Germans and capturing thirty others. It quickly estab-

Browning Automatic rifle (BAR). Originally developed in 1917, it was used as a support weapon by US infantry squads.

lished a perimeter defence and cut the communications cable running up to Cherbourg. The other two battalions had further to go in establishing a defence line and seizing the crossings over the Merderet. The 2nd Battalion, responsible for the former task, would, however, be ordered back to St-Mère-Église well after daylight as German pressure on the town increased. The success of the 1st Battalion in securing the crossings would be dependent on the other two regiments which landed west of the river.

The 507th and 508th Parachute Infantry Regiments were to drop between the Rivers Douve and Merderet and secure the west bank of the latter. This would then become the perimeter for the Utah beachhead. Because 91st Airlanding Division was already present in the drop area, the pathfinders were unable to mark the DZs. Consequently, the aircraft crews were unable to identify them and overshot. The result was a very scattered drop, with many of the paratroopers landing in the marshy ground bordering the Merderet. The one recognisable feature was the embankment which carried

(Left) The 82nd Airborne Division's principal task was to secure crossings over the River Merderet, but the scattered nature of its drop made it initially impossible to achieve. Luckily a reasonable number of men did land in or around the DZ near St-Mère-Église, making it the first French village to be liberated on D-Day. Thereafter it became the cornerstone of the paratroop's defence.

the railway running from Carentan to Cherbourg and it was to this that the men headed and began to gather. One group, under Brigadier-General James A. Gavin, the Assistant Divisional Commander, did try to move down along the edge of the marshes, but were unable to make any progress before dawn, because of the time it took to locate and extricate heavy equipment. As for those on the embankment, which numbered some 600 men from a variety of units, they began to move south towards the crossing at La Fiere. Many others found themselves fighting for their survival and were unable to progress to their objectives. The initial drops had caught

US paratroops moving towards their RV in Normandy. They had numerous minor clashes with Germans on D-Day. Hence the anxious expression of the man covering the rear.

the Germans by surprise, but they soon began to recover, although General Wilhelm Falley, commanding 91st Airlanding Division, was killed. He had been on his way to the map exercise at Rennes when the intensity of air activity caused him to turn back. Shortly before reaching his HQ, he heard machine gun fire and got out of his staff car to investigate. A few moments later he was shot dead by a paratrooper of the 508th. At 4am the first wave of US glider-borne troops came in to land. These were vital, since they had the heavier weapons which the paratroopers would need to hold the perimeter. However, the now thoroughly alert Flak defences opened up a heavy fire and a number of the tug aircraft were shot down. Some three-quarters of the gliders did manage to reach the landing zones, but many of them crashed into the marshes or ran up against thick hedgerows and stone walls. Casualties in personnel were surprisingly

The Division's overall task was to secure the area between the Rivers Dives and Orne, so that this could become the left flank of the Allied beachhead. It was therefore crucial to seize the bridges over the Dives to prevent counter-attack by elements of Fifteenth Army. Once 9th Parachute Bn had destroyed the Merville battery, it was sent to help hold the southern line defences. The Division remained in France until the end of August 1944.

light, although the Assistant Commander of the 101st Airborne was among the killed. Many of the jeeps and artillery guns were, however, lost. Now, with the coming of daylight and the American landings at Utah soon to take place, the German Seventh Army began to organize operations to seal the American lodgement and eradicate it. The 709th Division, with a regiment of the 91st under its command, was ordered to clear the area to the east of the Merderet, while the remainder of the 91st attacked in the

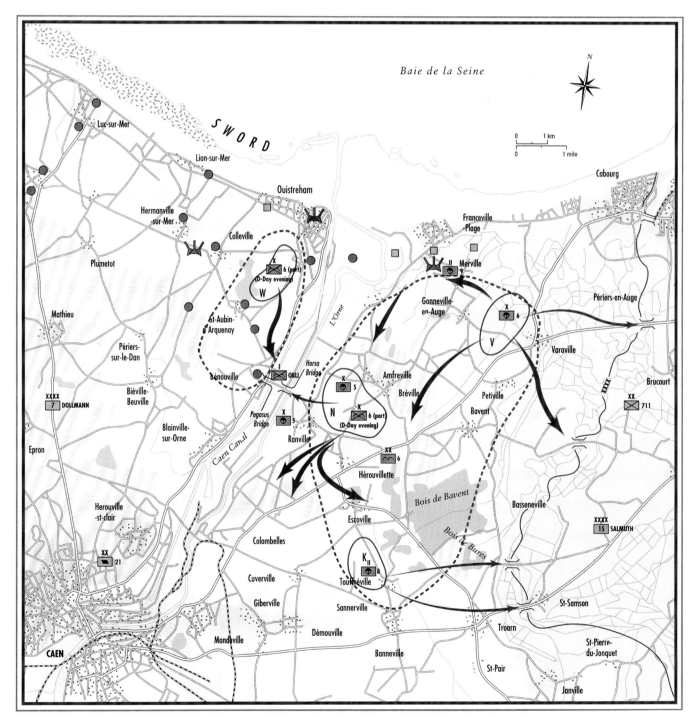

British 6th Airborne Division 6 June 1944

- Intended landing zones
- Actual landing zones
- Bridge captured
- Bridge destroyed
- Battery destroyed
- German strong points
- German resistance points

west. Von der Heydte's 6th Parachute Regiment was placed under command of the 91st and would attack from the south. The question now was whether the US paratroopers in their largely disorganized state could fend off these attacks and link up with the troops of the 4th Infantry Division on Utah.

Far to the east, at the other end of the Allied landing beaches, the British 6th Airborne Division had experienced similar problems to the Americans. General Richard ('Windy') Gale had the mission of landing between the Rivers Dives and Orne, securing bridges over both and providing a shoulder for the landings on Sword Beach so that German reserves approaching from the east and south-east could be blocked. He also had to capture and destroy a coastal battery at Merville, which could fire into the flank of the Sword landing. Pathfinders from the 22nd Independent Parachute Company landed between twenty and thirty minutes after midnight. High winds caused dispersal and, once on the ground, they found that many of their Eureka beacons did not function. One of those that did was set up in the wrong place.

The next phase was a daring glider operation. A company of the 2nd Oxfordshire and Buckinghamshire Light Infantry under the command of Major John Howard took off in six gliders, their objective the bridges over the River Orne and Caen Canal at Bénouville. Three gliders were allocated to each bridge and all would land on the narrow strip between the two waterways. They were 'to finish their landing run as close to the bridges as is consistent with avoiding injury to the gliderborne troops', as the operational order laid down. The pilots themselves carried out extensive flying practice by night. They also had a detailed model of the area and a film made from air photographs, which simulated the approach to the target. The three gliders bound for the canal bridge landed within yards of it and, after a brief fire fight, seized it. Two out of the other three landed by the river bridge, which again was quickly captured. The third

was released at the wrong cast-off point and came to rest by a bridge over the River Dives, seven miles away from the correct bridge. The troops on board secured this and then made there way to their original objective. It was, as Trafford Leigh-Mallory stated, 'one of the most outstanding flying operations of the war'.

The tasks of the 5th Parachute Brigade were to send one battalion to reinforce Howard's men on the Canal and Orne bridges, while the other two captured Ranville and the adjacent high ground just east of the Orne. Many of its men were

Gliders after landing. It was necessary to remove the tail section to extract vehicles and heavy weapons.

blown off course, and only some 200 could be gathered to help Howard, although more trickled in during the night. The other two battalions managed to capture Ranville, although, as at Sainte-Mère-Eglise, a number landed in the town and were killed or captured, and by daylight were also dug in around La Bas de Ranville. Many men of the 3rd Parachute Brigade landed in the flooded area bordering the

River Dives, four of whose bridges they had to demolish. Nevertheless, they succeeded and then dug in around Le Mesnil and Bois Bavent. One battalion, Lieutenant-Colonel Terence Otway's 9th, had a more challenging job, the destruction of the Merville Battery. This was well protected by concrete and earth, minefields and barbed wire and was defended by 130 Germans, armed with machine guns and 20mm cannon. Otway and his men carried out numerous

![Pegasus Bridge map]

The real achievement was landing the gliders so close to the bridges and it was this that enabled Major John Howard's men to achieve complete surprise. Howard himself led the capture of Pegasus Bridge and was later relieved by Commandos, while the Ranville Bridge group was relieved by 7th Parachute Battalion.

rehearsals on a 1:1 scale model. The plan was that they should drop out of sight of the battery, which would have been pounded by some 100 Lancaster and Halifax bombers to destroy the barded wire and at least some of the mines. Gliders carrying engineers with their heavy equipment would land and clear lanes through the minefield, after which the 9th Parachute Battalion would make its attack. Three gliders were simultaneously to crash-land on top of the battery.

Like the other drops, that of the Battalion was scattered and Otway was only able to assemble one quarter of his 600 men. Worse, the bombing had been inaccurate and the barbed wire and minefield were largely intact and the gliders carrying the engineers had landed well away from their prop-

er Landing Zone. Of the three gliders due to land on the battery itself, one's tow rope broke and it was forced to return to England, while the second was hit by flak and landed 200 yards away and those inside found themselves engaging a German patrol, which prevented them from taking part in the assault. The third managed to land within 50 yards. In spite of all this, Otway was determined to carry on. Sappers with him cleared lanes by digging for mines with their bayo-

The British Bren light machine gun. It was much lighter and easier to handle than the US BAR.

nets and, after silencing six of the ten machine guns defending the battery, Otway's men passed through and reached its entrance. After a short but grim hand-to-hand battle, the guns were in their possession. Instead of being of 150mm calibre, as expected, they turned out to be small-calibre Czech guns of 1914–18 origin. The paratroops destroyed them with plastic explosive and withdrew to the area north of Bréville and dug in. While the stragglers of the Division attempted to join up with their units, the remainder, like their US counterparts, prepared for the inevitable German counter-attack and hoped that they would be reinforced by troops from Sword Beach before it came.

There were other necessary preliminaries to the actual beach landings. First, bombers of RAF Bomber Command attacked the coastal batteries, dropping almost 5,000 tons of bombs, which included those used against the Merville Battery, mostly through cloud. The bombers overcame this to a degree through the use of Oboe, a radar system fitted to Mosquitoes, which would mark the target for the bombers. With the coming of daylight, the US Eighth and Ninth Air Forces would join in, together with medium bombers, fighter-bombers and fighters of 2 ATAF. The results of the campaign over the past few months to destroy the Luftwaffe in northern France and the Low Countries were now to be revealed. During D-Day the Allies flew nearly 15,000 sorties, while the Germans were able to manage only 319.

It was now the turn of the Allied navies. Each of the five task forces was preceded by minesweepers. Such was the success of their operations in clearing mines in the Channel that only two vessels were sunk in it on D-Day, a destroyer and an LST. By 2 am on 6 June the minesweepers were off the beaches. They had two tasks, to clear the approaches of mines and also the lanes which the bombarding ships would use. They faced a problem in that the Germans had laid several delayed-action mines, which remained on the sea bottom until acti-

Commandos dig in by the gliders used to transport John Howard and his men to the bridges over the Caen Canal and River Orne.

vated. Consequently, continual sweeping was required and no stretch of water could be guaranteed to be totally free of mines. Indeed, this was the major cause of loss of Allied ships off Normandy.

The bombarding ships task was to silence the German coastal batteries and they were organized in three groups. The heavier vessels in each task force – battleships, monitors, cruisers – were positioned some 11,000 yards from the coast and operated in lanes parallel to the shoreline, in which they could manoeuvre. The destroyers, on the other hand, had to approach within 5,500 yards and then anchor. Although this made them more vulnerable to German fire, they would be less prone to falling victim to the delayed-action mines. The final group was the support landing craft, with their miscellany of weapons, which would go in with the assaulting troops. To provide some protection for the bombarding ships and for the landing craft as they neared the shore, Bostons of the RAF's No. 2 Group laid a smokescreen. As for the targets, every battery within range of the landing force was to be

engaged, from Villerville, near to the mouth of the Seine, in the east to Barfleur in the west. Fighter aircraft were to be used to spot for the ships' guns and control their fire.

There was a debate between the British and Americans on how long the opening bombardment should be. The British favoured opening fire two hours before the leading landing craft hit the shore to ensure that the batteries were silenced, while the Americans opted for forty minutes in hope of achieving some surprise. H-hour on the two US beaches was to be 6.30am and so the US-commanded Western Task Force would open fire at 5.50am. On the British beaches, fire would open at 5.30am, once it was light enough for the spotter aircraft to see their targets. H-hour here would be 7.15am for Sword and Gold, 7.20am for the right sector of Juno, and 7.30am for the left. In total, five battleships, two monitors, nineteen cruisers, and fifty-eight destroyers and gunboats would take part in the bombardment, with each of the larger ships designated a particular battery as its target.

As it happened, it was the Germans who opened fire first. With the coming of dawn, they began to spot ships through the murk. At 5.05am a battery opened fire on the destroyers USS *Fitch* and *Corry* off Utah. Twenty minutes later, the German guns engaged minesweepers operating off the same beach and the British cruiser HMS *Black Prince* returned fire. A duel now developed, and at 5.36am Admiral Morton L. Deyo, commanding Force U's bombardment group, decided to begin his bombardment. At 6.10am, the aircraft began to lay a smokescreen, but the plane which was to cover *Corry*

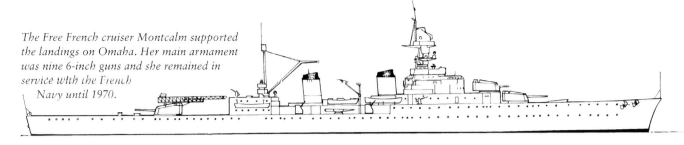

The Free French cruiser Montcalm supported the landings on Omaha. Her main armament was nine 6-inch guns and she remained in service with the French Navy until 1970.

was shot down, leaving her as the only vessel exposed to the shore. The full weight of the local German batteries turned on the destroyer. While manoeuvring to avoid their fire, she was struck by a mine, which broke her back. Two other

destroyers quickly moved in and rescued her crew, who suffered forty-six casualties. By now the ships of all five naval forces were engaging the batteries, while the destroyers off the American beaches moved in to suppress strongpoints just

Launched in 1911, the USS Arkansas was the oldest US battleship to serve in World War 2. Her primary armament was twelve 12-inch guns and she supported the Omaha landings and the assault on Cherbourg.

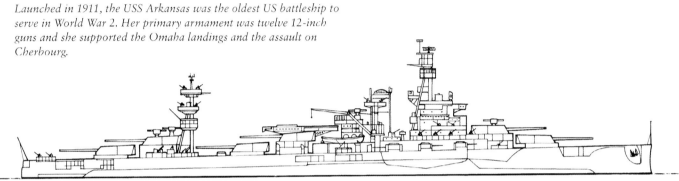

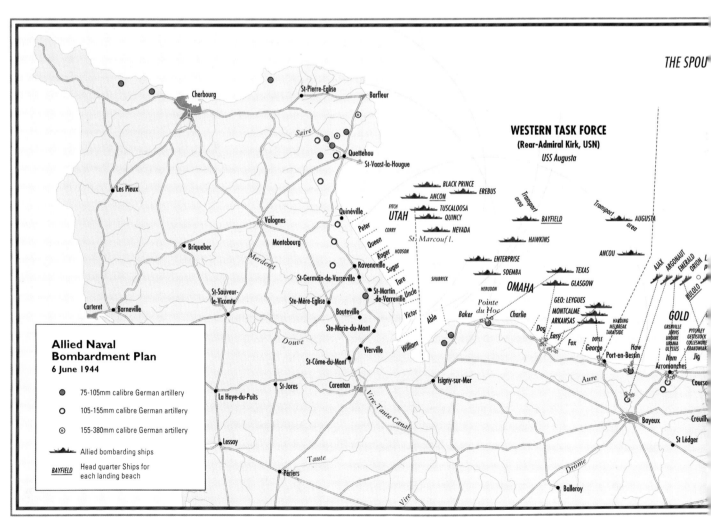

THE SPOU

WESTERN TASK FORCE
(Rear-Admiral Kirk, USN)
USS Augusta

Allied Naval Bombardment Plan
6 June 1944

- ● 75-105mm calibre German artillery
- ○ 105-155mm calibre German artillery
- ◎ 155-380mm calibre German artillery
- ▬ Allied bombarding ships
- *BAYFIELD* Head quarter Ships for each landing beach

beyond the beaches. Meanwhile, as H-hour approached, bombers launched more attacks.

For the assaulting troops, conditions during the Channel crossing had been uncomfortable and a number suffered from seasickness. All, though, were relieved that the time of waiting was finally over. Once dawn broke, the convoys were under constant fighter air cover, while on the flanks roamed maritime patrol aircraft watching for any signs of U-boats or German surface vessels. At sea, too, flotillas of anti-submarine vessels also kept constant watch.

Utah Beach was the responsibility of General J. Lawton Collins's US VII Corps. He was a veteran of the Pacific campaigns on Guadalcanal and New Georgia and was known as 'Lightning Joe' from the divisional patch of the 25th Division, which he had commanded against the Japanese. He was tasked with cutting off the Cotentin peninsula and securing Cherbourg. Utah itself was less than a mile and a half long and was characterized by gently sloping sand

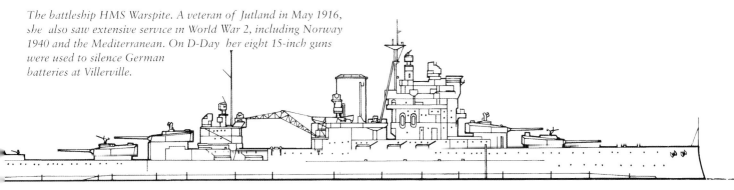

The battleship HMS Warspite. A veteran of Jutland in May 1916, she also saw extensive service in World War 2, including Norway 1940 and the Mediterranean. On D-Day her eight 15-inch guns were used to silence German batteries at Villerville.

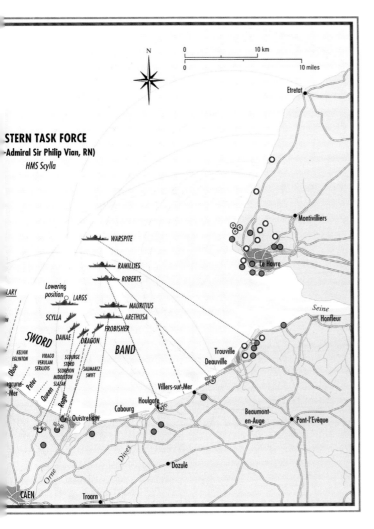

backed by a sea wall, between four and twelve feet high. Behind the beach there was some flooding, which made the causeways leading inland from the beach vital. Because the beach was relatively narrow, Collins decided that the initial landing would be made by just one reinforced Regimental Combat Team (RCT) of the 4th Infantry Division. This was to advance off the beach to the River Merderet and link up with the airborne troops. Eighty-five minutes after H-hour, a second RCT would land and move north to secure the high ground around Quinéville. The 4th Division's final RCT would land at H+4 hours, advance north-west and seize a crossing over the Merderet. Finally, a reserve RCT, from 90th Division, would also land. Sherman DD tanks would also swim ashore to support the first waves ashore. Collins himself, together with General Raymond O. Barton, commander of the 4th Division, were on board the HQ ship USS *Bayfield*.

Eleven miles from the shore, the troops trans-shipped to their landing craft, not an easy task given the sea state, but one in which they had received much training. The run to the

The underlined ships' names represent HQ ships, one for each main landing beach. They had elaborate radio communications and had the naval and landing force commanders on board. The channels had been swept of mines and the larger warships anchored offshore, each given a particular coastal battery to engage. Destroyers (indicated on the map just by their names) engaged the shore defences and helped to shoot the landing craft into the shore.

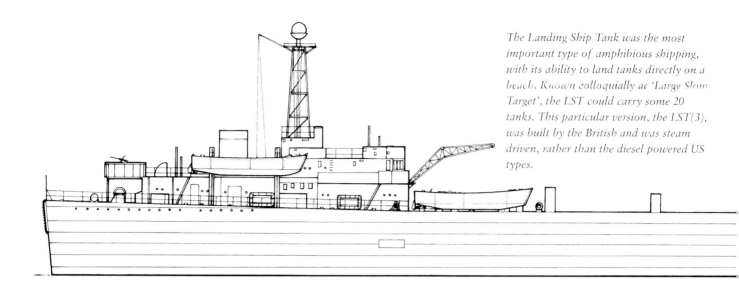

The Landing Ship Tank was the most important type of amphibious shipping, with its ability to land tanks directly on a beach. Known colloquially as 'Large Slow Target', the LST could carry some 20 tanks. This particular version, the LST(3), was built by the British and was steam driven, rather than the diesel powered US types.

Landing Craft Tank (Rocket). This was a variant of the LCT, with the tank deck occupied by a battery of either 792 or 1,080 5-inch rockets. These were fired electrically in salvoes and were designed to pulverize beach defences.

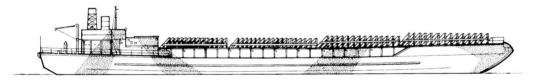

shore was long and uncomfortable in the rough sea. Not until they were halfway there could those on board the landing craft see the French coast, but they were guided by craft equipped with radars and radios. The intention was to release the tanks into the water from their Landing Craft Tank (LCT) five miles from the shore, but progress through the water was slow. En route, one of the patrol craft responsible for guiding them to the beach was sunk, as was an LCT,

both victims of mines. With time being lost, it was decided not to launch the tanks until they were one mile from the shore. The naval and air bombardment, together with the smokescreen, reduced visibility. As the leading waves of landing craft closed to the shore two pairs of Landing Craft Gun, armed with 4.7-inch guns, deployed to the flanks to provide supporting fire. Then, there was a hail of rockets from the seventeen LCT(R) supporting the assault.

Landing Craft Infantry (Large) was of British design but built in the USA. Each was capable of carrying some 200 troops.

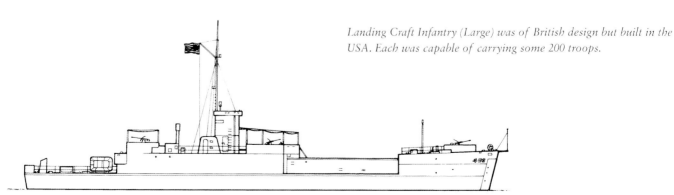

US troops crossdeck to their landing craft prior to landing.

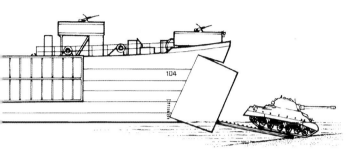

On shore, one battalion of the 709th Division was responsible for Utah, with another in depth behind it. Its defences were still incomplete. Indeed, only one of the Division's thirty-four planned strongpoints had been finished. The beaches were not mined and had few obstacles, with those below the waterline not having any explosives attached. The defenders on Utah were also dazed from the bombing and naval bombardment, which had cut their communications. Indeed, it would not be until the afternoon that the German higher command became aware of the Utah landings. This was as well for the attackers, since they found themselves having to

Barrage balloons were used to protect these LSTs en route to Normandy against low-level air attack.

wade ashore through some 100 yards of water. Landing with them was the Assistant Divisional Commander of the 4th Division, Brigadier-General Theodore Roosevelt Jr, son of the President and a veteran of not only North Africa and Sicily, but World War 1 as well, during which he had been twice wounded. He and others quickly realized that none of the features of the beach were recognizable. Because of the obscuration and a strong current, they had landed 2,000 yards south of where they should have been. Roosevelt reacted quickly to the changed circumstances, which were helped by the fact that the defences on this beach were much weaker than on the correct one. He adjusted the attack plans and diverted the follow-up waves. The surviving DD tanks, twenty-eight in all, got ashore ten minutes after H-hour.

Roosevelt saw that there were two priorities, pushing

inland and securing the correct beach. The latter proved a problem, mainly because the German gun line on a ridge overlooking the beach could not be overrun. Even so, the beach was secured, although the troops were not able to advance much towards Quinéville to the north. Better progress was made with the advance inland. One causeway proved to be both undefended and mine-free. Four others were already in the hands of 101st Airborne. The troops were therefore able to advance, with the DD tanks protecting their flanks, and link up with the paratroopers. Much of the 101st's effort had been directed on capturing Pouppeville, which fell at midday. The Germans here retreated towards the beaches and were caught by the advancing elements of 4th Division. The remainder of the 101st were holding a line on

Part of the invasion fleet at sea. In all nearly 6500 vessels, ranging from battleships to tugs, took part.

forced away from it by a determined German counter-attack. General Ridgway himself decided to anchor his defence on St-Mère-Église and established blocking positions on the roads leading into it. This enabled him to restore some cohesion, but, as night fell on D-Day, the 82nd was still isolated.

On the evening of 6 June, the second wave of gliders arrived carrying elements of the airborne divisions' Glider Infantry regiments with much needed heavy weapons. This time, the landings went better, largely because the gliders landed away from the fighting and had fighter cover, which was able to suppress much of the flak. Even so, over 60 per cent of the gliders were write-offs and some 200 men were killed, although this time most the jeeps and guns were saved. The salient result of the day, however, was that the troops who had landed at Utah were firmly ashore and had achieved this with less than 200 casualties. Teddy Roosevelt, whose

the River Douve north of Carentan. Luckily, the Germans did not put in any form of concerted counter-attack, partly because the Carentan canal was the boundary between 709th and 352nd Divisions and there appear to have been co-ordination problems. The 82nd Airborne was in a very much more parlous state. Scattered groups were still west of the Merderet and under increasing pressure from the Germans. The bridge at La Fiere was taken, but the Americans were

quick and clear thinking and calm courage had single-handedly restored order from what might have become total chaos, was awarded the Congressional Medal of Honor. Sadly, he was to die of a heart attack five weeks later just as he was about to be given command of a division.

If Utah was reasonably successful, even though the D-Day objectives were only partially achieved, Omaha came close to disaster. It was six miles long and the only possible landing beach between the Carentan estuary and Arromanches, which represented the western end of the British beaches. It was in the shape of a gentle crescent bounded at each end by cliffs. At low water there was a stretch of some 200–300 yards of sand littered with obstacles, but at high tide this was reduced to a few yards of shingle backed by a sea wall up to twelve feet in height. Behind this there was a shelf some 200 yards wide, on which, in the eastern half, ran a coast road. An anti-tank ditch had been constructed here. Beyond the shelf were cliffs some 150 feet high on which were situated numerous strongpoints. Two German regiments from 352nd Division held this sector, which was the most heavily defended of all the Allied beaches.

Clarence R. Huebner's 1st Infantry Division, 'the Big Red One', was to carry out the landings. His overall mission after landing was to advance in step with the British south towards St Lô. For this he would come under the orders of General Leonard T. Gerow's V Corps, which was responsible for the Omaha plan. The intention was to land two RCTs abreast, the 16th on the left and the 116th, which had been detached from 29th Division, on the right. The 18th Regimental Combat Team would be the follow-up. Omaha was more exposed to the weather than Utah. Even so, trans-shipping to the landing craft would take place at the same distance from the shore, ie, eleven miles. Likewise, the DD tanks, which were to land first, together with armoured bulldozers and demolition engineers, would be released 5,500 yards from the coast. All this was because of the threat of the coastal batteries. It was, however, hoped that the air and naval bombardment would neutralise them sufficiently to enable the troops to get over the cliffs and

secure the four entrances to the beach that ran through them. The nearest battery was at Pointe du Hoc, three miles east of Omaha, and, it was believed, consisted of five or six 155mm guns. This was of particular concern because it could shoot into the flank of the landing flotilla. While it was to be the target of the battleship USS *Texas*, it was decided to make doubly sure that it could not influence events, by landing two Ranger battalions to destroy the guns.

One blessing for Force O, the ships off Omaha, was that the Germans had laid no delayed-action mines in the area. They were in position by 2.20am and the transports carrying the assault troops were ready to begin trans-shipping them half an hour later. The sea, with a strong north-west wind blowing, was much rougher than off Utah and caused much discomfort to the troops once they were in their landing craft, but by 4.30am they were en route for the shore. At

The dominant bluff, defences and beach obstacles all helped to make Omaha the most problematic of the D-Day beaches.

5.30am a battery at Port-en-Bessin opened up on the battleship USS *Arkansas*. It was joined by other batteries, which engaged the destroyers, but that at Pointe du Hoc remained strangely silent. It was light enough for a spotter plane to be present and it was able to ensure that the batteries were neutralized just as the main bombardment opened at 5.50am.

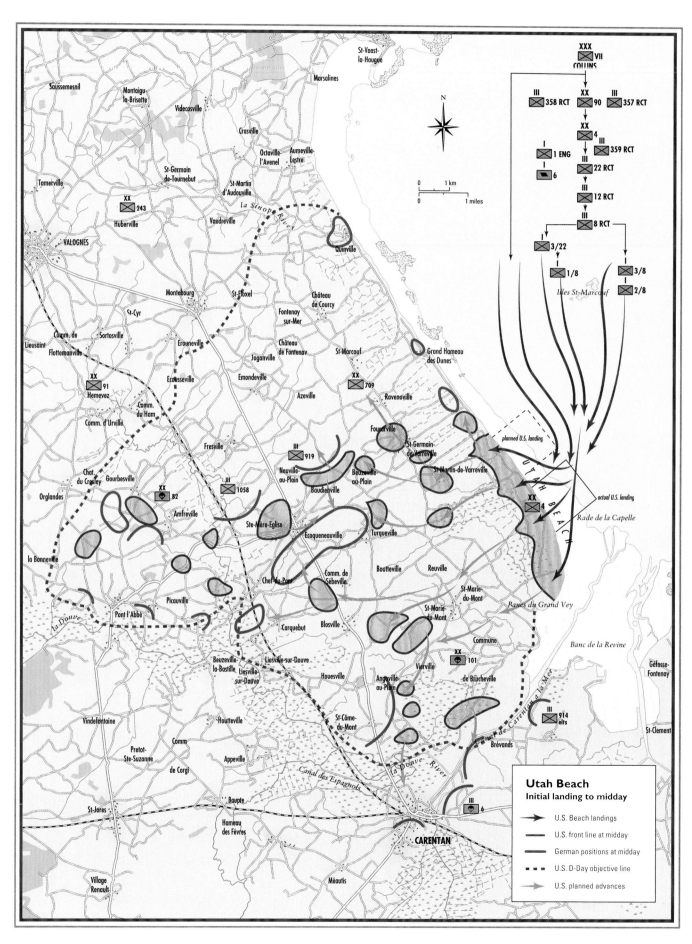

Utah Beach
Initial landing to midday

→ U.S. Beach landings

— U.S. front line at midday

— German positions at midday

- - - U.S. D-Day objective line

→ U.S. planned advances

(Left) The 4th Infantry Division landed on the wrong beach, but quickly adjusted to this. The key early success was securing the causeways leading inland from the beach. This enabled it to link up with elements of 101st Airborne, but much of this and 82nd Division were still very scattered and the Germans were setting about dealing with isolated pockets. The 4th Division's efforts to advance northwards were also being frustrated by heavy fire.

Ten minutes later, 480 B-24 Liberators flew over and dropped their bombs. As on Utah, there was a thirtysecond delay before bomb release to avoid hitting the landing craft and none of the coastal defences were touched. Meanwhile, the DD tanks supporting 116 RCT were launched. Almost immediately, some began to founder in the rough sea and only five out of thirty-two eventually reached the shore. Three of them survived only thanks to the LCT commander pulling up his ramp when the first of the tanks he was carrying drowned. Those carrying the tanks to support the other RCT also ran into the shore and landed them one minute before H-hour. Some of the landing craft in the leading waves were swamped during the run-in and as a result almost all their supporting field artillery was lost. Obscuration and the current played its part, as on Utah, with troops landing in the wrong place and being disorientated. Many landed shoulder-deep in water and struggled to get ashore with all the equipment they were carrying. Under intense German fire, many fell. Those who did make it onto dry land sought shelter under the sea wall or among the beach obstacles, but found that many of their radios did not work. Officers running between groups to try to restore cohesion were shot down and confusion reigned. Out at sea in their HQ ship, Gerow and Huebner had little idea of what was happening.

The Rangers, who were under command of 116 RCT, also had their problems. The idea was that Lieutenant- Colonel James E. Rudder's 2nd Ranger Battalion would make the initial attack on Pointe du Hoc, a small triangular cape some 120 feet high with almost vertical cliffs. The shingle beach below was covered by numerous machine guns and it appeared a suicidal mission. Rudder devised an ingenious way of surmounting the cliffs, using landing-craft-mounted

rocket launchers, which would fire ropes and rope ladders with grapnels attached to the end to anchor the ropes and ladders to the top of the cliffs. His men also had extension ladders, some borrowed from the London Fire Brigade. The landing craft became so swamped during the run-in that the Rangers had to use their helmets as bailers. Two even sank, including the one carrying their stores. The navigating launch then mistook another feature for the Pointe du Hoc. Rudder realized the error just in time, but the little flotilla

US troops start to move off the beach at Utah.

then had to beat its way up the coast in the face of a head wind. It was also being engaged by machine gun fire from the shore. A British and then a US destroyer laid down suppressive fire and the Rangers finally reached their objective at 7.08am, when they should have landed at 6.30am. With the destroyer USS *Satterlee* and the navigating launch providing covering fire, the rope grapnels were fired. Many held and 150 Rangers quickly began to scale the cliffs. Once on top, they fanned out over the point, discovering that the guns they had come to spike were mere telegraph poles put there until the battery casemates could be completed.

The plan was for the captors of Pointe du Hoc to now be reinforced by the balance of the 2nd Rangers and the whole of the 5th Rangers, but Colonel Max Schneider, commanding the group, was not told of their success. Hence, he adopted the secondary plan, which was to land with 116 RCT on the westernmost Omaha beach. On Pointe du Hoc itself, Rudder's men continued mopping up operations and also patrolled as far as the Grandcamp–Vierville road. One of these patrols discovered four of the Pointe du Hoc guns camouflaged in a field and rendered them inoperable with thermite bombs. The Germans were, however, well aware what had happened and launched a series of counter-attacks, the third of which forced the Rangers back onto the point. By the end of D-Day, Rudder was in a critical situation, with a third of his men casualties and ammunition running low.

Back on Omaha, at 7am the follow-up waves had begun to

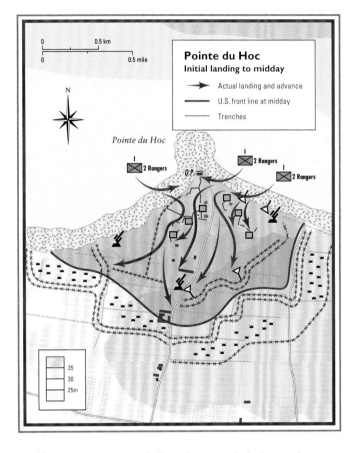

Rudder's Rangers' approach from the sea took the battery by surprise and circumvented most of its defences. They successfully secured the position by midday, but discovered that the actual guns had been removed. Their intention now was to exploit inland, but, because of the setbacks on Omaha, they were to find themselves isolated.

land, but the incoming tide was now up to the shingle below the sea wall. This caused growing congestion and at 8.30am the beachmaster was forced to order that no more vehicles be landed. As it was, he had had to divert some equipment carrying landing craft to less congested beaches, which added to the confusion. Even so, by this time the COs of the two lead-

Liberators overfly the invasion fleet. Their target was coastal batteries but cloud hampered them.

ing RCTs had landed, as well as the Assistant Divisional Commander of 29th Division, and some semblance of order began to be established. Men began to infiltrate the gaps in the cliffs behind the beach and knock out the strongpoints on them. At noon elements of 116 RCT, including the Rangers, had secured Vierville and in the late afternoon the balance of 29th Division began to land. Before nightfall the headquarters of V Corps had been established, but the situation was still serious. The Americans held a beachhead some 4,000 yards long and 1,000 yards deep. A concerted counter-attack could still drive them back into the sea.

There was better fortune on the British beaches, although there was still frustration. Some six miles east of Omaha was the westernmost of these beaches, Gold. The terrain here was somewhat different to Omaha. The beach was fringed merely by low sand dunes and behind it lay somewhat boggy ground intersected by dykes. One problem was that much of the foreshore was made up of blue clay, which made it difficult for vehicles to traverse. Gold lay in the eastern part of 352nd Division's sector and was covered by two battalions, supported by the Division's mobile reserve, which consisted of a further three battalions. The beaches had both underwater and exposed obstacles, which included mines attached to posts. There were also plenty of strongpoints overlooking the beach and the villages were well fortified. The area behind the beach was also littered with anti-tank obstacles.

The 50th (Northumbrian) Division, also known as the

Tyne and Tees, contained men largely from the north-east of England. For D-Day, however, it had been given an additional infantry brigade, 231, which was made of battalions from the south-west of England, 8th Armoured Brigade, a battalion of flail tanks for mine clearance, some flamethrower tanks, and 47 Royal Marine Commando. There were also Centaur tanks mounting a 95mm howitzer from the Royal Marines Support Group. Major-General Douglas Graham, the divisional commander, had already taken part in the Salerno landings, during which he had been wounded. His plan was to land with two brigades up, 231 in the west and 69 Brigade in the east, and

US naval demolition teams dealing with beach obstacles, many of which had explosives attached to them. Drawing by American artist Mitchell Jamieson (1915-76).

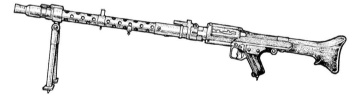

German MG42 machine gun. At 1200 rounds per minute it had a significantly faster rate of fire than Allied types.

then to use his other two brigades as follow-up. The Royal Marine Commando was given a special task of landing on the extreme right flank of 231 Brigade and then advancing west to seize Port-en-Bessin and link up with the Americans on Omaha. Once ashore, the Division's main objective was to secure the high ground south of Bayeux by the end of D-Day.

The air and naval bombardments followed much the same pattern as on the other beaches, although, of course, the naval bombardment was to last for two hours. Force G, however, had no battleships and was built around four British cruisers. They opened fire at 5.30am and the cruiser HMS *Ajax* found itself engaged in a duel with the coastal battery at Longues, which was not subdued until 8.45am. Otherwise, there was very little response from the shore. Because of the rough seas it was decided not to swim the DD tanks of 8th Armoured Brigade

ashore. They would be landed instead, together with the Centaurs. The first waves landed at 7.25am, five minutes before H-Hour. On Jig beach, the right-hand lead battalion of 231 Brigade, the 1st Hampshires, had a grim time. Because of the decision not to swim them, they arrived on the beach with no Sherman DDs. Only five out of the ten Centaurs allocated to it were landed, the others having been sunk, and these five were quickly knocked out on the beach. A number of the flail tanks fell victim to the blue clay. The Hampshires' primary task was to capture Le Hamel, but the preliminary bombardment had left it virtually unscathed. The defenders were full of fight and the Hampshires suffered heavy casual-

Troops struggle ashore on Omaha Beach after their landing craft has sunk. The weather conditions did not help in an already difficult situation.

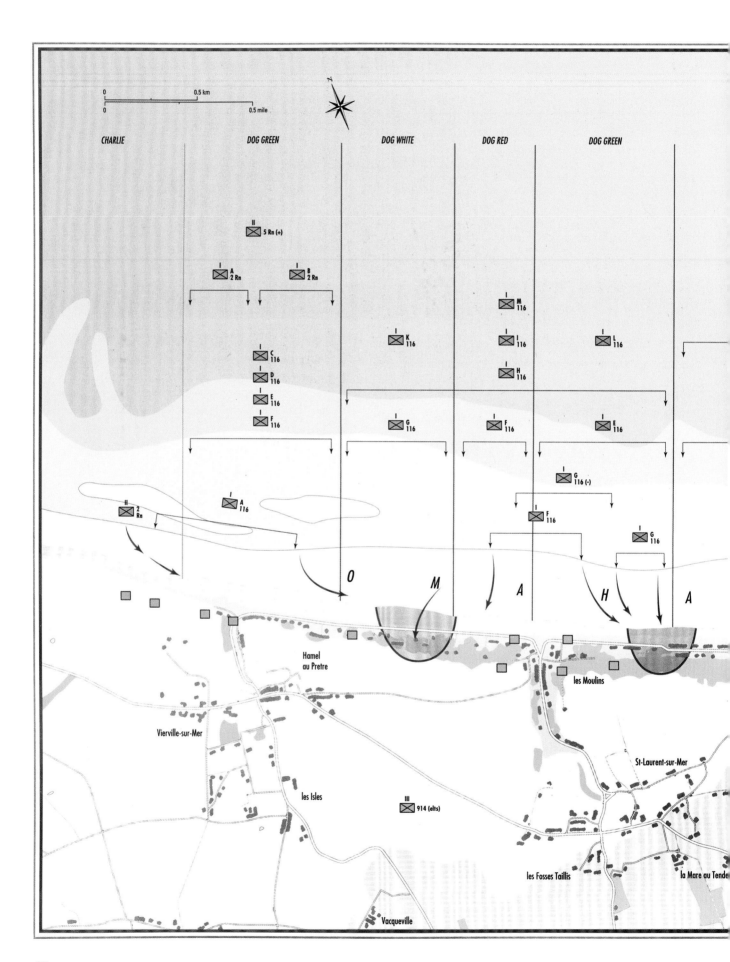

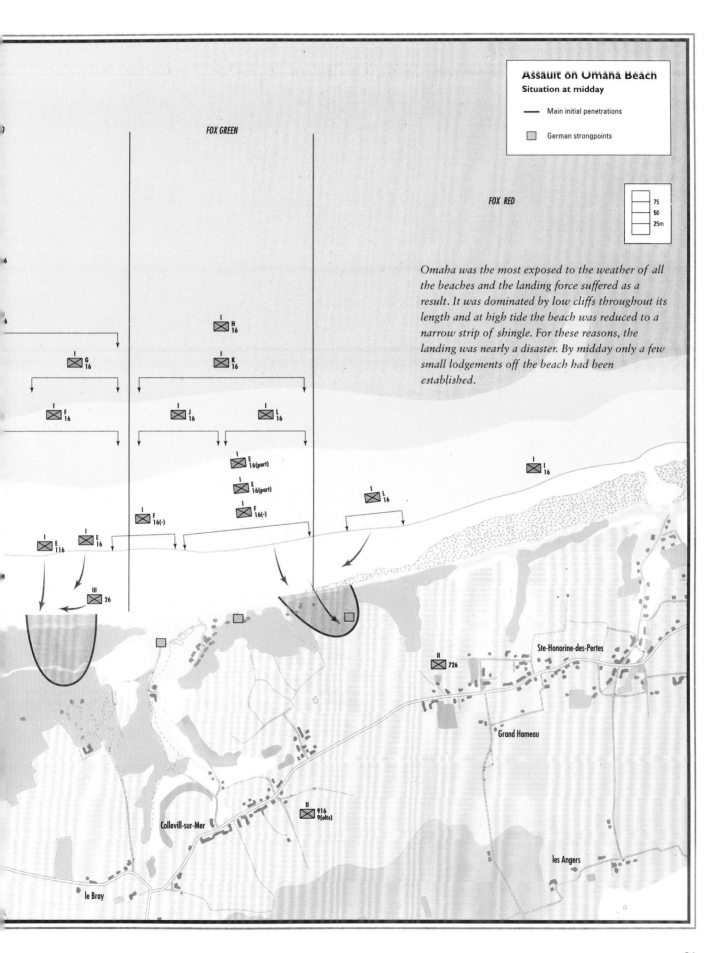

Assault on Omaha Beach
Situation at midday

— Main initial penetrations

German strongpoints

FOX GREEN

FOX RED

Omaha was the most exposed to the weather of all
the beaches and the landing force suffered as a
result. It was dominated by low cliffs throughout its
length and at high tide the beach was reduced to a
narrow strip of shingle. For these reasons, the
landing was nearly a disaster. By midday only a few
small lodgements off the beach had been
established.

75
50
25m

H 16

K 16

G 16

F 16

J 16

L 16

E 16(part)

E 16(part)

F 16(-)

I 16

L 16

F 16(-)

E 116

E 16

III 26

Ste-Honorine-des-Pertes

726

Grand Hameau

Collevill-sur-Mer

916
9(elts)

les Angers

le Bray

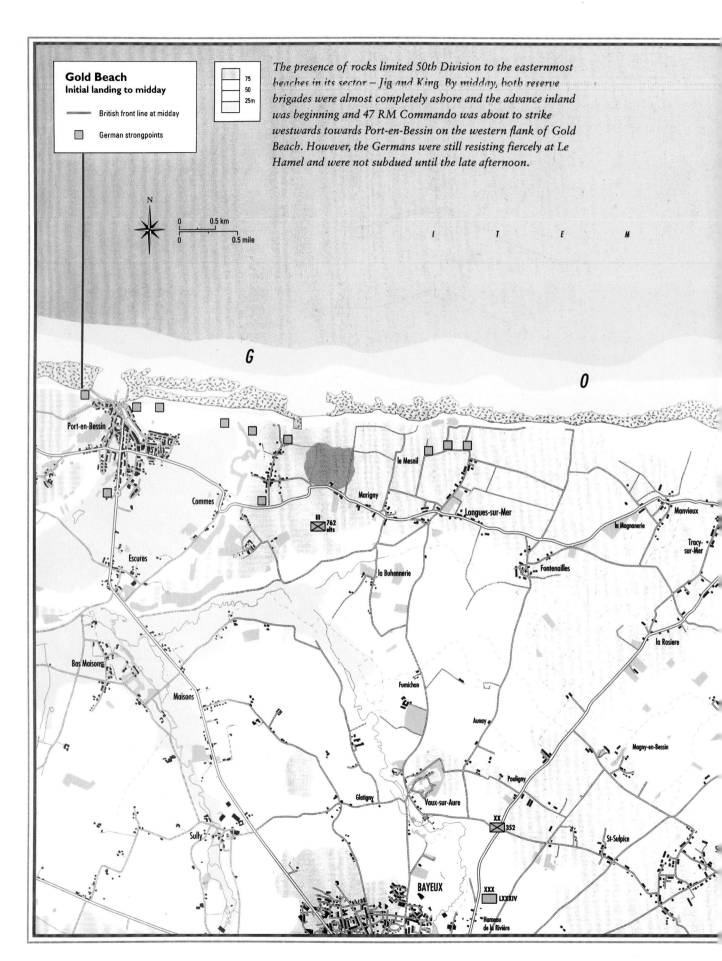

Gold Beach
Initial landing to midday

——— British front line at midday

▢ German strongpoints

75
50
25m

The presence of rocks limited 50th Division to the easternmost beaches in its sector – Jig and King. By midday, both reserve brigades were almost completely ashore and the advance inland was beginning and 47 RM Commando was about to strike westwards towards Port-en-Bessin on the western flank of Gold Beach. However, the Germans were still resisting fiercely at Le Hamel and were not subdued until the late afternoon.

N

0   0.5 km
0   0.5 mile

I   T   E   M

G

O

Port-en-Bessin

le Mesnil

Marigny

Longues-sur-Mer

Manvieux

Commes

la Magnanerie

III 762
elts

Tracy-
sur-Mer

Escures

la Buhennerie

Fontenailles

Bas Maisons

la Rosiere

Fumichon

Maisons

Aunay

Magny-en-Bessin

Pouligny

Glatigny

Vaux-sur-Aure

St-Sulpice

XX
352

Sully

XXX
LXXXIV

BAYEUX

Hameau
de la Rivière

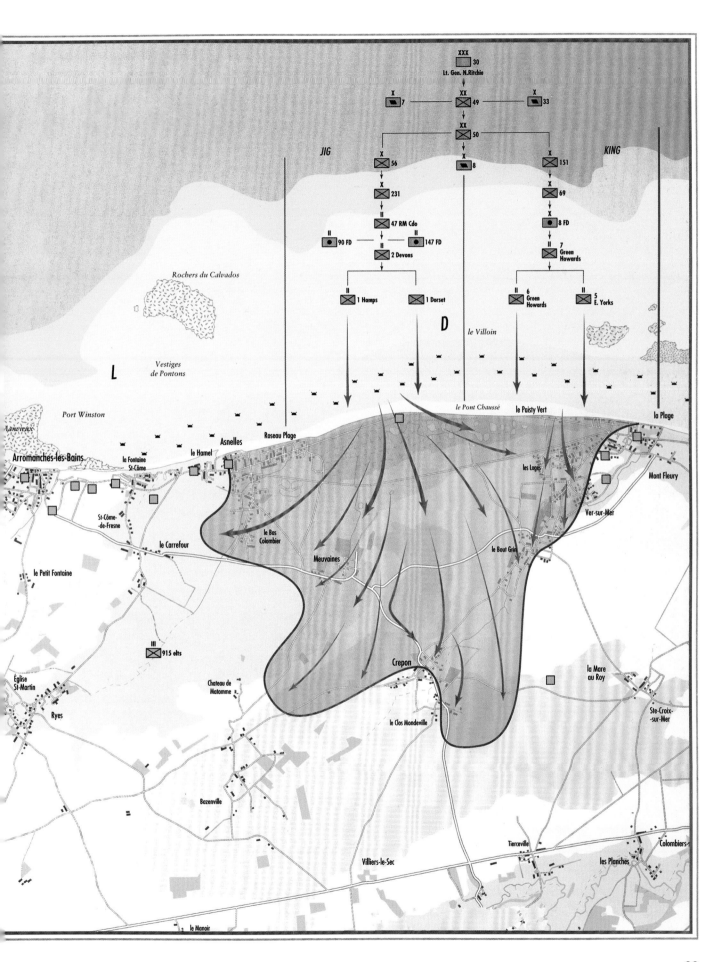

Rochers du Calvados

Vestiges de Pontons

JIG

KING

L

D

le Villoin

Port Winston

Manvieux

Arromanches-les-Bains

la Fontaine
St-Côme

le Hamel

Asnelles

Roseau Plage

le Pont Chaussé

le Paisty Vert

la Plage

les Logés

Mont Fleury

St-Côme-de-Fresne

le Carrefour

le Bas Colombier

Meuvaines

le Bout Grin

Ver-sur-Mer

le Petit Fontaine

915 elts

Crepon

la Mare au Roy

Ste-Croix--sur-Mer

Église St-Martin

Ryes

Chateau de Matomme

le Clos Mondeville

Bazenville

Tierceville

Colombiers-s

Villiers-le-Sec

les Planches

le Manoir

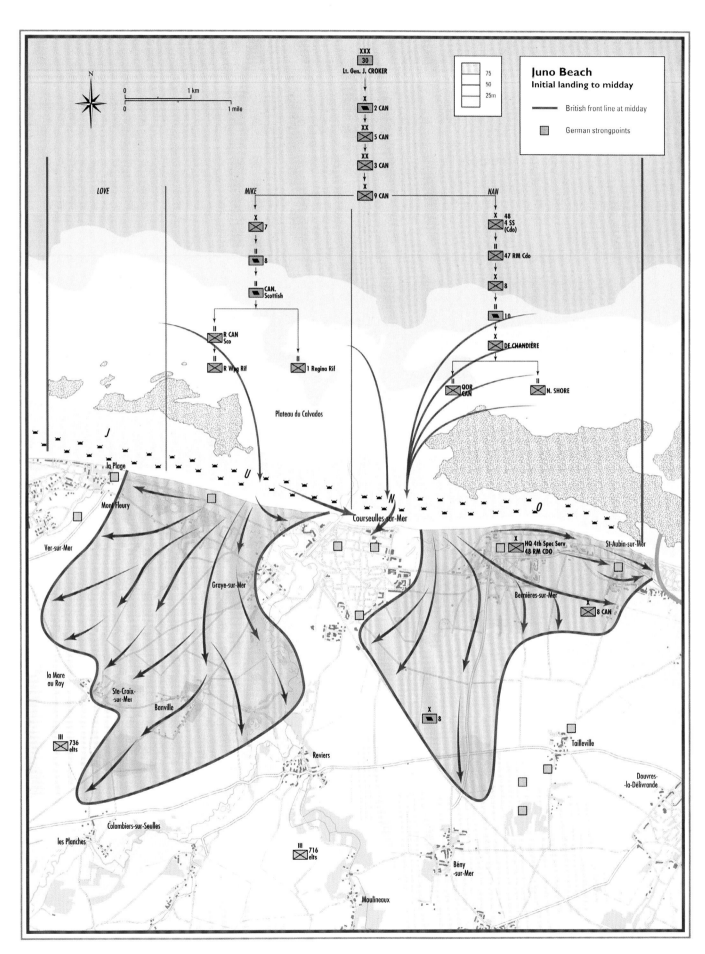

Juno Beach
Initial landing to midday

British front line at midday

German strongpoints

XXX
30
Lt. Gen. J. CROKER

X
2 CAN

XX
5 CAN

XX
3 CAN

X
9 CAN

LOVE

MIKE

NAN

X 7

II 8

II CAN.
Scottish

II R CAN
Sco

II R Wpg Rif

II 1 Regina Rif

X 48
4 SS
(Cdo)

II 47 RM Cdo

X 8

II 10

X DE CHANDIÈRE

II QOR
CAN

II N. SHORE

Plateau du Calvados

J

la Plage

Mont Fleury

Ver-sur-Mer

U

Graye-sur-Mer

la Mare
au Roy

Ste-Croix-
-sur-Mer

Banville

III 736
elts

N

Courseulles-sur-Mer

X HQ 4th Spec Serv
48 RM CDO

Bernières-sur-Mer

O

St-Aubin-sur-Mer

X 8 CAN

X 8

Tailleville

Douvres-
la-Délivrande

Reviers

III 716
elts

Colombiers-sur-Seulles

les Planches

Bény
-sur-Mer

Moulineaux

(Left) As with Gold Beach, offshore rocks resulted in a narrow landing area. This did cause increasing congestion once the reserve brigade began to land at 11.40 am. The two assault brigades, even though they landed behind schedule, were quickly off the beaches. Only the strongpoints in and around Courseulles-sur-Mer presented any significant problems.

ties, including both the CO and Second-in-Command killed. The 1st Dorsets experienced fewer problems on the left part of Jig Beach. Flail tanks and Armoured Vehicles Royal Engineers (AVREs) landed with the leading waves, providing immediate armoured support. They quickly cleared the beach obstacles and were soon advancing inland, skirting round east of Le Hamel. On King Beach the story was much the same as for the Dorsets, although the left -hand battalion of 69 Brigade was pinned down for a while under the sea wall and had to call in naval fire support to extricate itself.

At 8.15am the follow-up battalion of 231 Brigade landed and incurred casualties from Le Hamel. It sent one company to assist the Hampshire, while the remainder began to advance southwest. Immediately afterwards, the Royal Marine Commandos came ashore, but not before three out of their five landing craft had been holed by underwater obstacles. The survivors had to swim ashore, but No 47 quickly reorganised and was soon advancing to Port-en-Bessin. They fought a sharp action for the village of La Rosière and reached a piece of high ground just south of Port-en-Bessin and dug in for the night. Meanwhile the follow-up battalion of 69 Brigade had also

Sherman Duplex Drive (DD). The turret and upper part of the hull were protected by a canvas screen, with the propellor providing propulsion. Once on shore, the screen and duplex could be removed.

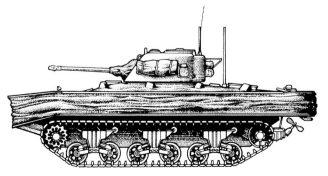

landed and this was followed by the other two brigades in the Division, although 56 Brigade had to be allocated a different beach because of the threat from Le Hamel. Both these brigades were completely on shore by midday. The 50th Division now began to advance inland, forcing the Germans back with heavy casualties. Le Hamel was eventually secured and by nightfall the Division had penetrated over three miles inland, although it was stopped short of Bayeux.

Canadian troops come ashore on Juno Beach. They are clearly one of the follow-up waves but they are still under fire. Hence the tension in the men's faces.

Juno Beach was a Canadian affair and was to be assaulted by Major-General Rod Keller's 3rd Canadian Division. The main problem with the beach itself was offshore reefs, which restricted the entrances to it, to just one for Mike and one for Nan beaches. Indeed, while H-hour for Mike was 7.35am, that for Nan was ten minutes later to allow time for the tide to cover rocks off it, although these in the end proved to be just seaweed. Behind the beaches, the ground generally rose inland. The sector was part of that of the German 716th Division. One battalion covered the beaches themselves, with an 'East' battalion of doubtful quality in support. The further battalions provided depth to the defence and there was a mobile reserve in the shape of a Panzer Grenadier battalion of 21st Panzer Division. There

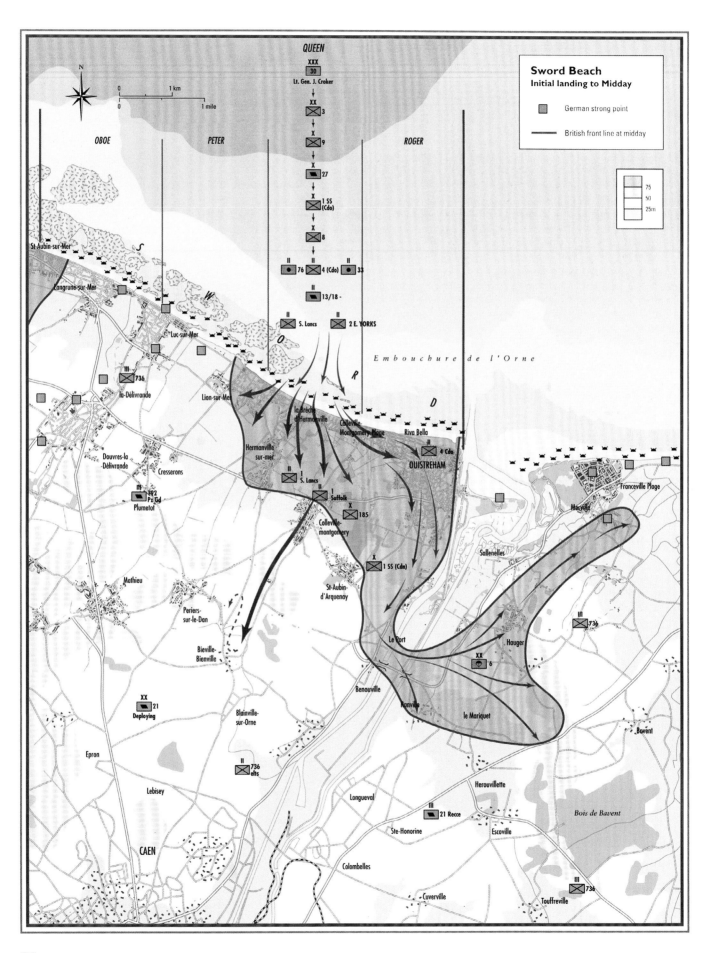

QUEEN

XXX
30
Lt. Gen. J. Croker

XX 3

X 9

X 27

X 1 SS (Cdo)

X 8

76 | 4 (Cdo) | 33

13/18 -

S. Lancs | 2 E. YORKS

OBOE

PETER

ROGER

Sword Beach
Initial landing to Midday

German strong point

British front line at midday

75
50
25m

St-Aubin-sur-Mer

Langrune-sur-Mer

Luc-sur-Mer

la-Délivrande

736

Douvres-la-
Délivrande

Cresserons

192 Pz Gd
Plumetot

Mathieu

Periers-
sur-le-Dan

Bieville-
Bienville

21
Deploying

Blainville-
sur-Orne

Epron

Lebisey

736
elts

Longueval

CAEN

Colombelles

Cuverville

Lion-sur-Mer

la Brèche
d'Hermanville

Hermanville
sur-mer

S. Lancs

Suffolk

185

Colleville-
montgomery

St-Aubin-
d'Arquenay

1 SS (Cdn)

Le Port

Benouville

Ranville

Embouchure de l'Orne

Colleville-
Montgomery-Plage

Riva Bella

OUISTREHAM

4 Cdo

Sallenelles

le Mariquet

Ste-Honorine

Herouvillette

21 Recce

Escoville

Franceville Plage

Merville

736

Hauger

6

Bavent

Bois de Bavent

Touffreville

736

(Left) By midday, the British 3rd Division was firmly ashore. 185 Brigade was poised to advance on Caen, but was still awaiting its supporting tanks, which were held up on the exits of the beach. The Commandos of 1 Special Service Brigade were racing to relieve Howard's men on Pegasus Bridge. On the German side, 21st Panzer Division was beginning to deploy for a counter-attack, but was reacting to events much too slowly.

was also an anti-tank battalion deployed on the high ground south of Creully. As on the other beaches, the coast was protected by a number of strongpoints.

Keller's D-Day task was to secure the high ground west of Caen inclusive of the Caen–Bayeux road. In particular, he was to capture Carpiquet airfield. He planned to land with two brigades abreast, with the third landing on whichever beach had shown the most progress. This would then advance

follow-up brigade. Twenty-eight AVREs were also available for beach obstacle clearance. The Canadians had the smallest of the naval bombardment forces, with just two cruisers and eleven destroyers.

An initial problem occurred on the approach of Force J to the swept channels, with four of its groups straying into the wrong channels. Consequently, H-hour was postponed by ten minutes, but the naval bombardment opened on time. The swell and current also slowed the run-in to the shore. The two DD tank companies supporting 7 Brigade on the right were to be launched in the water 7,000 yards from the shore, but it was decided to reduce this to 4,000 yards. Twenty-two out of thirty-eight got onto the beach ahead of the infantry. They immediately began engaging strongpoints, but a number

to the railway line running just south of the Caen–Bayeux road and prepare to meet the expected German counter-attack. Keller was also given No. 48 Royal Marine Commando. This was to land on the extreme left flank, capture Langrune-sur-Mer, and link up with Sword Beach. There was also a Canadian armoured brigade, one battalion of which would land with each of the leading brigades, with two tank companies swimming ashore and the other being landed dryshod. The third tank battalion would support the

Commandos, with bicycles to improve their mobility, come ashore on Sword Beach.

became trapped by the incoming tide and were immobilized. The infantry landed at 8.10am, twenty-five minutes after the amended H-hour, because of the sea conditions and the fact that a number of landing craft were lost to underwater obstacles. They then had a fierce battle on their hands to clear the strongpoints around Courseulles. The 8 Brigade DD tanks were released even closer in and found themselves merely having to wade ashore, but they arrived after the infantry, who themselves were just over fifteen minutes late. They, too, had a tussle to reduce the strongpoints on their beach. As on Gold, it was noted that the naval bombardment had a disappointing effect on these defences. The reserve battalions in each brigade arrived and were ashore by 9.30am, but the beaches, especially Mike, were beginning to suffer from congestion because of the limited exits from them. It was for this reason that 9 Brigade began to land on Nan at 11.30am, but its arrival immediately compounded the congestion.

No. 48 Commando landed at St-Aubin just before 8.45am. Two out of its six landing craft were caught on obstacles and some who tried to swim ashore were drowned. The other four beached at an angle, which meant that the men found themselves waist-deep in the sea. While organizing his men, the CO was wounded by mortar fragments, but continued in command. The Commandos then began to clear the houses on the beach and set up a base 1,000 yards inland from which they could attack Langrune. They managed to seize a strongpoint and houses in Luc-sur-Mer, just to the south, but Langrune itself held out and at dusk the Commandos were ordered to take up a defensive position. Thus, they were unable to make contact with the 3rd British Division on Sword. As for the main 3rd Canadian Division thrust inland, 9 Brigade was not able to begin doing this until 4pm, because of the beach congestion. It advanced towards Carpiquet airfield, but was held up by stiff resistance in the villages of Villons-les-Buissances and Ainsy. In the east, 7 Brigade made good contact with 50th (Northumbrian) Division and then also pressed southwards. Time, however, was against them and just before dusk they dug in for the night, although one troop of tanks did get to within one and a half miles of the final objective before being recalled. As it was, 3rd Canadian Division was roughly on the line of its intermediate D-day phase line. It could, however, take comfort from the fact that it had destroyed a good part of the German 716th Division.

It is at this point that tribute must be paid to the two British midget submarines (X-craft), positioned as navigation beacons off Juno and Sword. As a result of the post-

ponement of D-Day, they were forced to spend no less than sixty-four hours submerged off the beaches. Yet, at 5am on 6 June they were still in their correct positions and began flashing their green lights to guide in the Canadian and British assault forces. It was, as Admiral Sir Bertram Ramsay commented, a feat of 'great skill and endurance'.

Sword itself presented many of the same problems as Juno when it came to suitable landing points. It was divided into four sub-sectors – Oboe, Peter, Queen and Roger. Rocks prevented access to Oboe, Peter, and the western end of Queen. Roger, too, was beset by shoals. Thus, Queen was the only possible landing beach and it meant that only one brigade could be landed at a time. Behind the beaches the ground was generally low-lying, apart from on the east flank, where high ground ran south to Caen. A ridge from this projected into the Sword sector and covered the direct routes leading from the coast to Caen. Sword was defended by the right half of 716th Division. This had three German and one 'East' battalions. The bulk of 21st Panzer Division provided the reserve, although it also had the secondary task of combating airborne landings. There was the usual pattern of underwater and beach obstacles, as well as strongpoints.

Major-General Tom Rennie, a Scotsman, who had fought with distinction in France 1940, where he was captured but escaped, North Africa and Sicily, commanded 3rd British Division. His D-Day task was to secure the high ground above Caen and, if possible, capture the city itself. First, his 8 Brigade would land with two battalions up, and supported by a battalion of DD tanks. The brigade was to secure Hermanville and St Aubin. Then, Lord Lovat's 1st Special Service Brigade of three Army and one Royal Marine Commando, together with two troops of French Commandos, would land, charged with relieving the airborne troops and John Howard's men on the bridges over the Caen Canal and River Orne. The second brigade of the Division, 185, would now come ashore and make the thrust to Caen, supported by a tank battalion from 27 Armoured Brigade. Finally, 9 Brigade would fill the two and a half-mile gap that had been created between 3rd Division and the Canadians and then advance in step with 185 Brigade. H-hour was to be 6.45am.

Force S had a powerful bombardment element, with two

battleships, a monitor, five cruisers and thirteen destroyers. The battleships and monitor were to neutralize the coastal batteries east of Sword, while the cruisers took on those covering Sword itself. The destroyers and support landing craft, which included 3rd Division's artillery, would engage the beach defences until the first landing craft touched down and then switch their fire to the flanks. Fire opened some five minutes earlier than scheduled and there was little response from the shore. Almost at the same time, the Germans enjoyed their one naval success of the day. Three E-boats had set out from Le Havre. They fired two torpedoes at the battleships *Warspite* and *Ramillies*, but missed. A third struck the Norwegian destroyer *Svenner*, sinking her, although her crew were rescued. *Warspite* then blew one E-boat out of the water and the others withdrew under a smokescreen. A similar attempt to disrupt the American landings was thwarted by bad weather. In the meantime, the LCTs carrying the DD tanks had reached the lowering position, but because of the sea condition, it was decided to release them 5,200 yards from the shore. At 7.30am the first tanks reached the shore, with thirty-one out of forty actually making the beach. AVREs and Centaurs also arrived.

The first infantry now landed and the Germans opened a heavy fire on the beach, killing, among others, the CO and two company commanders of the 1st South Lancashires. Even so, within forty minutes of landing the first clear lane up the beach had been opened and at 8.30am, the lead battalions began to move inland, securing Hermanville by 9am. Lovat's Commandos had begun to land and also took casualties. They cleared Ouistreham and then set off for the bridges, spurred on by messages that the paratroops were still holding them. They had to advance over four miles in three hours through territory held by now-thoroughly alert Germans. Remarkably, they reached the bridges just two minutes behind schedule. Back on the beaches themselves, six out of the eight planned lanes were open by 9.45am and 185 Brigade began to land. It was on shore within twenty-five minutes, but it took time to organize the troops in their assembly area prior to advancing on Caen and the vehicles were held up at the exits from the beach. General Rennie himself landed at 10.30am and soon afterwards the bulk of his division's artillery was ashore. By 2.45pm the reserve brigade was

also complete. Meanwhile, 185 Brigade had been awaiting its supporting tanks, which had been delayed by the congestion on the beaches. At noon, the brigade commander decided to press on towards Caen. Meanwhile one of the battalions of 8 Brigade faced a difficult task in subduing a strongpoint codenamed Hillman, which was the HQ of the german 736th Regiment. It incurred heavy casualties and did not eventually overcome the position until the evening. This caused some delay in fully deploying the troops off the beaches. Warned that German tanks were advancing north from Caen, 185 Brigade continued its advance. At 4pm, after finally being joined by the tanks, its lead battalion secured Bieville, just two and a half miles north of Caen. Thirty minutes later, the Germans counter-attacked.

One of the significant features of D-Day was the

The Norwegian destroyer Svenner (formerly HMS Shark) was one of the few warship victims on D-Day. She was hit amidships by an E-boat torpedo off Sword Beach and immediately broke in two.

A German S-boat (Schnellboot 'fast boat'), known by the Allies as an E-boat (Eilboot 'boat in a hurry'). This particular model was armed with two torpedo tubes and two 20mm cannon. They were capable of speeds of up to 40 knots.

German failure to launch a timely armoured counter-attack against at least one of the beaches. By 1.45am, as a result of the airborne landings, both the German Seventh and Fifteen Armies had been placed on maximum alert. At 4.25am von Rundstedt's headquarters requested that OKW release the Panzer reserves, but General Alfred Jodl, the Chief of Staff OKW, stated that Hitler was in bed, after taking a sleeping draught, and could not be woken. Even so, von Rundstedt agreed that the 12th SS Panzer Division could be placed under the control of Army Group B and it began to concentrate at Lisieux, thirty miles east of Caen.

Rommel, too, had left orders that the two Panzer divisions in Fifteenth Army's area were not to be moved, since landings in Seventh Army's sector were likely to be a diversion from the main landings in the Pas-de-Calais. This left 21st Panzer Division, whose subordinate units were scattered. As early as 1.20am on D-Day, General Wilhelm Richter, commanding 716th Division, ordered 21st Panzer to carry out its secondary role of tackling the paratroops dropping east of the River Orne. With Feuchtinger, its commander,

Because of the delays in Hitler's agreeing to the release of the reserve Panzer divisions, the only mobile formation in the landing area was 21st Panzer Division, which was deployed on both sides of the River Orne. At 8 am it began to attack the British 6th Airborne Division, but was then ordered to counter-attack Sword and Juno. The first attack, at about 4 pm, was hampered by Allied aircraft and beaten off by 185 Brigade. However, that evening 192 Panzer Grenadier Regiment did advance up the gap between the two beachheads before withdrawing, fearing it would be cut off.

still away, indecision seems to have gripped his staff and it was not until 6.30am that the orders were given, and it was a further ninety minutes before units began to deploy. By now Feuchtinger had returned, but before his troops could really make contact with 6th Airborne Division he was

German PzKw IV. The Panzer divisions in Normandy were largely equipped with this tank. It was armed with a 75mm gun, but, unlike the heavier Panther and Tiger, it was matched by Allied tanks.

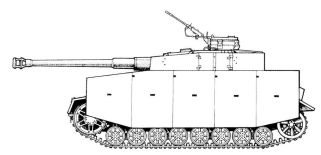

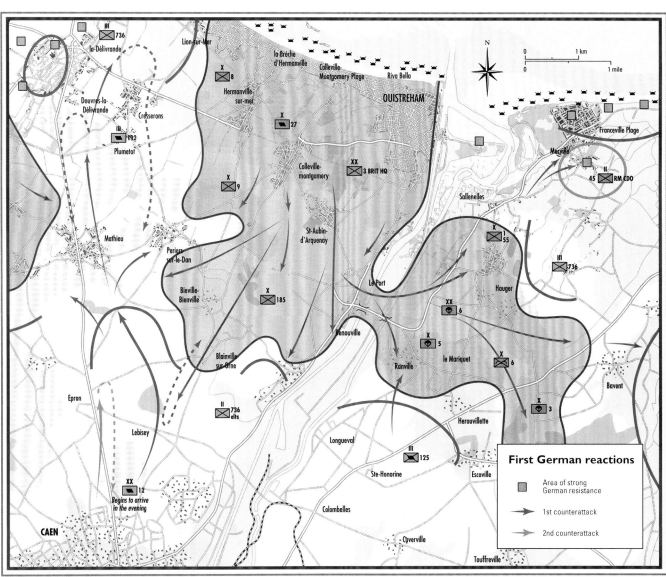

given fresh orders. These came from General Erich Marcks, commander of LXXIV Corps, who had lost a leg in the opening days of the invasion of Russia in June 1941 and was now facing the landings on the British beaches. Army Group B had placed 21st Panzer Division under his command and at midday he ordered Feuchtinger to counter-attack the forces coming ashore on Sword and Juno. Feuchtinger left a Panzer Grenadier Regiment to deal with the airborne threat and began to redeploy the remainder, which, given the overwhelming Allied presence in the skies above, proved to be no easy task.

Von Rundstedt's HQ continued to badger OKW for an answer on the Panzer reserves and eventually received an answer at 2.30pm. The 12th SS Panzer Division was released to him, together with the Panzer Lehr, an elite formation made up of staffs from the various armour schools and based in the Le Mans area, and 17th SS Panzer Grenadier Division. The last-named had only been formed in October 1943 and was still very deficient in equipment. It was carrying out its final collective training near Poitiers, south of the River Loire. Sepp Dietrich's HQ I SS Panzer Corps was to co-ordinate this attack and would come under Seventh Army's command. Given the distance that they had to travel, the adverse air situation, and the disruption to the roads and railways caused by the Allied bombing and French Resistance, which carried out demolitions on nearly one thousand cuttings during D-Day, it would take time for these divisions to come into action.

Feuchtinger eventually launched his attack at 4.30pm. It was not a success. The 1st Suffolks at Bieville, supported by tanks and anti-tank guns, repulsed the main attack, quickly knocking out some twelve PzKw IVs. One Panzer Grenadier battalion did, however, manage to find the gap between the British 3rd and Canadian 3rd Divisions and at 8pm actually reached the coast. Soon after this the Airlanding Brigade of 6th Airborne Division began to arrive by glider. Some of the gliders landed south of where the Panzer Grenadier battalion was positioned and, fearing that it might be cut off, Feuchtinger ordered it to withdraw. Meanwhile, although harassed by Allied aircraft en route, 12th SS Panzer Division began to concentrate near Noyers, south-west of Caen. Sepp Dietrich had established his HQ near Falaise. He and his chief of staff then went

forward to HQ 21st Panzer Division, which had also been placed under his command, to assess the situation. To his fury, Feuchtinger had gone off to see General Richter of 716th Division, but had failed to take a radio with him. Thus, the German efforts to immediately drive the Allies back into the sea on D-Day had proved a damp squib.

While they had failed to secure many of their D-Day objectives, the Allies could feel reasonably content. They had succeeded in landing some 150,000 men in Normandy at a cost of 9,000 casualties, considerably less than many had feared. The experience gained during the previous four years of amphibious operations had proved invaluable. But much still needed to be done. The five beach-heads had to be linked up and expanded. Follow-up forces needed to be landed quickly so that the initial success

British Commandos move inland from Sword Beach to relieve the Airborne troops on the bridges over the Caen Canal and River Orne.

could be exploited. At the same time, while a major German counter-attack had not materialized on D-Day itself, it was certain to come soon. As for the Germans, the day had been a bewildering one, catching many initially by surprise. Yet they were still unconvinced that Normandy was the invasion area. An assault elsewhere was still possible. They were cheered to learn that, having driven back from Germany, Rommel had returned to his headquarters on the evening of D-Day. With a significant armoured force now gathering, there was still time to defeat the Allies.

4
The
Beachhead
Battles

Erwin Rommel bids farewell to Field Marshal Gerd von Rundstedt and his Chief of Staff, General Günther Blumentritt, after a visit to his HQ at La Roche Guyon.

On the night of D-Day General Bernard Montgomery set sail from Portsmouth in the destroyer HMS *Faulknor*. Next morning, after the destroyer had missed its way and found itself off Cherbourg, he arrived off the invasion beaches. The main concern was Omaha, one that General Omar Bradley, commanding the US First Army, shared. Apart from the fact that its beachhead was the shallowest of the five, there was a yawning gap between it and the British Second Army which could be easily exploited by Rommel. Montgomery therefore decided that he would have to postpone US VII Corps's advance to Cherbourg from Utah. Instead, it was to link up with Omaha. To keep the Germans distracted, the British and Canadians were to continue to advance inland. To Rommel, sitting in his headquarters at the La Roche Guyon château on a loop in the Seine near Bonnières, Caen and Cherbourg were the two principal areas of interest. As long as both were held, the Allies would have neither a firm left flank nor a port. To do this, he would have to launch counter-attacks, although these could only be limited because his resources were already stretched. His main hopes rested on

the armoured attack being prepared against the British and Canadians. Kurt ('Panzermeyer') Meyer and his 25th SS Panzer Grenadier Regiment had already deployed to block the Canadian advance on Carpiquet airfield and before dawn on 7 June a plan had been worked out for 21st Panzer and 12th SS Panzer Divisions to attack side by side to drive the Allies back into the sea. H-hour was planned for noon, but delays in the arrival of 12th SS Panzer Division's tanks meant that it had to be put back until 4pm.

On the Allied side, the Canadians had resumed their advance at 6.15am, with orders from General Keller to achieve

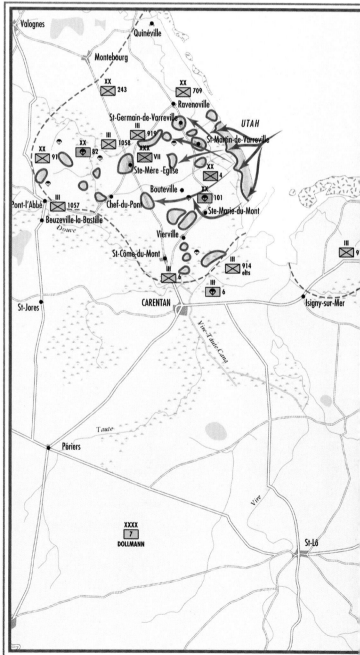

their D-Day objectives. Opposition was initially slight and, on the right, 7 Brigade advanced swiftly and secured the villages of Putot, Bretteville-l'Orgueilleuse and Norrey shortly after midday. Their objectives achieved, the Brigade dug in, ignoring a perfect opportunity to outflank Meyer's men covering Carpiquet airfield. On the left, 9 Brigade resumed its advance somewhat later. Again, the initial progress was promising. The Canadians entered Buron shortly before midday and just over an hour later they were in St-Authie, only two-and-a-half miles north of the airfield. They were now out of range of their own artillery. Worse, Meyer had spotted them. He decided to allow the Canadians to advance a little further, to Franqueville, where their flanks would be even more exposed, and then strike. His men caught the lead Canadian battalion and its supporting tanks totally off balance. They quickly recaptured St-Authie and by late afternoon had forced the Canadians out of Buron.

Although they had not achieved any of their ultimate D-Day objectives, the Allies could be well pleased with progress. Only Omaha had been a cause of real concern. The main tasks now were to link up the beachheads, unite US VII Corps with 82nd and 101st Airborne Divisions, and continue to advance inland. On the German side, the focus was on gathering sufficient armoured strength in the Caen area for an early and effective counter-attack.

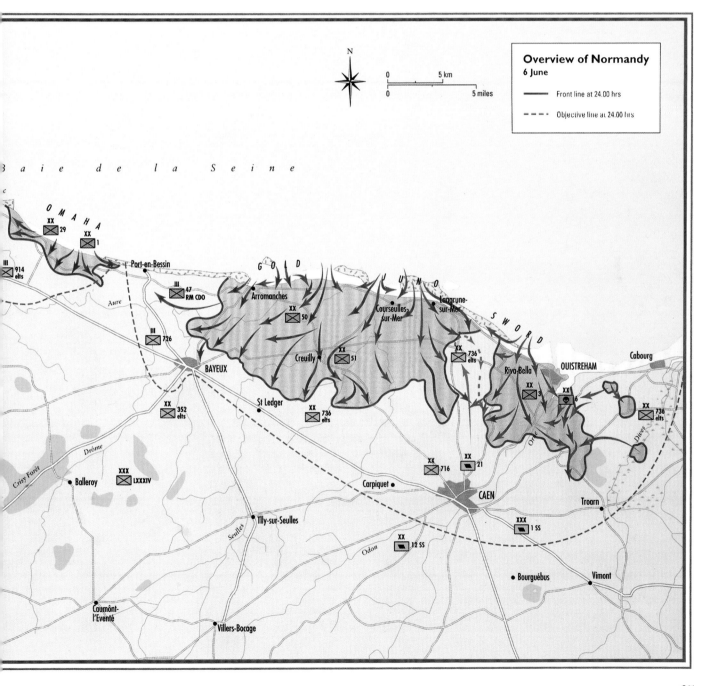

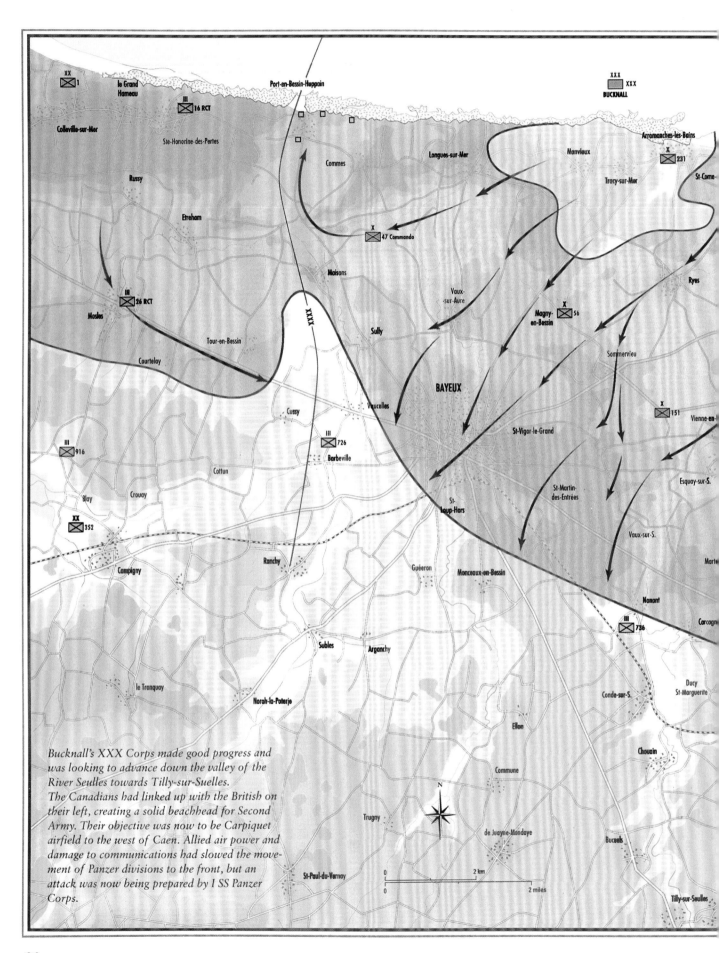

le Grand Hameau

Port-en-Bessin-Huppain

BUCKNALL

Colleville-sur-Mer

Ste-Honorine-des-Pertes

Commes

Longues-sur-Mer

Manvieux

Arromanches-les-Bains

Tracy-sur-Mer

St-Come-

Russy

Etreham

47 Commando

Maisons

Vaux-
-sur-Aure

Ryes

Magny-
en-Bessin

56

Mosles

26 RCT

Sully

Sommervieu

Tour-en-Bessin

Courtelay

BAYEUX

St-Vigor-le-Grand

151

Vienne-en-

Cussy

Vaucelles

916

726

Barbeville

Cottun

St-Martin-
des-Entrées

Esquay-sur-S.

Blay

Crouay

St-
Loup-Hors

352

Vaux-sur-S.

Marte

Campigny

Ranchy

Guéeron

Monceaux-en-Bessin

Nonant

736

Carcagno

Subles

Arganchy

Ducy
St-Marguerite

Condé-sur-S.

le Tronquay

Norah-la-Poterje

Ellon

Chouain

Bucknall's XXX Corps made good progress and was looking to advance down the valley of the River Seulles towards Tilly-sur-Suelles.
The Canadians had linked up with the British on their left, creating a solid beachhead for Second Army. Their objective was now to be Carpiquet airfield to the west of Caen. Allied air power and damage to communications had slowed the movement of Panzer divisions to the front, but an attack was now being prepared by I SS Panzer Corps.

Commune

Trugny

N

de Juayne-Mondaye

Bucools

St-Paul-du-Vernay

0   2 km
0   2 miles

Tilly-sur-Seulles

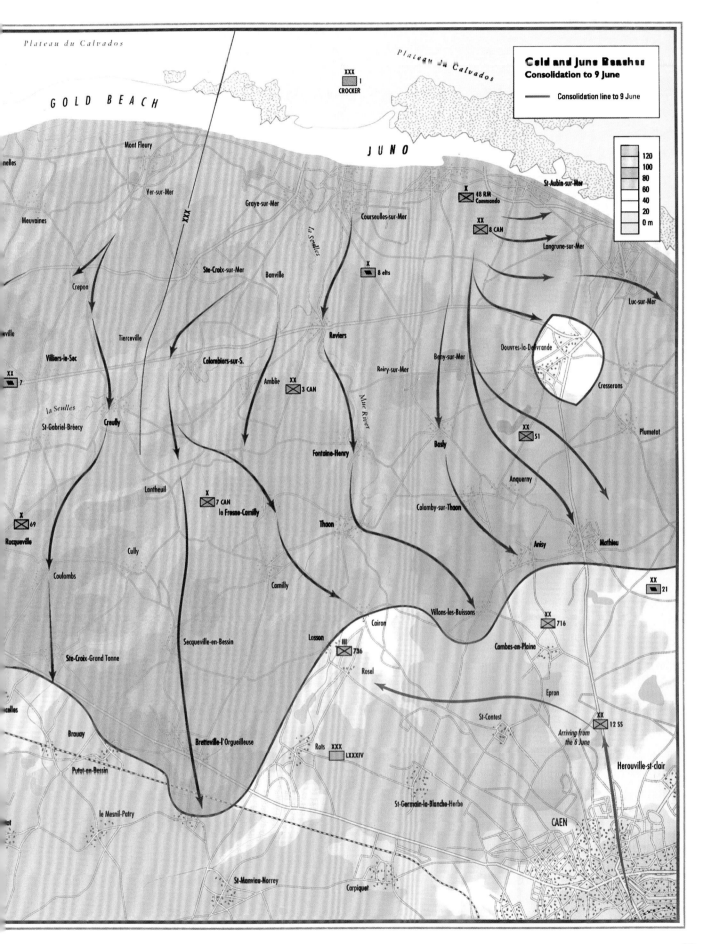

Plateau du Calvados

Cold and June Beaches
Consolidation to 9 June

Consolidation line to 9 June

XXX
1
CROCKER

Plateau du Calvados

GOLD BEACH

J U N O

St-Aubin-sur-Mer

X 48 RM
Commando

XX 8 CAN

Langrune-sur-Mer

Luc-sur-Mer

Mont Fleury

Ver-sur-Mer

Graye-sur-Mer

Courseulles-sur-Mer

Meuvaines

X 8 elts

Crepon

Ste-Croix-sur-Mer

Banville

Reviers

Douvres-la-Delivrande

Cresserons

Villiers-le-Sec

Tierceville

Colombiers-sur-S.

Reiry-sur-Mer

Beny-sur-Mer

XX 7

Amblie

XX 3 CAN

la Seulles

St-Gabriel-Bréecy

Creully

Lantheuil

Fontaine-Henry

Basly

Plumetot

Anquerny

XX 51

Colomby-sur-Thaon

Anisy

Mathieu

X 7 CAN
le Fresne-Camilly

Thaon

X 69
Rucqueville

CulI y

Camilly

Villons-les-Buissons

XX 21

Coulombs

Secqueville-en-Bessin

Losson

Cairon

Cambes-en-Plaine

XX 716

Ste-Croix-Grand Tonne

III 736

Rosel

Epron

cclles

Brouay

Bretteville-l'Orgueilleuse

Rots XXX
LXXXIV

St-Contest

St-Germain-la-Blanche-Herbe

XX 12 SS

Arriving from
the 6 June

Herouville-st-clair

Putot-en-Bessin

le Mesnil-Patry

CAEN

St-Manvieu-Norrey

Carpiquet

120
100
80
60
40
20
0 m

These troops then withdrew to Les Buissons, around which the remainder of 9 Brigade were digging in.

The fighting also spilled over into the British 3rd Division's sector, halting the advance on Caen. But, in spite of Meyer's success in halting the advance, the planned counterstroke with 21st Panzer Division had proved abortive. Feuchtinger's division was under too much pressure to go over to the offensive. Furthermore, the Panzer Lehr was experiencing great difficulty in its move to the coast. Destroyed bridges necessitated diversions and during the daylight hours Allied air attacks were frequent. It was clear to Sepp Dietrich, commanding I SS Panzer Corps, that no concerted armoured counterattack would be possible until 8 June.

On Gold Beach, 50th Division enjoyed a better day than that of the other two British beaches. On the left, 69 Brigade

Canadian troops entering a village D+1.

managed to get across the Caen–Bayeux road and linked up with the Canadians. Tanks from 8 Armoured Brigade then passed through and began to advance on Villers-Bocage, but became embroiled in the Canadians' fight with Panzermeyer's SS men. In the west, Bayeux was captured and the high ground to its south-east secured, but the German defences on the River Drôme, which runs west of Caen, could not be forced. No. 47 Commando RM spent the day attempting without success to secure Port-en-Bessin, which would enable a link-up to be made with the Americans on Omaha. Here the remainder of 29th Infantry Division got ashore during the day, while the 1st Division managed to secure two bridgeheads over the River Aure, but could not reach Port-en-Bessin. Efforts to relieve

Rudder's hard-pressed Rangers on Pointe du Hoc also failed. Even so, the German 352nd Division was beginning to buckle under the pressure, in spite of being reinforced by a brigade of cyclist troops during the day. Utah, too, faced problems. True, on the night 6/7 June a patrol from the beleaguered 82nd Airborne Division in Ste-Mère-Église managed to make contact with the US 4th Infantry Division, enabling some co-ordination. This was just as well, since the Germans had been gathering reinforcements, including a Panzer battalion, for an attack against the lightly armed paratroopers. When it did come, a US tank battalion was quickly deployed and played a major part in breaking up the assaults. But these attacks prevented 82nd Airborne from achieving its D-Day objective, securing crossings over the Merderet. The 101st Airborne also faced counter-attacks, which succeeded in isolating those groups which had reached the north bank of the Douve. As for the 4th Infantry Division, it continued to experience great difficulty in exploiting to the north. Nevertheless, the Allied beachheads were very much more secure than they had been the previous day and, with reinforcements being landed, the chances of the Germans being able to drive the Allies back into the sea were receding by the hour.

During the night of 7/8 June, at HQ I SS Panzer Corps Sepp Dietrich was doing his best to try to cobble together another attack. He was aware that 21st Panzer Division remained under pressure and was still in no position to take part. Likewise, only the leading elements of the Panzer Lehr had arrived in the area of Fontenay-le-Pesnel and Tilly-sur-Seulles and the Division was thus in no position to strike. This left only 12th SS Panzer Division, but this was also incomplete. Fritz Witt, the divisional commander, realized that to have any chance good jump-off positions needed to be secured and as early as 3am his men began to attack the Canadians once more. They enjoyed mixed success. While they failed to drive the Canadians out of Norrey, one battalion did capture Putot, although it was forced out again that night. Elements of the Panzer Lehr did become embroiled, but suffered severely from artillery and more notably naval gunfire. Indeed, during the early days of the campaign, the Germans came to respect the power of the guns of the capital ships even more than Allied supremacy in the air. But while the attack achieved no significant gains, it did halt the Canadian advance and the thrust towards Villers-Bocage.

D-Day +2 also saw the link-up between Gold and Omaha beaches as a result of Port-en-Bessin being secured. The Rangers on Pointe du Hoc were finally relieved and the 29th Division advanced south and secured Isigny by nightfall, leaving the left flank of the German 352nd Division in the air. 101st Airborne Division was given the task of capturing Carentan, but the flooded area around the River Douve and the Carentan Canal restricted its operations. Furthermore, Von der Heydte's 6th Parachute Regiment, reinforced by elements of 77th Division,

The last German position close to the beaches to fall was the radar station at Douvres, which the British decided to leave to soak rather than attack it. The thrust by the British 3rd Division towards Caen was frustrated by stiff German resistance.

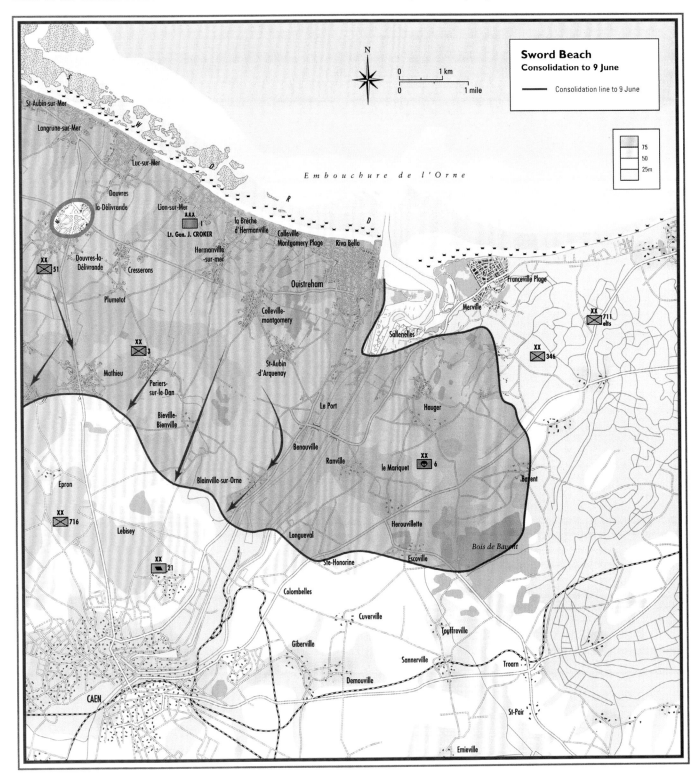

which had moved from Brittany on D-Day itself, was not prepared to give the town up without a fight and it did not fall until 12 June. Finally, on the following day VII Corps on Utah linked up with V Corps on Omaha, providing the Allies with one solid continuous beachhead across the whole front. Meanwhile, on 10 June, 90th Division, which had begun to land on Utah towards the end of D-Day, began to attack through 82nd Airborne with the aim of cutting off the base of the Cotentin peninsula, which Montgomery and Bradley had agreed was the best alternative to striking directly for Cherbourg.

The 90th Division, which had only arrived in Britain in April and was now experiencing its first combat, was soon in difficulties. Not least was a problem that all the Allied ground

mounting the banks enclosing the fields. Many found it a bewildering experience which had not been covered in their training, whose emphasis had been on getting ashore rather than dealing with what the troops could expect once they advanced inland off the beaches. The 90th also suffered from poor leadership, which General Lawton Collins, the corps commander, recognized. Within a few days he sacked the divisional and two regimental commanders, but not before the Division had suffered nearly 3,000 casualties.

Over in the east, Rommel was still striving to concentrate his armour, while organizing local counter-attacks at the same time. I SS Panzer Corps had now been placed under Panzer Group

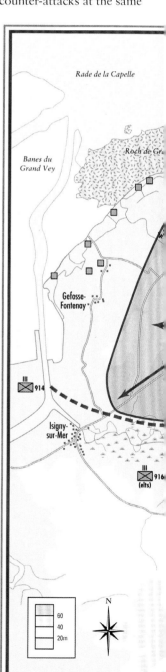

troops were facing – the unique nature of the terrain in Normandy. Although there were areas of open countryside, notably in the east, much of the region was dominated by the *bocage*, small fields bounded by banks topped with hedges. It provided a claustrophobic atmosphere and one that favoured the defence. Infantry were highly vulnerable to concealed machine guns and snipers, while armour advancing down the narrow and twisting lanes was easy prey for tank and anti-tank guns. When the tanks did try to get off the road and into the fields they were still liable to fall victim, especially when

LSTs on one of the US Normandy beaches. Until the Mulberry harbours had been established, all reinforcements and supplies had to be landed directly onto the beaches.

After its D-Day difficulties, V Corps began its advance inland and reached its 6 June objectives on the 8th. On the same day, 47 RM Commando finally entered Port-en-Bessin, thus achieving a link-up between Omaha and Gold beaches. The priority now was to achieve a similar link-up with V11 Corps to the west.

West and Rommel visited Geyr von Schweppenburg on 10 June. Movement during daylight hours was now becoming nigh on impossible because of the air threat. This especially affected replenishment, with supply convoys often having to travel over 100 miles because of the destruction of forward dumps and bridges. In the afternoon of the 10th, shortly after Rommel had departed, the Panzer Group West HQ was hit by an air attack after being pinpointed by Ultra. Most of Geyr's staff were killed, and planning for a major counter-offensive came to a halt. Even so, Rommel continued to move armour into Normandy. The 2nd Panzer Division came from the Pas-

de- Calais, leaving 116th Panzer to deal with any Allied assault north of the Seine, which the Germans had still not totally discounted. Furthermore, Hitler's favourite formation, the 1st SS Leibstandarte Panzer Division, which provided his own household troops, was en route from Belgium. This enabled Rommel to create another Panzer Corps, von Funck's XLVII, which deployed west of I SS Panzer Corps. He accepted, however, that there was little that he could do about the Cotentin peninsula except fight a delaying action to keep the Americans away from Cherbourg for as long as possible. Rather, he concentrated on thwarting the British Second Army.

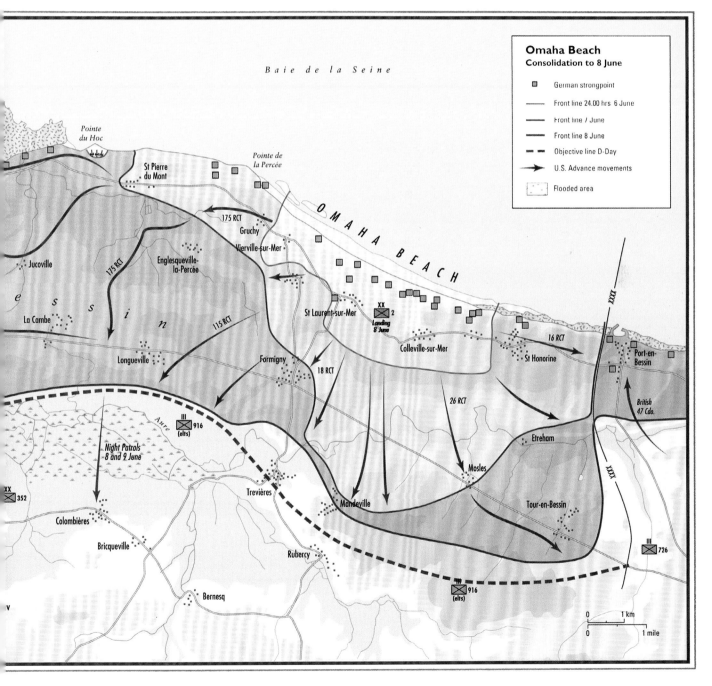

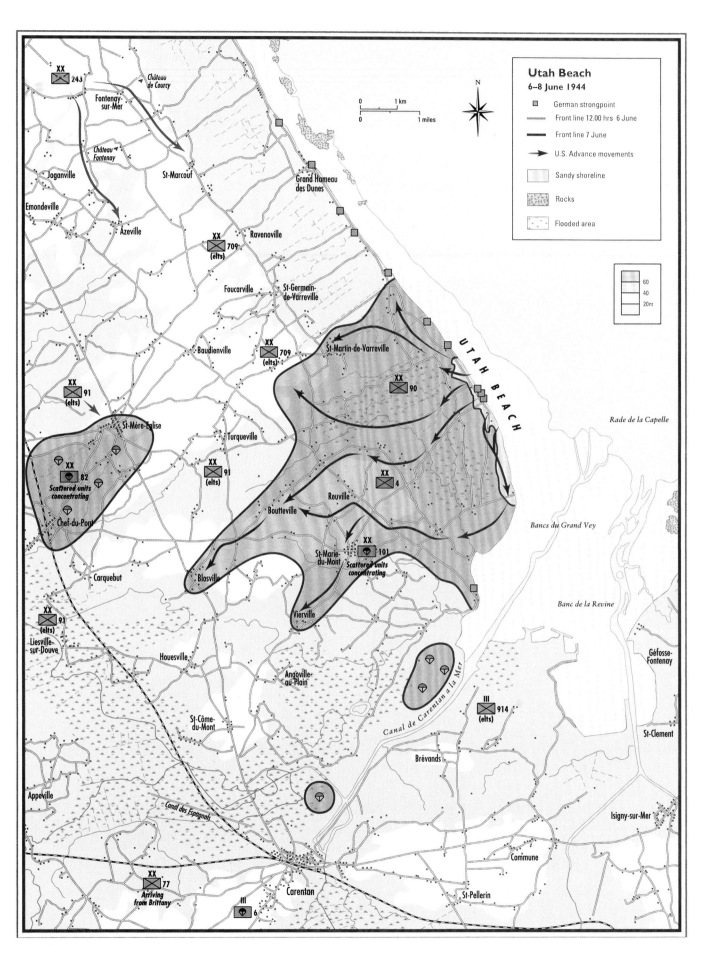

Utah Beach
6–8 June 1944

- German strongpoint
- Front line 12.00 hrs 6 June
- Front line 7 June
- U.S. Advance movements
- Sandy shoreline
- Rocks
- Flooded area

60
40
20m

UTAH BEACH

Rade de la Capelle

Bancs du Grand Vey

Banc de la Revine

Géfosse-Fontenay

St-Clement

243
Château de Courcy
Fontenay-sur-Mer
Château Fontenay
Joganville
Emondeville
Azeville
St-Marcouf
Grand Hameau des Dunes
709 (elts)
Ravenoville
Foucarville
St-Germain-de-Varreville
709 (elts)
Baudienville
St-Martin-de-Varreville
90
91 (elts)
St-Mère-Eglise
Turqueville
82
Scattered units concentrating
91 (elts)
4
Reuville
Chef-du-Pont
Boutteville
St-Marie-du-Mont
101
Scattered units concentrating
Carquebut
Blosville
Vierville
91 (elts)
Liesville-sur-Douve
Houesville
Angoville-au-Plain
914 (elts)
St-Côme-du-Mont
Brévands
Appeville
Canal de Carentan a la Mer
Canal des Espagnols
Isigny-sur-Mer
77
Arriving from Brittany
Carentan
Commune
6
St-Pellerin

The first significant British threat came on 13 June, from the veteran 7th Armoured Division, the Desert Rats. The previous day its tanks reached Caumont and General George Erskine saw an opportunity to swing east and cut off the Panzer Lehr by securing Villers-Bocage. His leading tanks and mounted infantry occupied the village without resistance the following morning and then began to advance along the road to Caen. Unbeknown to them, a company from the 101st Heavy SS Tank Battalion had recently arrived in the area and was lying up in woods overlooking the road. Michael Wittmann, the company commander had four Tigers and one PzKpfw IV under his command. He was also a renowned tankman, with a high score of 'kills' from the Eastern Front. Rather than pick off the British advance guard, Wittmann decided on the bold approach of driving into Villers-Bocage itself. En route, he destroyed four

Recently relieved US paratroopers with a trophy.

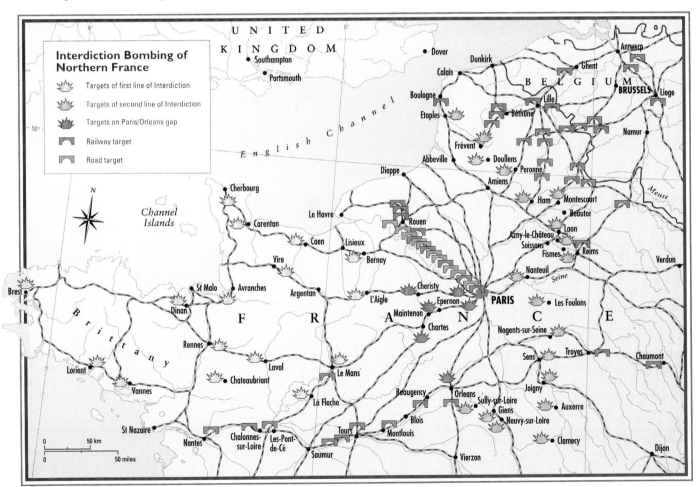

(Left) While VII Corps completed its link-up with 101st Airborne Division, 82nd Airborne was still virtually isolated and under pressure. 90th Infantry Division was now ashore and 101st was ordered to capture Carentan. Because of the marshy terrain and fierce resistance from the German 6th Parachute Regiment, now being reinforced by elements of 77th Division, this proved a difficult operation.

(Above) It was once the Allies were ashore in Normandy that the effectiveness of the air campaign against communications, which had begun in earnest in April 1944, became critical. Aided by the French Resistance, the aim was to seal off Normandy itself and also develop an outer 'cordon' to hinder the movement of German reinforcements from Fifteenth Army to the east and from southern France.

Cromwell tanks and then, after charging through the village, shot up a column of tanks and other armoured vehicles, causing chaos and confusion. The British recovered and four Cromwells deployed in the village to prepare for Wittmann's return. When he did they ambushed him, knocking out his own Tiger, another one and his PzKpfw IV. Wittmann, however, managed to escape on foot to fight another day. What he had done was to single-handedly block a yawning gap, which, if properly exploited, could have unpinned the whole German defence. As it was, 2nd Panzer Division now began to deploy to fill the void and 7th Armoured Division, feeling dangerously exposed, pulled back.

The affair at Villers-Bocage caused Montgomery to rethink his strategy. He decided to abandon attempts to envelop Caen from the east and west. Instead he would go over to the defensive on the eastern flank and concentrate his efforts on the Villers-Bocage and Caumont sector. What concerned him was the arrival of 2nd Panzer Division and the danger that it might be employed against the Americans. Indeed, elements of it had clashed with the US V Corps in the Caumont area. Montgomery therefore decided that the British must maintain pressure here in order to tie down the German armour. Likewise, the concern expressed by General Leonard T. Gerow, commanding US V Corps, at the appearance of German tanks in his sector put paid to the concept of launching a break-out simultaneously with clearing the Cotentin peninsula and seizing Cherbourg. The American effort must be dedicated to the latter, Montgomery decided.

On the peninsula, the ill-fated US 90th Division was relieved by 82nd Airborne and 9th Infantry Divisions. In spite of the *bocage*, they pressed forward and reached the west coast on 18 June, thus isolating the German forces in the northern part of the peninsula. The capture of Cherbourg was now a mere matter of time, but the Allied supply problem had already begun to be eased by the deployment of the Mulberry harbours. The first Mulberry convoys had set sail on D-Day itself and work began on the construction of the breakwaters on the following day. The American Mulberry A was open for business on the afternoon of 16 June, but that at Arromanches (Mulberry B) took longer to put in place and work on it was interrupted by a three-day storm which blew up on 19 June. Worse, this almost destroyed the US Mulberry and resulted in the loss of some 600 vessels of all types. The storm drastically

Landing at a forward airstrip in Normandy. These were quickly established to ensure that the ground troops had the most effective tactical air support. The conditions show how unseasonably wet Normandy was in June 1944.

reduced the rate of supply and reinforcement of the beachhead, but, thanks to superhuman efforts, the Arromanches harbour was functioning on 29 June. The damage to Mulberry A had, however, been so severe that, apart from re-establishing the breakwater off Omaha, it was not rebuilt and parts of it were used in the completion of Mulberry B. At much the same time, PLUTO also came on stream and was soon delivering 8,000 tons of fuel per day into the beachhead.

The storm proved very much more effective than the German Navy in hampering the Allies. True, torpedo boats based at Cherbourg did have a few successes against the Americans before Admiral Theodor Krancke, commanding the German naval forces in the West, ordered the evacuation of the port after the Cotentin peninsula had been cut off. Great numbers of these vessels were based in the French Channel ports and presented a threat to shipping off the British beaches. This was largely nullified by air-power. RAF Coastal Command shadowed the ports, while RAF Bomber Command mounted a series of attacks on them. These were so successful that Krancke noted in despair at the end of June: 'The naval situation in the Bay of the Seine has completely deteriorated. It will be impossible to start the planned operations with the forces that have survived.' Air-power, too, played a significant role in removing the U-boat threat. Initially, the Germans deployed sixteen U-boats in the English Channel and a further nineteen in the Bay of Biscay to guard against an Allied landing on the French Atlantic coast. During the first two nights after the landings Allied aircraft sank four of the latter and damaged five others. As for those in the Channel, after three U-boats were sunk during the first three days of the landings Krancke laid down that only those equipped with *schnorkels*, enabling them to remain submerged for longer, should be used. This radically cut down the numbers of U-boats which could be employed. They did, however, have a few successes, sinking a British frigate and a destroyer on 15 June, while U-984 sank four American LSTs on 29 June. These, however, were merely pinpricks and, given the massive Allied maritime and air supremacy, there was little that the German Navy could do.

In Normandy itself, von Rundstedt and Rommel faced a real dilemma. They realized that the only way that they could defeat the Allies was by launching a major armoured counterstroke, but so stretched were the defences that all the available Panzer divisions were in the line and they lacked the infantry reserves to replace them so that they could be concentrated for the attack. They pleaded with Hitler to come and see for himself, which he did, holding a meeting with the two Field Marshals on 17 June in a bunker complex which had been constructed at Margival near Soissons for Hitler to oversee the invasion of Britain. Hitler first declared that Cherbourg must be held at all costs and ordered its garrison to be reinforced. Von Rundstedt then made some introductory remarks and handed the floor over to Rommel. He gave a detailed account of the situation and pointed out that the fall of Cherbourg was inevitable. He told Hitler that he believed that the Allied intention was to break out in the Caen–Bayeux area and advance to Paris, with a subsidiary operation to clear Brittany. To counter this, Rommel proposed to withdraw the Panzer divisions and strike the Allied thrust in the flanks. As a precursor to this it was essential to withdraw the German line so that it was out of range of naval gunfire. He then went on to plead for reinforcements and, with von Rundstedt's support, demanded freedom of action in the West without interference from Hitler's headquarters. Hitler appeared to ignore what Rommel told him and launched into a monologue on the V-1 flying-bomb offensive against England which had opened four days earlier. Rommel asked him if the V-1s could be used to attack the Allied beachheads and the English South Coast ports from which supplies and reinforcements were flowing to Normandy. Again, Hitler ignored him, launching another tirade which culminated with the boast that V-1s and jet aircraft would devastate Britain.

But while von Rundstedt was depressed by what had transpired, Rommel appeared uplifted. General Alfred Jodl, Chief of Operations at OKW, had told him that Paul Hausser's

II SS Panzer Corps was en route from Russia and other reinforcements were also being sent to France. Hitler had also agreed to visit Rommel at his HQ the following day. This never took place, however. On the evening of the conference a rogue V-1 exploded close to Margival. It was too much for Hitler. He left immediately for Germany without informing von Rundstedt or Rommel. Two days later, Hitler ordered von Rundstedt to prepare a major armoured counter-attack in the Caumont area with the object of splitting the British from the Americans, but the time it was taking for reinforcements to arrive at the front meant that such an operation could not be

A British Vickers machine-gunner.

mounted immediately. Allied air-power and the French Resistance were imposing considerable delays on movement.

Take, for example, the case of the 2nd SS Panzer Division Das Reich. It had received its marching orders on 8 June to deploy to Normandy from the Toulouse area. It took ten days for the Division to reach its assembly area near St-Lô, but its heavy PzKpfw V Panther tanks were held up south of Angers and did not join the Division until the end of the month. So frustrated did the men of the Division become that they took their revenge on the inhabitants of the village of Oradour-sur-Glane near Limoges, herding them into the church and various barns, to which they then set light. Six hundred and forty-two men, women, and children perished and the village was totally burnt. Likewise, the communications leading out of Brittany were virtually severed, making it very difficult to redeploy formations from there. In consequence of this, von Rundstedt warned Hitler that the attack could not take place before 5 July.

The Cromwell tank was the most recent member of the British tank family.

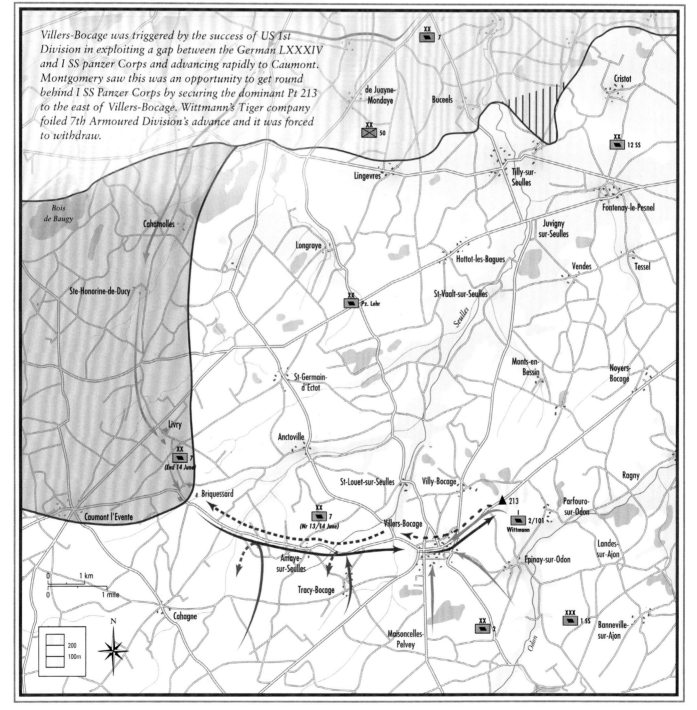

Villers-Bocage

11–14 June 1944

—— Front line 24.00 hrs 11 June	
—— Front line 24.00 hrs 14 June	
⬋ Advance of 7th Armoured Division 12 June to 24.00 hrs	
⬋ Advance of 7th Armoured Division 13 June	
⬋ German counter-attacks 13 June	
⬅ Retreat of 7th Armoured Division 13 June	
⬅ German counter-attacks 14 June	
⬅ Retreat of 7th Armoured Division 14 June	
||| British withdraw from salient 12 June	

Villers-Bocage was triggered by the success of US 1st Division in exploiting a gap between the German LXXXIV and I SS panzer Corps and advancing rapidly to Caumont. Montgomery saw this was an opportunity to get round behind I SS Panzer Corps by securing the dominant Pt 213 to the east of Villers-Bocage. Wittmann's Tiger company foiled 7th Armoured Division's advance and it was forced to withdraw.

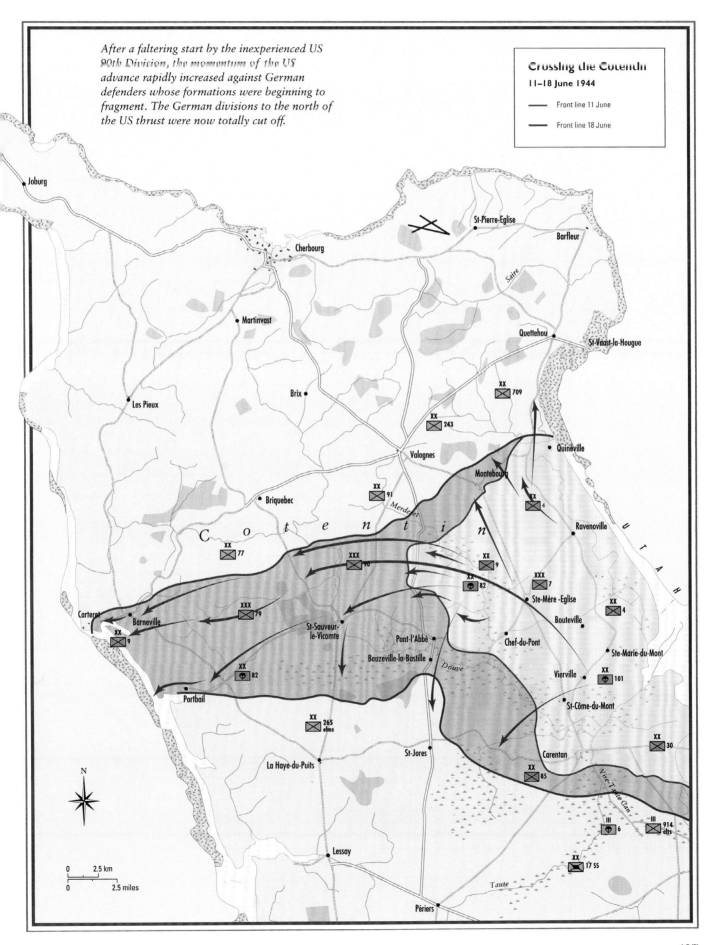

After a faltering start by the inexperienced US 90th Division, the momentum of the US advance rapidly increased against German defenders whose formations were beginning to fragment. The German divisions to the north of the US thrust were now totally cut off.

Crossing the Cotentin

11–18 June 1944

—— Front line 11 June

—— Front line 18 June

Joburg

St-Pierre-Eglise

Barfleur

Cherbourg

Saire

Martinvast

Quettehou

St-Vaast-la-Hougue

Brix

XX 709

XX 243

Valognes

Quinéville

Monteboug

Les Pieux

XX 4

Ravenoville

Briquebec

XX 91

Merderet

C o t e n t i n

XX 77

XXX 90

XX 9

XXX 7

Carteret

Barneville

XXX 79

Ste-Mère-Eglise

XX 82

Bouteville

XX 4

XX 9

St-Sauveur-le-Vicomte

Pont-l'Abbé

Chef-du-Pont

Ste-Marie-du-Mont

Beuzeville-la-Bastille

Douve

Vierville

XX 101

XX 82

Portbail

St-Côme-du-Mont

XX 265 elms

St-Jores

Carentan

XX 30

La Haye-du-Puits

XX 85

Vire-Taute Can

III 6

III 914 elts

Lessay

XX 17 SS

N

0   2.5 km

0   2.5 miles

Taute

Périers

107

US infantrymen fight their way through a French village.

On 24 June, the same day that the Commander-in-Chief West gave Hitler the unwelcome news about the armoured counter-attack, Hitler demanded another counter-attack be launched, this time against the Americans closing on Cherbourg. Von Rundstedt replied that this was impossible, but Hitler kept pressing. As it was, the port was protected by three defence lines, each based on a ridge and with 40,000 defenders, although some were East battalions of doubtful quality, and morale was, overall, low. The US VII Corps began to close on Cherbourg on 22 June, while Hitler exhorted the garrison to 'defend the last bunker and leave to the enemy not a harbour but a field of ruins'. Three days later, the assault proper began, supported by the guns of three battleships, four cruisers, and eleven destroyers. By the end of the day, the defences on the left and right wings had collapsed. Next day, having located the commander of Cherbourg, General Karl-Wilhelm von Schlieben, in a tunnel on the southern outskirts, the Americans demanded that he surrender. Von Schlieben refused, but rounds fired by tank

German prisoners of war from Normandy are marched through the port of Dover on arrival in England.

destroyers into two of the entrances to the tunnel soon brought him, and the naval commander at Cherbourg, out, but he continued to refuse to surrender the whole of the city and port. But, as word got about that he had personally surrendered, other Germans began to put their hands up. The port capitulated on 28 June and German resistance on the peninsula ceased on 1 July. So the Allies now had their port, but much of its infrastructure had been destroyed by the Germans and it would take two months of repair work to make it fully operational.

While the battle for Cherbourg continued, Montgomery had been preparing a new attack designed to pave the way for

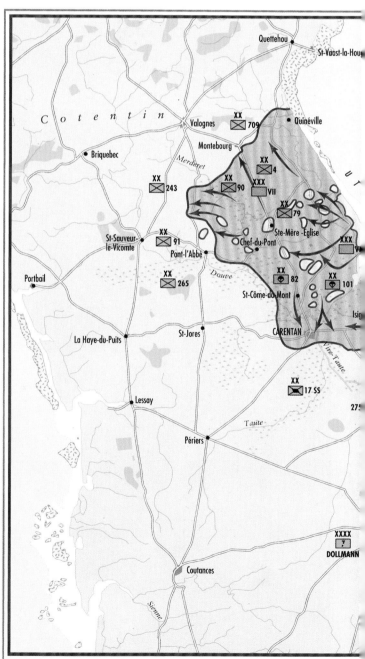

the American break-out. Again, it was to the west of Caen and the idea was to advance south and then east to seize the high ground south of the city. Montgomery's original intention was to launch the assault on 22 June, but the great storm which so damaged the Mulberries forced a postponement and it was not until 25 June that Operation Epsom got underway. The three days' grace that it gave Rommel was invaluable, enabling him to shore up his defences. The recently arrived 49th West Riding Division made the initial assault, which aimed to secure the right flank of the British VIII Corps and was partially successful. On the following day, the main attack stepped off,

with 15th Scottish Division in the lead. Its task was to advance five miles to the River Odon, secure bridges over it and then allow 11th Armoured Division to pass through. The weather, however, was still poor and meant that little tactical air support could be provided because of the cloud cover. Resistance was fierce, notably from the now-battle-hardened young soldiers of the 12th SS Panzer Division, many of them ex-Hitler Youth members. Indeed, the Division's subsidiary title was the Hitlerjugend Division. Just after midday, General Dick O'Connor, commanding VIII Corps, released 11th Armoured Division in an effort to speed up momentum. It, too, was unable

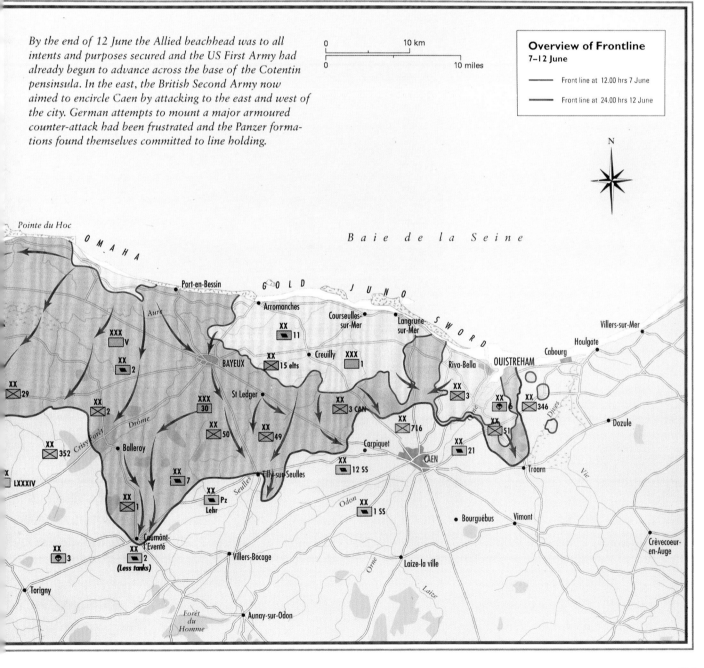

By the end of 12 June the Allied beachhead was to all intents and purposes secured and the US First Army had already begun to advance across the base of the Cotentin pensinsula. In the east, the British Second Army now aimed to encircle Caen by attacking to the east and west of the city. German attempts to mount a major armoured counter-attack had been frustrated and the Panzer formations found themselves committed to line holding.

Overview of Frontline
7–12 June

Front line at 12.00 hrs 7 June

Front line at 24.00 hrs 12 June

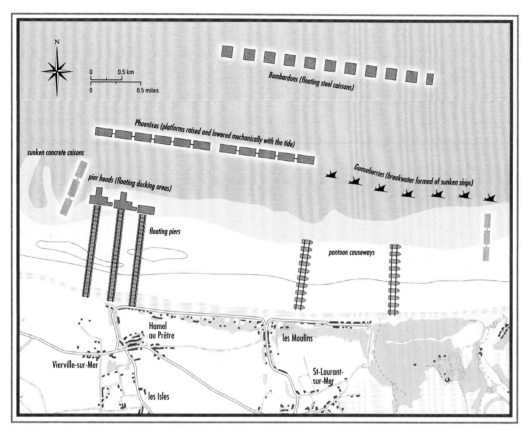

Mulberry Harbour A
at St Laurant-sur-Mer
largely destroyed in the storm
of 19-21 June 1944

The US Mulberry appeared well protected, with its system of artificial breakwaters. On 18 June, the day that it opened for business, the weather was perfect. That evening the barometer began to fall and next day the waves and the wind began to increase. By 20 June it was blowing Force 6, and the Bombardons were only designed to resist winds up to this strength, while the Gooseberries could resist even less. Consequently, Mulberry A and the incomplete British Mulberry B began to break up.

to make much progress and at 6pm 15th Scottish once more took up the baton. Nightfall found its men struggling to gain the ridge north of the Odon. It was not the 'blitz' attack that Montgomery had envisaged, but it was keeping the German armour tied down.

During the night, 43rd Wessex Division was brought up to relieve 15th Scottish so that it could press on again next day. The weather was still poor, but, in spite of several German counter-attacks, the Division did succeed in capturing one intact bridge over the Odon. In the early evening 11th Armoured started to pass over it. By the time darkness fell it had secured the northern part of Hill 112, two miles south of the river. O'Connor was conscious, however, that several villages north of the Odon were still in German hands. Even so, on 28 June 11th Armoured struggled to secure the remainder of Hill 112, but with little further success. O'Connor then ordered it to halt, while the rear was tidied up. On 29 June, II SS Panzer Corps mounted a furious counter-attack from Villers-Bocage. The attack was repulsed, but marked the end of

Epsom. The final element of it was to withdraw 11th Armoured Division from its exposed position on Hill 112.

Thus the German defence still proved firm and Montgomery was aware that fresh Panzer divisions were beginning to appear. Hopes that Omar Bradley might be able to begin his break-out had also been dashed by the great storm which had delayed the arrival of the US VIII Corps, whose participation was crucial to the operation. Undeterred, on 30 June Montgomery expounded his concept of the break-out to his subordinate commanders. While the British Second Army tied down the Germans between Caen and Villers-Bocage, the Americans would advance southwards and eastwards in a wide sweep so as to cut off the withdrawal of the German forces south of Paris. In the meantime, the pressure had to be kept up and Montgomery focussed again on Caen. He wanted to capture it by attacking on both sides to create a double envelopment.

On the German side, von Rundstedt and Rommel were becoming increasingly frustrated over Hitler's interference in the conduct of the campaign, in particular with his refusal to allow them to withdraw their forces out of range of the Allied naval guns. On the evening of 27 June both received a summons to Hitler's Bavarian mountain retreat at Berchtesgaden. They were not allowed to fly or go by train and had to face a 600-mile journey by car. Hitler once more harangued them, boasting of his 'miracle weapons', which would turn the tide in the West. All that von Rundstedt and Rommel needed to do was to halt the Allied advance and clear up their beachhead. The naval gunfire problem could be eradicated by the use of glider-bombs, which the Germans had already begun to employ against ships, and maximum employment of the German surface and sub-surface naval forces. Ground reinforcements were hardly mentioned, and for a very good reason. On 22 June the Russians had launched a major offensive on the Eastern Front, Operation Bagration. It had already thrown Army Group Centre into disarray and there was a very real danger that the Russians would tear an enormous hole in the German defences. In the face of this growing catastrophe, little could be spared for the West. Hitler had also instituted a witch hunt over the fall of Cherbourg and it seemed as though he blamed General Eugen Dollmann, the commander of Seventh Army. On the day that the two Field Marshals arrived at Berchtesgaden, Dollmann died of a heart

How a Mulberry harbour was laid out in theory. The key was the artificial breakwaters, which provided shelter for the vessels unloading at the piers.

What a Mulberry looked like in practice.

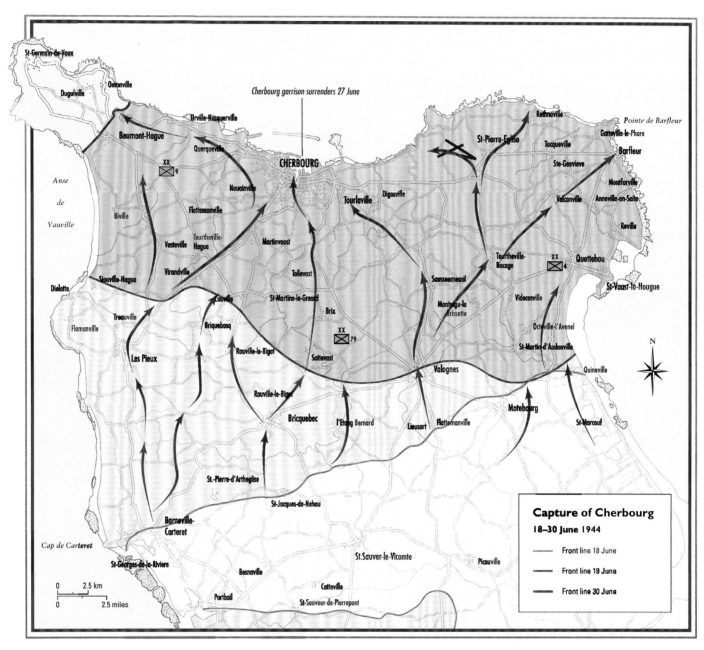

Capture of Cherbourg

Capture of Cherbourg
18–30 June 1944

Cherbourg garrison surrenders 27 June

St-Germain-de-Vaux
Omonville
Dugulville
Urville-Nacqueville
Beumont-Hague
Querqueville
CHERBOURG
Anse
de
Vauville
Nouainville
Biville
Flottemanville
Vasteville
Teurtheville-
Hague
Martinvaast
Tollevast
St-Martine-le-Greand
Virandville
Siouville-Hague
Dielette
Treouville
Couville
Brix
Briquebosq
Flamanville
Les Pieux
Rauville-le-Bigot
Sottevast
Rauville-le-Bigot
Bricquebec
l'Etang Bernard
Barneville-
Carteret
St.-Pierre-d'Artheglise
Cap de Carteret
St-Georges-de-la-Riviere
St-Jacques-de-Nehou
St.Sauver-le-Vicomte
Besnaville
Catteville
Portbail
St-Sauveur-de-Pierrepont

Tourlaville
Digosville
Sausseemesnil
Montaigu-la-
Brissette
Valognes
Lieusart
Flottemanville
Motebourg
Picauville

Rethnaville
St-Pierre-Eglise
Pointe de Barfleur
Gatteville-le-Phare
Tocqueville
Barfleur
Ste-Geevieve
Montfarville
Valconville
Anneville-en-Saire
Reville
Teurtheville-
Bocage
Quettehou
St-Vaast-la-Hougue
Videcosville
Octeville-i'Avenel
St-Martin-d'Audouville
Quineville
St-Marcouf

N

	Front line 18 June
	Front line 19 June
	Front line 30 June

0   2.5 km
0   2.5 miles

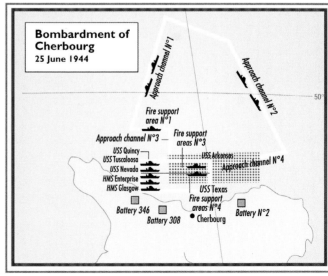

Bombardment of Cherbourg
25 June 1944

Approach channel N°1
Approach channel N°2
50°
Fire support
area N°1
Approach channel N°3
Fire support
areas N°3
USS Quincy
USS Tuscaloosa
USS Nevada
HMS Enterprise
HMS Glasgow
USS Arkansas
Approach channel N°4
USS Texas
Fire support
areas N°4
Battery 346
Battery 308
Cherbourg
Battery N°2

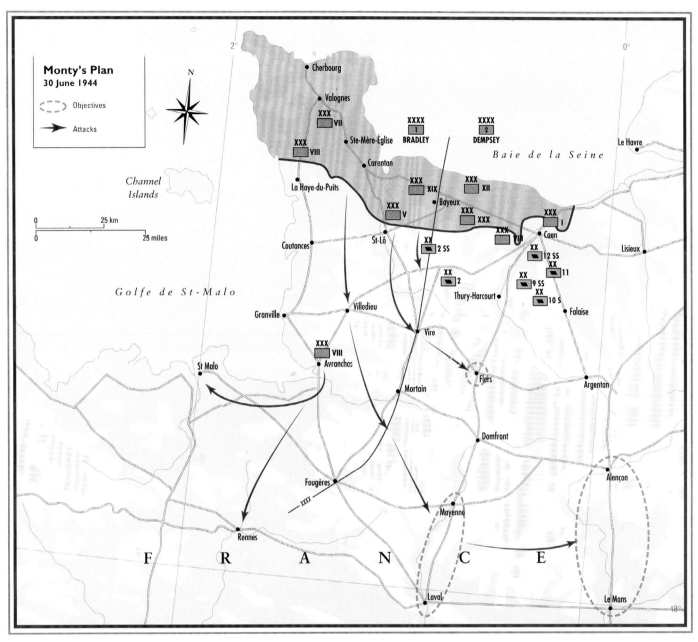

Monty's Plan
30 June 1944

Objectives

Attacks

*Channel
Islands*

Golfe de St-Malo

Baie de la Seine

Cherbourg

Valognes

Ste-Mère-Église

Carentan

La Haye-du-Puits

Bayeux

Coutances

St-Lô

Caen

Lisieux

Le Havre

Granville

Villedieu

Vire

Thury-Harcourt

Falaise

St Malo

Avranches

Flers

Argentan

Mortain

Domfront

Alençon

Fougères

Mayenne

Rennes

Laval

Le Mans

F   R   A   N   C   E

0   25 km
0   25 miles

N

(Left) Although Hitler ordered Cherbourg to be defended to the last man, the shattered German divisions defending it offered only half-hearted resistance. The naval bombardment of the coastal batteries marked the end of Operation Neptune (see lower map), since the Allied ground forces in Normandy were now almost out of range of naval gunfire. The extreme north-west corner of the Cotentin peninsula was liberated on 1 July.

General Karl-Wilhelm von Schlieben, commanding Cherbourg, surrenders in the tunnel that was his HQ.

attack. Von Rundstedt and Rommel demanded that the investigation be halted so that no slur would be attached to Dollmann's memory.

Further orders from Hitler awaited them when they arrived back at their respective headquarters late on 30 June. The

(Above) While the British Second Army kept as many Panzer divisions pinned down in the east, Bradley was to break out southwards and then send one corps to clear Brittany and secure its ports, while the remainder swung eastwards in a deep outflanking move designed to cut off the German withdrawal routes south of Paris.

salient over the Orne must be eradicated at once and on no account was Seventh Army to be driven out of the *bocage*. Simultaneously came a request from Geyr von Schweppenburg and SS General Paul Hausser, who had taken over Seventh Army, to be allowed to withdraw out of range of naval gunfire. Von Rundstedt immediately informed OKW and told Rommel to put in train preparations for this to happen. The answer came back from OKW that there was to be no withdrawal. It was the last straw for von Rundstedt. He immediately phoned Field

Marshal Wilhelm Keitel, Hitler's obsequious Chief of Staff at OKW, and told him that the only option was to make peace and that he himself had had enough. Hitler immediately relieved him and he was succeeded by Hans von Kluge, recently recovered from serious injuries received in a car crash on the Eastern Front.

Meanwhile, the Allies continued to grind on. West of Caen, the Canadians attacked on 3 July, their objective Carpiquet airfield. They managed to secure the village of the same name, but their old adversary 12th SS Panzer Division denied them the airfield. This, however, was a mere preliminary to the main assault on Caen. General Miles Dempsey, commanding the British Second Army, decided that maximum fire-power was the key that would unlock the door. Not only did he concentrate all

A recently captured officer briefs Americans on German disposi-tions. Prisoners were often willing to give information if interro-gated soon after capture, when they would still be suffering from shock.

the artillery that he could bring to bear, but he also intended to use naval gunfire and RAF Bomber Command to clear the way. Caen was in the sector controlled by Panzer Group West, now commanded by General Heinrich Eberbach, since Geyr von Schweppenburg had been sacked at the same time as von Rundstedt. North and west of the city was held by his dependable SS Panzer troops, while the east was defended by a Luftwaffe field division of more doubtful quality, but supported by elements of 21st Panzer Division. In the late afternoon of 7 July the battleship HMS *Rodney* engaged a hill just north of the city, which was

considered a key point in the defences. That night 450 heavy bombers blasted the northern outskirts. At 11pm the artillery opened fire, pounding the German positions. At 4.20am on the 8th, ninety minutes before sunrise, the D-Day veterans of 3rd Infantry Division and the newly arrived 59th Division attacked. Numbed by the ferocity of the preparatory bombardment, the Germans in the forward defences succumbed quickly. The 3rd Canadian Division now began to attack from the west. By the end of the day it and 3rd British division had advanced two and a half miles, but 59th Division's progress was not as good, resulting in a two-mile gap between the former two formations. But the pressure on 12th SS Panzer Division had become almost unbearable and that night Eberbach agreed that all German forces around and in the city could withdraw to the south bank of the Odon. The British advance resumed at 3am on the following day, but the rubble in Caen, combined with a skilful rearguard action by the one remaining SS battalion north of the river meant that it took all day to reach the Odon bridges. By that time all had been blown and heavy fire from the south bank meant that no further progress could be made.

The Americans, too, had begun to press south. Montgomery's concept was for them to now swing south and east from Caumont and then attack into Brittany as well as breaking out eastwards. To Bradley the crucial first objective to enable all this to happen was the road communications centre at St-Lô. With his fourteen divisions now in place, outnumbering the Germans opposite First Army by at least three to one, it appeared straightforward. The terrain, however, was against him. Along the fifty miles of American front there were no open areas where he could deploy armour en masse. In the east the deep valley of the River Vire and the tenacious German hold on St-Lô itself gave him few

(Right) The Americans called it 'the battle of the hedgerows'. Advancing through some of the worst of the bocage and against desperate German resistance, the advance was slow compared to the recent operation in the Cotentin peninsula. Not until 18 July was St-Lô actually entered.

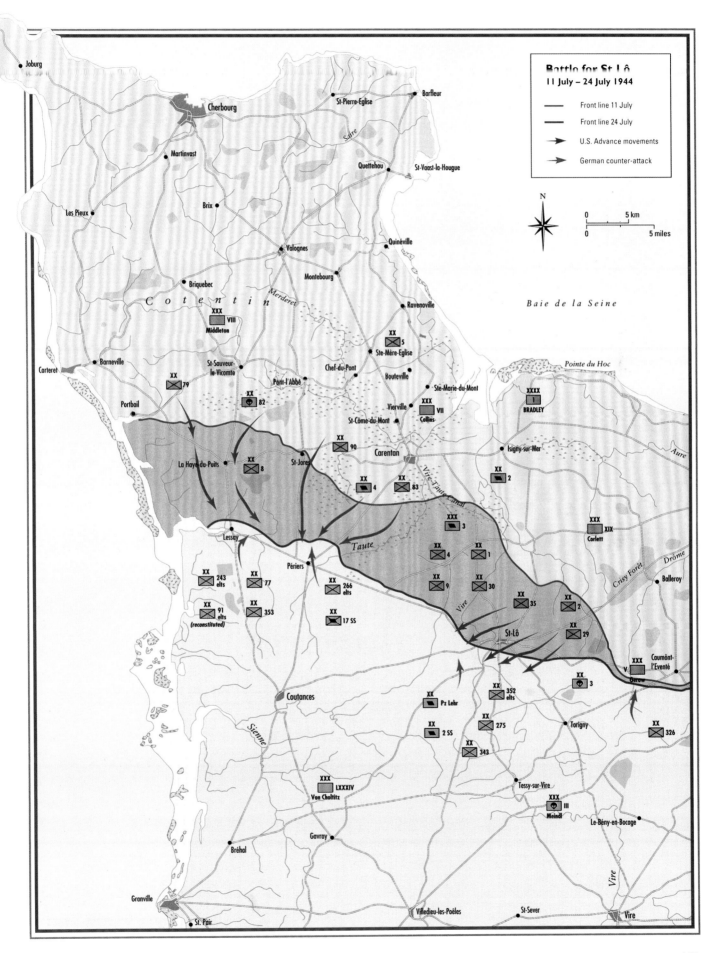

Battle for St Lô
11 July – 24 July 1944

Front line 11 July
Front line 24 July
U.S. Advance movements
German counter-attack

N

| 0 | 5 km |
| 0 | 5 miles |

Joburg

Cherbourg

St-Pierre-Eglise

Barfleur

Satre

Martinvast

Quettehou

St-Vaast-la-Hougue

Brix

Les Pieux

Quinéville

Valognes

Montebourg

Briquebec

Baie de la Seine

Merderet

C o t e n t i n

XXX VIII
Middleton

Ravenoville

XX 5
Ste-Mère-Eglise

Pointe du Hoc

Barneville

St-Sauveur-
le-Vicomte

Chef-du-Pont

Bouteville

Ste-Marie-du-Mont

Carteret

XX 79

XX 82

Pont-l'Abbé

Vierville

XXX VII
Collins

XXXX 1
BRADLEY

Portbail

St-Côme-du-Mont

XX 90

Carentan

Isigny-sur-Mer

Aure

La Haye-du-Puits

XX 8

St-Jores

Vire-Taute Canal

XX 2

XXX 3

XXX XIX
Corlett

Crisy Forêt

Drôme

Lessay

XX 4

XX 83

Taute

XX 4

XX 1

Balleroy

Périers

XX 243
elts

XX 77

XX 266
elts

XX 9

XX 30

Vire

XX 35

XX 2

XX 91
elts
(reconstituted)

XX 353

XX 17 SS

St-Lô

XX 29

XXX V
Gerow

Caumônt-
l'Eventé

XX 3

Coutances

XX Pz Lehr

XX 352
elts

XX 326

Torigny

Sienne

XX 2 SS

XX 275

XX 343

XXX LXXXIV
Von Choltitz

Tessy-sur-Vire

XXX III
Meindl

Le-Bény-en-Bocage

Gavray

Bréhal

Vire

Granville

St-Pair

Villedieu-les-Poêles

St-Sever

Vire

115

options. The centre of the sector was dominated by flooding with just one decent road, that running from Carentan to Périers, while the west was covered with thickly wooded hills and ridges. Nevertheless, to Bradley the right flank seemed to offer the best prospects, and it was here that the US VIII Corps kicked off the offensive on 3 July. Its opponent was the German LXXXIV Corps, formerly commanded one by one-legged General Erich Marcks, who had been killed by a US fighter-bomber on 12 June, and now under General Dietrich von Choltitz. He took maximum advantage of the terrain to make the American advance slow and costly. The US XIX and VII Corps experienced much the same frustration and by 10 July

An ammunitions truck takes a direct hit during the Canadian advance to Falaise.

Bradley was forced to call a halt, with St- Lô still firmly in German hands. But the attrition was having its effect. LXXXVIII Corps warned: 'The struggle cannot be maintained with the present forces for any length of time.'

Von Kluge had taken up his post as Commander-in-Chief West after a pep talk from Hitler which had fired him with the

(Right) Epsom was in pursuit of Montgomery's plan to envelop Caen. The key objective was Hill 112, which was part of a ridge which dominated the area and which General Paul Hausser, commanding II SS Panzer Corps at the time, called 'the key to the back-door of Caen'. In the event, the British found themselves being attacked in the flanks of their narrow salient and, apart from a narrow bridgehead, were forced to withdraw north of the River Odon.

Operation Epsom
24–30 June 1944

Front line 24 June

Front line 25 June

Front line 26 June

Front line 30 June

Allied advance

German counter-attacks

German retreat

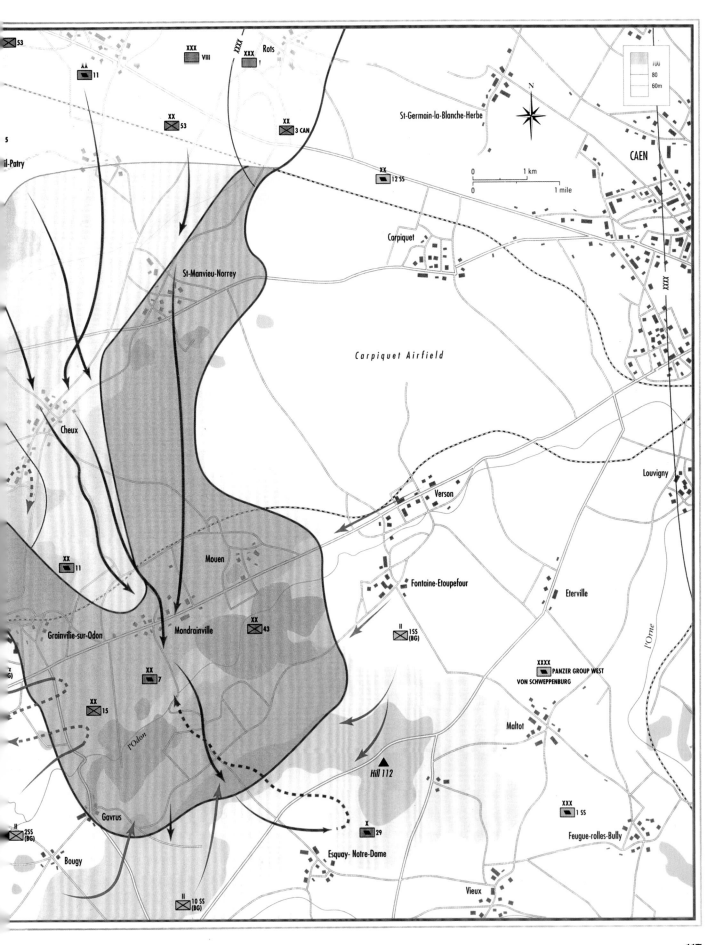

CAEN

St-Germain-la-Blanche-Herbe

Carpiquet

Carpiquet Airfield

Rots

St-Manvieu-Norrey

Cheux

Louvigny

Verson

Mouen

Fontaine-Etoupefour

Eterville

Grainvilie-sur-Odon

Mondrainville

l'Odon

l'Odon

l'Orne

PANZER GROUP WEST
VON SCHWEPPENBURG

Maltot

Hill 112

Gavrus

1 SS

Bougy

Feugue-rolles-Bully

Esquay- Notre-Dame

Vieux

il-Patry

5

belief that the problems that von Rundstedt and Rommel had described had been overemphasized. Consequently, his first meeting with Rommel at La Roche-Guyon on 3 July had served merely to get the latter's back up, especially when von Kluge told him that he was to obey his orders to the letter. It did not take long for the scales to be lifted from von Kluge's eyes. He began to appreciate how the sheer mass of Allied fire-power was wearing the defence down and came round to Rommel's viewpoint, especially after several further discussions with him. Encouraged by this, Rommel submitted a memorandum to his superior on 16 July. He pointed out that there had been 117,000

Caen at the end of Operation Charnwood. There was little left of it by the end of the campaign and it had to be totally rebuilt.

German casualties since D-Day, but that only 10,000 replacements had been sent. Army Group B was close to breaking point. Von Kluge passed this on to OKW, but it made little difference.

If there was frustration in the German high command in France, the Allies were also experiencing it. In spite of the pressure which they had been applying, Caen was still partially in German hands and St-Lô remained just outside the American grasp. There appeared to be stalemate. Certainly, Eisenhower thought this and began to query Montgomery's strategy, pointing out that the terrain in the west made it almost

impossible for the Americans to break out. Rather, he suggested, Montgomery should consider a break-out in the east. Churchill, too, was becoming increasingly impatient. At the lower levels, morale was flagging and such was the growing belief that the German weapons systems were superior that Montgomery forbade mention of the matter in after-action reports. The troops, at least those who had been in Normandy from the beginning, were becoming very tired and casualties were increasing. Those among the British infantry were of particular concern, since there was a growing shortage of replacements in Britain.

Yet Montgomery remained self-confident. He reiterated his concept of the British keeping the German armour tied down while the Americans broke out. Bradley agreed to continue preparing for this, but expressed his concerns over the terrain in First Army's sector. Dempsey, who was present at this conference, held on 10 July, proposed that instead of an American attack, Second Army should take advantage of the good tank country around Caen and launch an all-out offensive there. Montgomery was initially undecided, but then agreed to allow Dempsey his head. He informed Eisenhower, who was delighted that Montgomery appeared to have listened to his advice, and offered all possible air support for Goodwood, as the operation was codenamed. But, while Eisenhower and Dempsey saw it as the Allied break-out, Montgomery took a more cautious approach. If it worked, well and good, but it was essential, in his eyes, that the eastern part of the beachhead be maintained as a 'bastion' on which the American operations could be anchored. Dempsey laid down his aim of establishing an armoured division in each of the Bretteville-sur-Laize, Vimont-Argentan and Falaise areas, but Montgomery deleted Argentan and Falaise, since he feared that this would over-extend Second Army and make it vulnerable to counter-attack. He saw Goodwood as being much more about wearing down the maximum German forces so as to facilitate the American break-out. In other words, he remained true to his original strategy.

The Goodwood attack was to take place just east of Caen. It would involve all three British armoured divisions – 7th, 11th and Guards. Their primary objective was the dominant Bourguébus Ridge, which ran north-west to south-east to the south-east of Caen. Once this had been secured, the armour would then advance towards Falaise. Simultaneously, 3rd Infantry Division would attack south-east and capture Troarn,

Charnwood's aim was finally to secure Caen. It marked the first significant use of allied carpet bombing. While this did numb the defenders, it reduced much of the northern part of Caen to rubble, which made it difficult for the attackers. By the end of the operation, the Germans were still holding the area of the city to the south of the River Odon.

Operation Charnwood
7–9 July 1944

——— Front line 7 July (eve)

✸ '3 map squares' bombing target area

✈ Lancasters and Halifax bombers

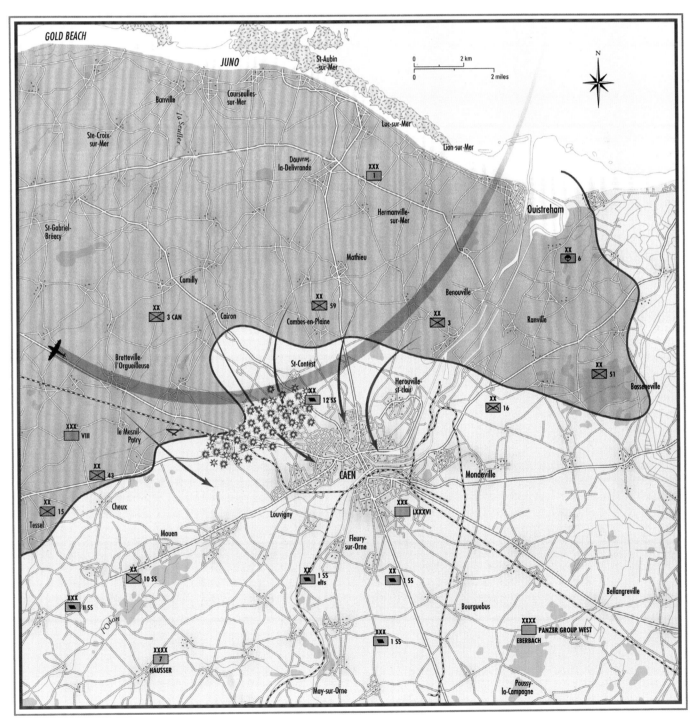

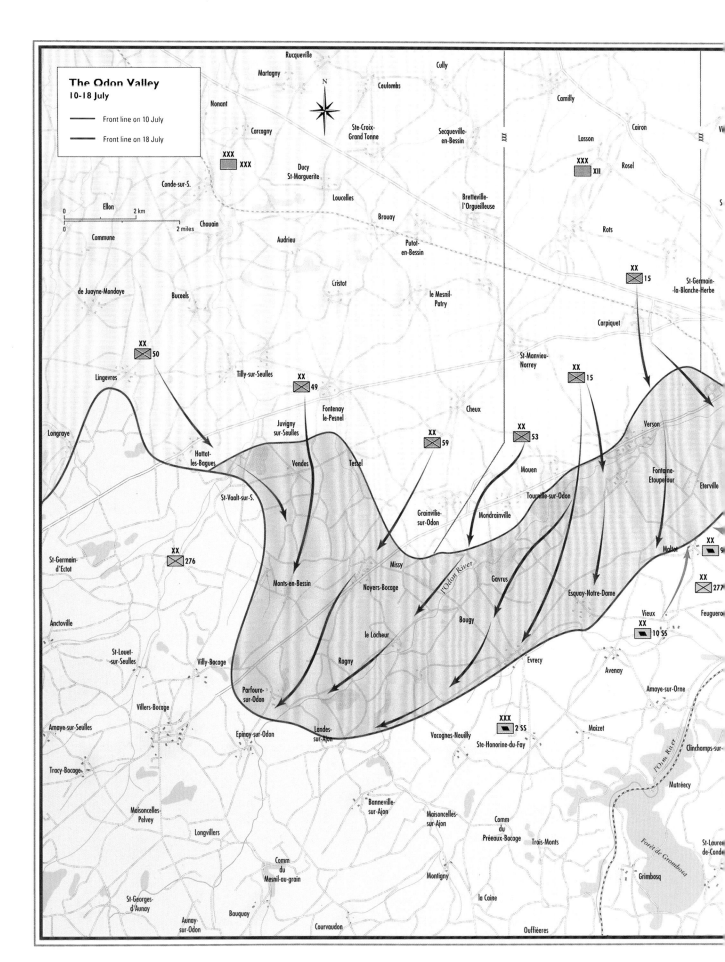

The Odon Valley
10–18 July

Front line on 10 July
Front line on 18 July

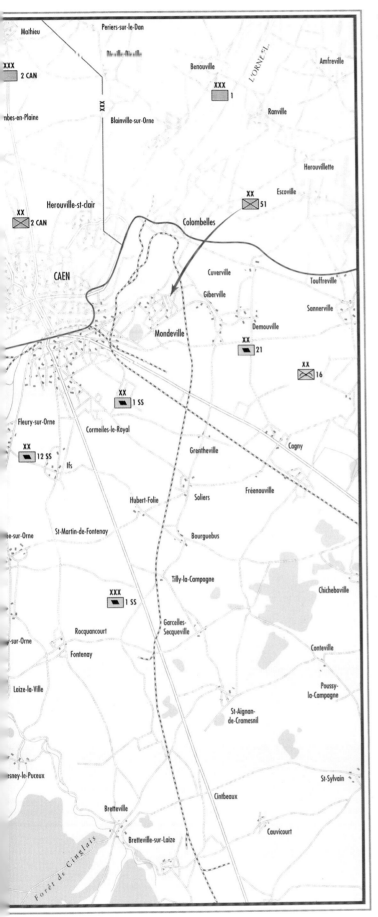

so as to secure the left flank of the armoured thrust, and the Canadian Corps would overrun the remainder of Caen and seize crossings over the River Orne to the south to enable the armour to advance towards Falaise. As to the area west of Caen, the remainder of the British Second Army had been continuing to maintain pressure and by 18 July, when Goodwood was mounted, had almost reached Villers-Bocage. Thus, Panzer Group West had been allowed little respite.

Rommel had read his opponent's mind well. The continuing attacks to the west of Caen were a good indicator, as well as the build-up of British armour in the sector. On 15 July he warned

(Left) No sooner had Charnwood ended, than the British Second Army renewed its attacks to the west of Caen. They were designed to maintain pressure on the Panzer divisions, while Bradley prepared his break-out operation.

Germans forming up for a local counter-attack.

the commander of 346th Division, which was east of Caen, of this, and did the same the following day to Panzer Group West and LXXXIV Corps. On 17 July he visited II SS Panzer Corps, which had recently suffered heavy casualties in the operations west of Caen, and then Sepp Dietrich's I SS Corps, which was east of the city. At about 4pm he left Dietrich's headquarters to return to his own, taking minor roads wherever possible to avoid the attentions of the ever-present Allied aircraft.

US troops make a local attack during the advance to St-Lô. The prone man in the foreground is about to fire a rifle grenade. The soldier on the extreme right is carrying an M1 anti-tank rocket launcher, commonly known as a Bazooka.

Unfortunately, he was forced to take the main road for part of the way and it was on a stretch of this that his car was attacked by an Allied fighter-bomber. Rommel's driver lost control and the car ended up in a ditch, with the Field Marshal unconscious from a severe fracture of the skull. It was to be the end of his active soldiering and, with the battle for Normandy about to enter its crucial phase, his presence would be sorely missed. As it was, he was not replaced and von Kluge took over command of Army Group B, while continuing to act as Commander-in-Chief West.

During the days before Goodwood the British armour had been deploying. Shortage of routes and the narrowness of the assembly area for the attack meant that the initial assault could only be carried out by one division. This was 11th Armoured commanded by General Pip Roberts, the youngest of the British divisional commanders and one who had fought throughout the North African campaign. The Guards Armoured Division would follow and come up on 11th Armoured's left, while 7th Armoured would move behind them and be prepared to lend its weight to either of the two lead divisions. Between 5.30am and 8.30am on 18 July, RAF Bomber Command, operating in clear conditions, with little flak and no German aircraft present, dropped no less than 5,000 tons of bombs on the villages east of Caen. Meanwhile, at 7.45am 11th Armoured Division began to advance under a rolling artillery barrage. So numbed were the defenders from 16th Luftwaffe Field Division and 21st Panzer Division, that there was initially little resistance. Indeed, not until the leading tanks reached Cagny, three-and-a-half miles from the start line, did the defence start to come alive. Sixteen tanks were quickly knocked out and the remainder veered away to the south-west, their

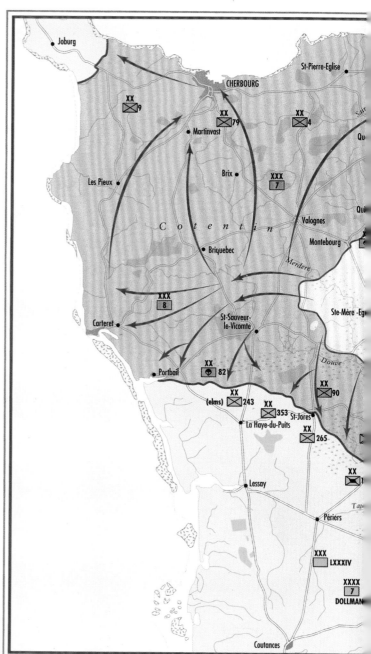

objective the dominant Bourguébus Ridge. The Division's infantry were, however, still trying to clear villages to the rear and the move of Guards and 7th Armoured Divisions had been delayed by traffic congestion on the few routes forward.

By now the Germans were recovering fast. Sepp Dietrich ordered 1st SS Panzer Division to move its tanks onto the Bourguébus Ridge and the Panthers of 501 SS Heavy Tank Battalion to the village of Frenouville on the eastern flank. As 11th Armoured Division's tanks crossed the Caen–Vimont railway line, they found themselves under heavy fire from the ridge to their front and from Frenouville on their flank. In addition, some of the villages to the rear had come alive again and were engaging both 11th Armoured and the two other divisions with anti-tank fire. Chaos began to reign and the advance ground to a halt. The British armour tried again on the following day, but made little progress. Indeed, Dietrich had now also brought 12th SS Panzer Division onto the ridge. Thunderstorms on 20 July were the last straw and the attack was halted.

The British breakthrough, if it was meant to be so, had failed at a cost of some 400 tanks. But there were consolations. The Canadians had succeeded in capturing the remainder of Caen,

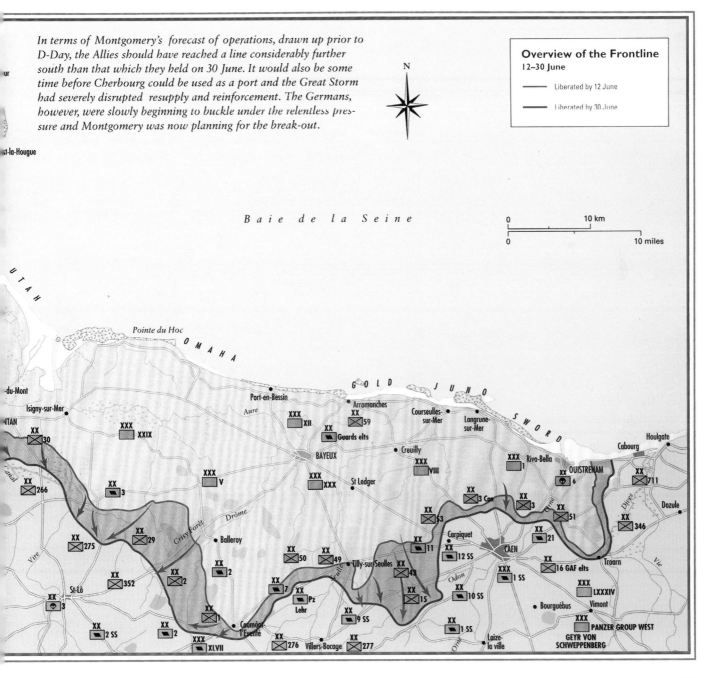

In terms of Montgomery's forecast of operations, drawn up prior to D-Day, the Allies should have reached a line considerably further south than that which they held on 30 June. It would also be some time before Cherbourg could be used as a port and the Great Storm had severely disrupted resupply and reinforcement. The Germans, however, were slowly beginning to buckle under the relentless pressure and Montgomery was now planning for the break-out.

Overview of the Frontline
12–30 June

——— Liberated by 12 June

——— Liberated by 30 June

American troops finally enter St-Lô, a knocked out Panther in their path.

although they then faced fierce counter-attacks. Bridgeheads over the Orne and Odon had been secured and six Panzer divisions had been kept tied down in the British sector. But Bradley's break-out operation, codenamed Cobra, had been scheduled for 20 July, which would have ensured that none of the Panzer divisions could be deployed to his sector in time. He was, as Dempsey had been for Goodwood, reliant on bombers

Greetings to the liberators.

paving the way for the initial assault, and the bad weather meant that they could not be used. Consequently, Cobra was postponed until 24 July. This meant an awkward pause, which could give the Germans time to recover.

Montgomery himself had been over-optimistic in his initial public utterances on the progress of Goodwood. Eisenhower and other senior officers at SHAEF were even more convinced that he had intended to break through. Now that he had failed, they were angry, especially at his protestations that the object of the exercise had been to tie down the German armour so as to facilitate Bradley's attack. Eisenhower felt that Montgomery had misled him and there were calls for him to be removed from command of 21st Army Group. On 20 July Churchill came over to France to see Montgomery, and some of his staff thought that it was to sack him. As it was, Montgomery took him into his Operations caravan and Churchill came out beaming with pleasure. Montgomery's position was still safe.

Churchill retired to spend the night on board the cruiser HMS *Enterprise*. The following morning he returned to 21st Army Group HQ, to be greeted with some astounding news.

(Right) The debate over whether Montgomery intended Goodwood to be a break-out operation has continued to this day. The main problems with it were that the approach routes for the three armoured divisions were too narrow and that Sepp Dietrich, commanding I SS Panzer Corps, reacted quickly, occupying the dominant Bourguebus Ridge before the British tanks could reach it.

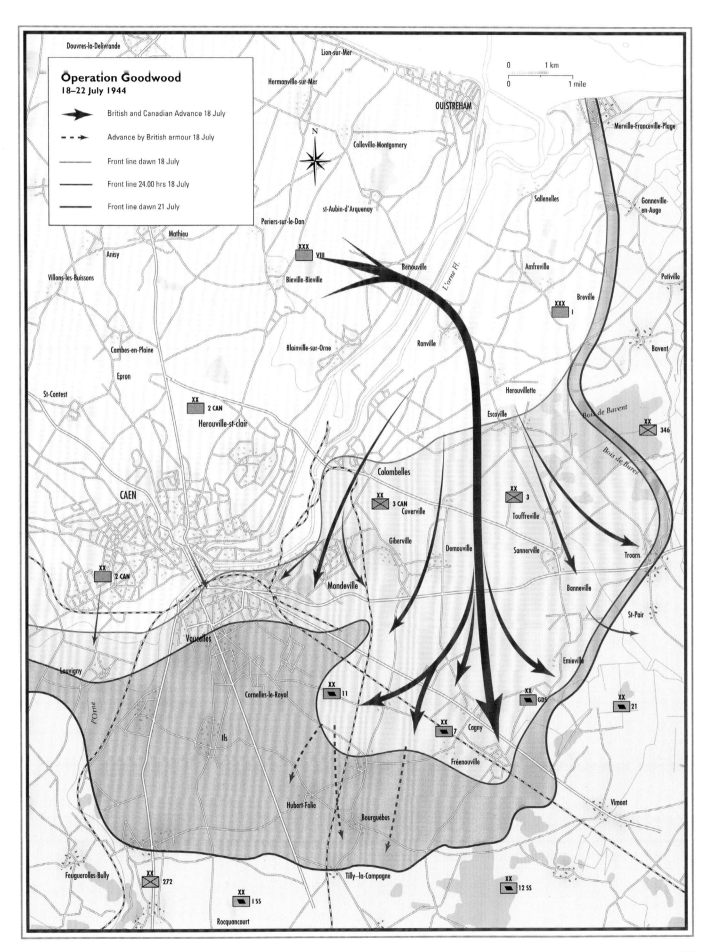

Operation Goodwood
18–22 July 1944

→ British and Canadian Advance 18 July

⇢ Advance by British armour 18 July

— Front line dawn 18 July

— Front line 24.00 hrs 18 July

— Front line dawn 21 July

N

0   1 km

0   1 mile

Douvres-la-Delivrande

Lion-sur-Mer

Hermanville-sur-Mer

OUISTREHAM

Merville-Franceville-Plage

Colleville-Montgomery

Sallenelles

Gonneville-en-Auge

st-Aubin-d'Arquenay

Petiville

Periers-sur-le-Dan

XXX VIII

Benouville

Amfreville

Mathieu

Bieville-Bieville

L'orne Fl.

Breville

Anisy

XXX I

Villons-les-Buissons

Blainville-sur-Orne

Ranville

Bavent

Cambes-en-Plaine

Herouvillette

Bois de Bavent

Epron

Escoville

XX 346

St-Contest

2 CAN

Bois de Bures

Herouville-st-clair

Colombelles

XX 3

CAEN

3 CAN
Cuverville

Touffreville

Giberville

Demouville

Sannerville

Troarn

2 CAN

Mondeville

Banneville

Vaucelles

St-Pair

Louvigny

Emieville

l'Orne

Cornelles-le-Royal

XX 11

XX GDS

XX 21

Ifs

XX 7

Cagny

Fréenouville

Hubert-Folie

Vimont

Bourguèbus

Feuguerolles-Bully

XX 272

Tilly-la-Campagne

XX 12 SS

XX I SS

Rocquancourt

An M5 Stuart (known by the British as a Honey) passes the victims of an earlier tank clash, a Sherman and a Panther.

Ultra intercepts had revealed that there had been a coup against Hitler the previous day. What had actually happened was that Colonel Claus von Stauffenburg, a staff officer from the headquarters of the German Reserve Army, had visited Hitler's headquarters at Rastenberg in East Prussia, the so-called Wolf's Lair, for a conference. He carried a briefcase with a bomb concealed in it, which he placed under the conference table. He then excused himself, saying that he had to make a telephone call. The bomb duly exploded, killing some and wounding others present, but Hitler, apart from being very shaken, escaped the blast. Von Stauffenburg did not know this and telephoned his fellow conspirators in Berlin to say that the Führer was dead. They hesitated to organize the occupation of key buildings in Berlin until they had confirmation that this was so. They did spread the news of the bomb, including to the

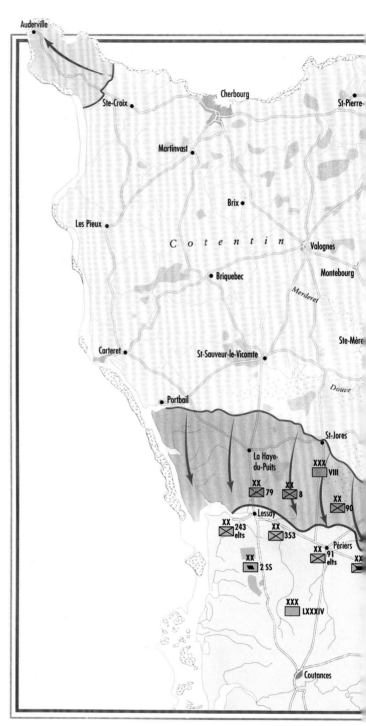

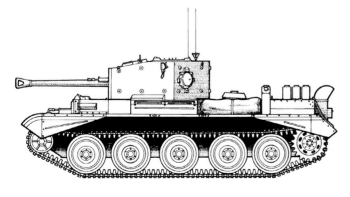

The British Cromwell tank, which had recently come into service with 11th Armoured Division. It had a 75mm gun, but its main drawback was its box-like armour, whose vertical faces made it easier to penetrate than sloped armour.

military governor of Paris, General Karl Heinrich von Stülpnagel, who was also in the plot. While the plotters in Berlin waited, von Stülpnagel immediately arrested Gestapo and SS members in the French capital. Word reached von Kluge of what had happened but, like the Berlin conspirators, he wanted confirmation and was not prepared to commit himself until he had it.

In Berlin, doubts still reigned. Keitel phoned the Commander of the Reserve Army in the mid-afternoon to assure him that Hitler was still alive. Even so, at 4pm the conspirators decided to

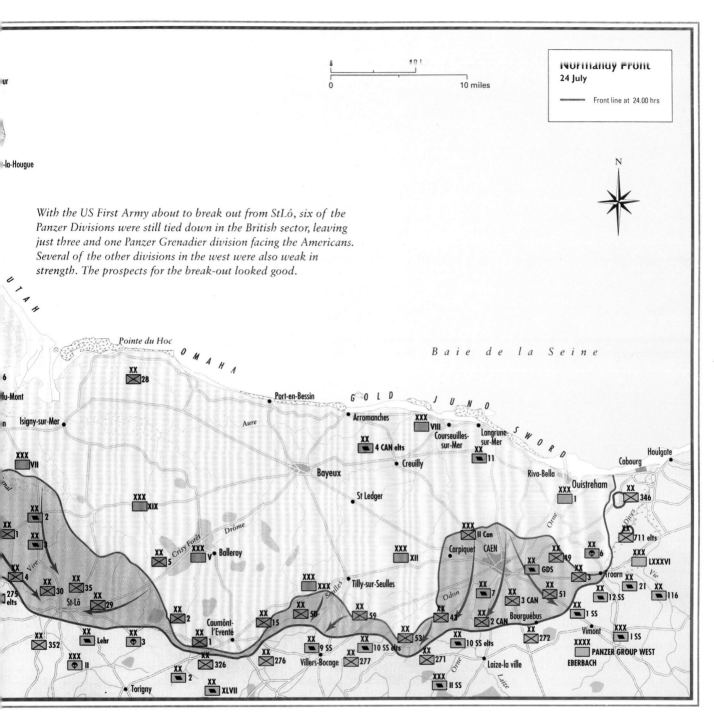

Normandy Front
24 July

Front line at 24.00 hrs

With the US First Army about to break out from StLô, six of the Panzer Divisions were still tied down in the British sector, leaving just three and one Panzer Grenadier division facing the Americans. Several of the other divisions in the west were also weak in strength. The prospects for the break-out looked good.

act. The commander of the Grossdeutschland Guard Battalion, Major Otto-Ernst Remer, was ordered to secure the official quarter of the city, which contained all the important government buildings. Unfortunately, one of propaganda minister Josef Goebbels' staff had been lecturing Remer's men that day and he suggested to Remer that confirmation be sought from Goebbels. In the meantime, Remer did as he had been told and deployed a cordon around the government buildings. He then received an order summoning him to Goebbels' office, where he was handed the telephone. Hitler was on the other end and ordered Remer to

arrest the plotters. It was the end of the coup. Von Stülpnagel was forced to release his prisoners, and von Kluge, realizing that it had failed, openly condemned the plot.

To Churchill and Montgomery, the putsch, even though it had proved abortive, was a sign that cracks were appearing in the Nazi regime. Montgomery immediately issued a new directive. It was largely a repeat of previous directives, with the emphasis on the Americans gaining the Brittany peninsula and also swinging south-east towards Paris. But now that the British had the whole of Caen in their possession, Second Army was in

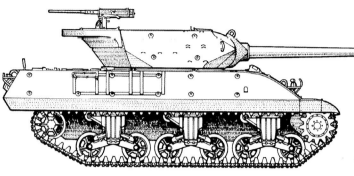

The US M10 Tank Destroyer. This mounted a 3-inch gun and had an open topped turret. The concept was to provide a highly mobile anti-armour force.

a good position to exploit any sudden development, including a regime collapse. In view of the delay imposed on mounting Cobra, it was essential that Dempsey kept the German armour tied down on his front. To this end, the newly created Canadian First Army was to take over the extreme eastern part of the front and drive the Germans back east of the River Dives, while the British Second Army was to push southwards from Caen towards Argentan and Falaise. In reply to a cable letter sent by Eisenhower on 21 July, which demanded that the British put the same effort into the offensive as the Americans were about to do, Montgomery assured him that 'there is not and never has been any intention of stopping

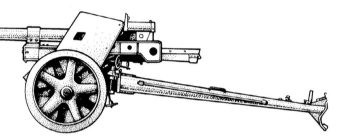

The PaK 40 75mm was the most widely used of the German anti-tank guns. While not having the same range as the '88', it was more manoeuvrable and easier to conceal.

A Sherman engages a water tower. Northern France was and still is littered with these, and they made very good observation posts.

The infamous 'Eighty-Eight'. It could destroy any Allied tank up to 2,000 yards and beyond, although this length of range was seldom achieved in the close country of Normandy.

offensive operations on the eastern flank'. For the time being, the ructions in the Allied camp had abated. All now looked to 24 July and for what they hoped would be the decisive battle which would bring the exhausting Normandy campaign to an end and even complete the destruction of the German forces in the West.

British infantry skirmish through the remains of a French farmhouse.

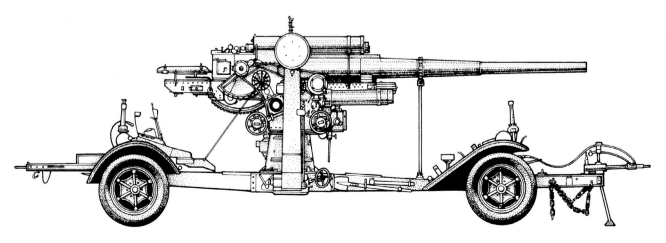

Break-Out

radley's plan for the break-out from Normandy was to attack on a 7,000-yard frontage just to the west of St-Lô. The task was given to Lawton Collins's VII Corps, which was swollen to four infantry and two armoured divisions. Three infantry divisions would carry out the initial break-in. Once they had achieved this, the remaining infantry division and the armour would thrust south-south-west towards Coutances with a view to trapping the bulk of the German Seventh Army with its back to the French Atlantic coast. It would then be the turn of General George S. Patton's US Third Army, which was assembling in the rear, to complete the break-out.

Crucial to the success of the initial phase of Cobra was the employment of 'carpet bombing' to numb the defenders, as it had done, at least temporarily, at the opening of Goodwood. Bradley himself was very keen that his troops should take maximum advantage of this and wanted them to withdraw no more than 800 yards from where the bombs would fall on the German defences. He also wanted the bombers to fly along the St-Lô–Périers road, which represented the start line for the attack. For safety reasons, the airmen wanted the forward troops to be

St-Lô after its capture.

yards for fighter-bombers and 1,450 yards for the heavy bombers. Eighty minutes before H-hour, 350 fighter-bombers would attack the 250-yard strip just south of the road. After twenty minutes of this nearly 1,600 B-17s and B-24s would plaster the area to a depth of 2,500 yards from the road. This would bring the time up to H-hour and, as the attacking troops crossed the start line, more fighter-bombers would appear, followed by medium bombers, which would concentrate on the southern part of the target area. It represented a massive weight of bombs, which was just as well. While Collins had some 1,000 guns available to support his attack, ammunition was short, and only definitely identified strongpoints would initially be engaged.

Although the weather forecast for 24 July was doubtful, there were indications that it would improve. Trafford Leigh-Mallory, the Allied air commander, therefore set the Cobra H-hour for 1pm and flew across to France to observe the air assault at first hand. On arrival, he saw no signs of the skies clearing and therefore

A B-24 Liberator during the carpet bombing which preceded Operation Cobra, the American break-out.

no closer than 3,000 yards from the target and were unhappy about attacking with a lateral approach to the front since they feared that this would caused congestion in the air. Rather, they proposed that they should fly in from the north so that the danger from flak and the Luftwaffe could be minimized. After some debate both sides agreed that the safety margin should be 1,200

(Right) After the delay in mounting the attack, because of bombing problems, it quickly gained momentum. The Germans did attempt armoured counterstrokes against its flank, but these were too weak to have any effect. With the critical communications centre at Avranches secured by 31 July, Patton's newly established Third Army was ready to exploit.

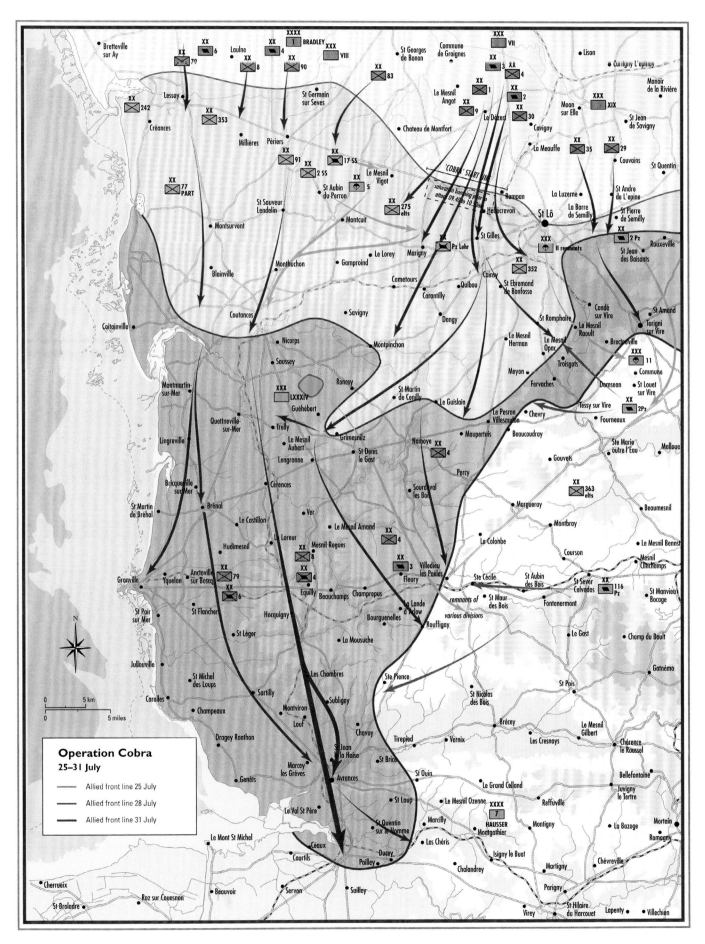

Operation Cobra
25–31 July

— Allied front line 25 July

— Allied front line 28 July

— Allied front line 31 July

Planning a counterstroke into the American flank. A PzKw V Panther waits in the background.

a better weather forecast, was determined that it be launched on the following day. The airmen were, however, insistent that it was too late to recast their plans for a lateral approach to the target. Indeed, the air plan was to be exactly the same as on the 24th, except that the fighter-bombers would begin their attacks at 9.38am. Then came the B-17s and B-29s, 1,500 of them. At first all went well, with the lead groups dropping their bombs on target, but, as the bombing continued, they began to fall closer to the Americans' positions and then on top of them. Both the 4th and the luckless 30th Divisions were hit; this time the casualties were considerably heavier than the previous day, some 600 in all. Even so, the attack went ahead.

In some cases, the Germans had occupied the safety area from which the Americans had withdrawn and they had to fight to reclaim it. Even though the bombing had dazed the defenders, they put up some stiff resistance, especially the Panzer Lehr, which bore the brunt of the attack. As a result, the Americans were restricted to an advance of less than two miles on the first day. The 2nd SS Panzer and 17th SS Panzer Grenadier Divisions were also beginning to threaten on the right flank, but Lawton Collins was determined to press on. The following morning, after further carpet bombing, he released his second wave. On the right, 1st Infantry Division, supported by part of 3rd

decided to postpone the attack. By then, the bulk of the US Eighth and Ninth Air Forces had taken off and were en route to the target, intending to approach from the north. Some of the fighter-bombers received the turn-back order, but others did not and carried out their attacks. There was no direct radio communication with the heavies, but the early groups, seeing the dense cloud, aborted on their own initiative. Unfortunately, many of the final group, consisting of some 300 bombers, saw some breaks in the cloud and pressed on. Worse, one of the lead bombardiers was having trouble with his bomb-release mechanism and dropped his bombs prematurely. Others followed his example and the result was that it was the forward positions of the 30th US Infantry Division which suffered, with nearly 160 casualties inflicted on its men. It was not a good start for the long-awaited break-out, with Bradley especially angered that the airmen had ignored his request to approach from the west.

Cobra, however, had to go ahead and Bradley, encouraged by

Fighting their way out of the bocage. A US patrol tries to locate a German sniper.

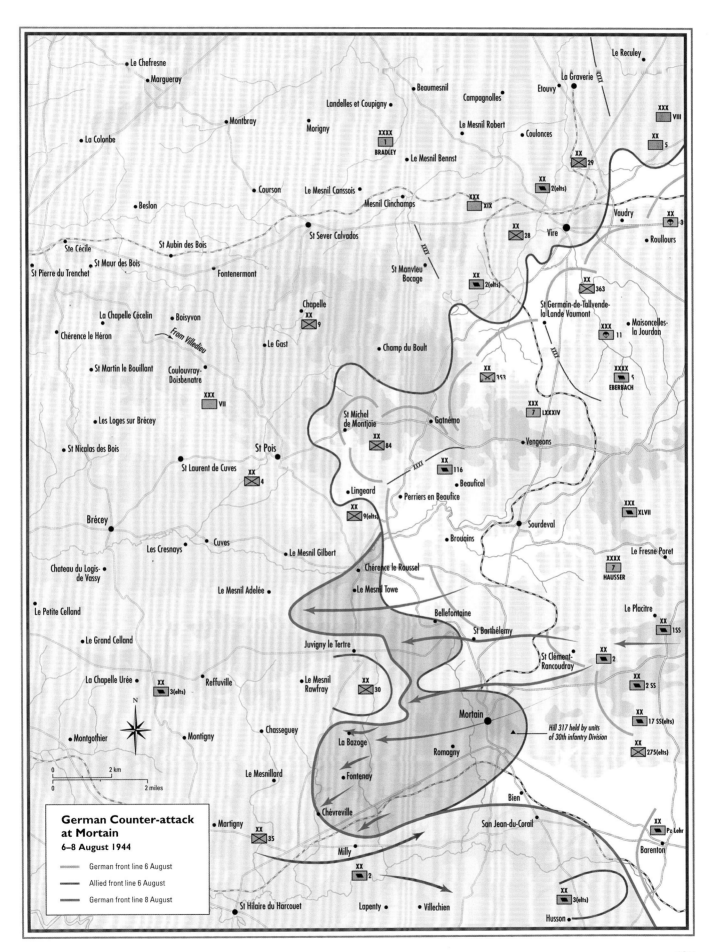

Le Reculey

La Graverie
Etouvy

Le Chefresne

Margueray

Beaumesnil

Campagnolles

VIII

Montbray

Morigny

Landelles et Coupigny

Le Mesnil Robert

XX 5

La Colonbe

XXXX
1
BRADLEY

Le Mesnil Bennst

Coulonces

XX 29

Courson

Le Mesnil Canssois

XX 2(elts)

Beslon

Mesnil Clinchamps

XXX XIX

Vaudry

St Sever Calvados

XX 28

Vire

XX 3

Roullours

Ste Cécile

St Aubin des Bois

St Maur des Bois

Fontenermont

St Manvleu Bocage

XXXX

XX 2(elts)

St Germain-de-Tallvende-la Lande Vaumont

XX 363

St Pierre du Trenchet

Chapelle

XX 9

Maisoncelles-la Jourdan

XXX 11

La Chapelle Cécelin

Boisyvon

Chérence le Héron

From Villedieu

Le Gast

Champ du Boult

XXXX
5
EBERBACH

St Martin le Bouillant

Coulouvray-Doisbenatre

XX 353

XXX
7 LXXXIV

St Michel de Montjoie

Gatnémo

Vengeons

Les Loges sur Brécey

XXX
VII

St Nicalas des Bois

St Pois

XX 84

XX 116

Beauficel

XXX XLVII

St Laurent de Cuves

XX 4

Lingeard

Perriers en Beaufice

Sourdeval

Brouains

Le Fresne Poret

Brécey

Cuves

XX 9(elts)

XXXX

Les Cresnays

Le Mesnil Gilbert

XXXX
7
HAUSSER

Chateau du Logis-de Vassy

Chérence le Roussel

Le Mesnil Adelée

Le Mesnil Towe

Le Placitre

Le Petite Celland

Bellefontaine

XX 1SS

Le Grand Celland

St Barthélemy

Juvigny le Tertre

XX 2

La Chapelle Urée

XX 3(elts)

Reffuville

Le Mesnil Rawfray

XX 30

St Clément-Rancoudray

XX 2 SS

Mortain

Hill 317 held by units
of 30th Infantry Division

XX 17 SS(elts)

Montgothier

Montigny

Chasseguey

La Bazoge

Romagny

XX 275(elts)

Le Mesnillard

Fontenay

Bien

San Jean-du-Corail

Martigny

XX 35

Chévreville

Milly

Pz Lehr

Barenton

German Counter-attack at Mortain

6–8 August 1944

XX 2

German front line 6 August

Allied front line 6 August

German front line 8 August

St Hilaire du Harcouet

Lapenty

Villechien

XX 3(elts)

Husson

N

0   2 km
0   2 miles

Armored Division, found it a struggle because of resistance from the two SS divisions and the cratering caused by the bombing, but 2nd Armored Division was able to punch through the remains of the Panzer Lehr and reached the St-Lô – Coutances railway by nightfall. By this time the Panzer Lehr itself had been reduced to a mere fourteen tanks. It was now noticeable that the Americans had learnt much from the previous weeks of *bocage* fighting. Co-operation between infantry and armour was very much closer than it had been. The tanks, too, were better able to cope with the terrain through the attachment of steel prongs to the front of them, an invention of a sergeant in a reconnaissance squadron. These were fitted to some sixty per cent of the US Shermans, which became known as Sherman Rhinos, and enabled them to cut their way through hedgerows and other obstacles. Another element was effective close air support. The AEAF fighter-bombers were now operating what was called the 'cab rank' system. It proved remarkably responsive, with aircraft constantly circling overhead until directed onto a target by a ground controller.

Von Kluge still believed that the main effort would be from the British sector. This was reinforced by a spoiling attack by the Canadians against the Bourguébus Ridge. Although it was unsuccessful, it dissuaded him from transferring Panzer divisions westwards during the first two critical days of Cobra. Not until the night of the 26/27, after the Canadians had called off their attack, did von Kluge order 2nd Panzer Division from the Orne sector and 116th Panzer Division from north of the Seine to move and strike at the eastern flank of the Americans, while 2nd SS Panzer and 17th SS Panzer Grenadier Divisions attacked from the west. It was too late.

On 27 July the US VIII Corps struck towards Coutances, threatening to annihilate the infantry divisions of LXXXIV

The PzKw VI Tiger, with its 88mm gun, was the most formidable tank in the German armoury. They fought in Heavy Tank battalions.

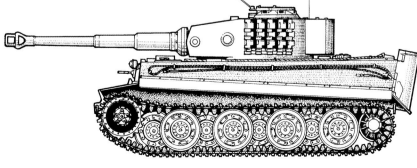

Given the nature of the terrain and its restricted routes, 43rd Division was given an over-ambitious objective in the Bois du Homme. As it was, it left 15th Division with a very exposed flank by the end of the day. 11th Armoured Division's progress was initially slow, but on 31 July it would accelerate as it infiltrated its way through the thinly held German defences.

Corps. The two SS mobile divisions had to turn to meet this new threat, while 2nd and 116th Panzer Divisions struggled in the face of constant air attack to deploy to the area of the break-out. The following day saw VII Corps capture Coutances and the remnants of LXXXIV Corps in danger of being trapped to the south-east of the town. Bradley had originally intended to pause and regroup at this stage, but such was the growing momentum of the advance that he ordered it to continue, handing over control of VII Corps to Patton, who now began to swing south-east, leaving VIII Corps to advance towards Avranches. The 2nd and 116th Panzer Divisions did their best to try to slow the American advance by attacking VII Corps in the flank, but to little effect. Avranches fell to VIII Corps late on 30 July and a despairing von Kluge announced that his complete left flank was now in a state of collapse. The only way that he could prevent the complete disintegration of the front was to attack into the eastern flank of the American penetration, but his two Panzer divisions already

A British Churchill VII infantry support tank. Heavily armoured and relatively slow moving, three Tank as opposed to Armoured brigades of these fought in Normandy.

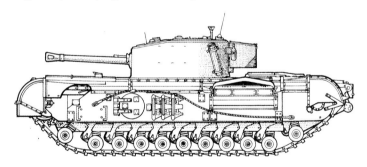

in this area were too deeply embroiled. He would have to transfer additional divisions from the eastern part of the front, but Montgomery now set in a motion an operation to prevent this from happening.

Apart from the Canadian attack east of Caen on the opening day of Cobra, Montgomery had planned further assaults to keep the German armour tied down. The British XII Corps was to attack west of Caen on 28 July towards Evrecy, followed two days later by a mainly armoured thrust by VIII Corps east of

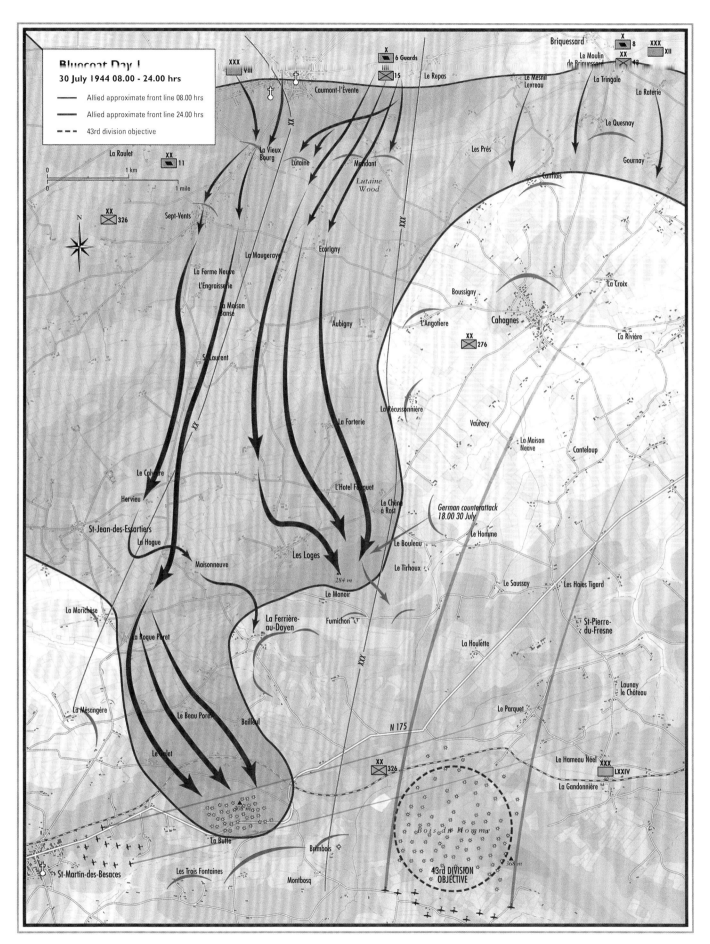

Bluecoat Day I

30 July 1944 08.00 - 24.00 hrs

——— Allied approximate front line 08.00 hrs

——— Allied approximate front line 24.00 hrs

- - - - 43rd division objective

0   1 km

0   1 mile

N

La Raulet

XXX VIII

Caumont-l'Évente

X 6 Guards

15

Le Repas

Briquessard

Le Moulin de Brinnessard

X 8

XXX XII

XX 43

Le Mesnil Levreau

La Tringale

La Raterie

XX 11

Le Quesnay

Gournay

La Vieux Bourg

Lutaine

Mandant

Lutaine Wood

Les Prés

Conflans

XX 326

Sept-Vents

La Maugeraye

Ecorigny

Boussigny

La Croix

XX 276

Cahagnes

La Rivière

La Ferme Neuve

L'Engraisserie

La Maison Bansé

St-Laurent

Aubigny

L'Angotiere

La Forterie

La Récussonnière

Vaurecy

La Maison Neave

Canteloup

Le Calvaire

Hervieu

St-Jean-des-Essartiers

La Hogue

Maisonneuve

L'Hotel Fouquet

Le Chêne à Rost

L'Hotel Fouquet

Les Loges

Le Bouleau

Le Tirhoux

284 m

Le Manoir

German counterattack 18.00 30 July

Le Homme

Le Saussay

Les Haies Tigard

St-Pierre-du-Fresne

La Morichèse

La Roque Poret

La Ferrière-au-Doyen

Fumichon

La Houlette

XXX

La Mésangère

Le Beau Poret

Bailleul

N 175

Launay le Château

Le Parquet

Le Hameau Néel

XXX LXXIV

Le Poulet

XX 326

La Gandonnière

La Butte

Brimbois

Bois du Homme

368 m

St-Martin-des-Besaces

Les Trois Fontaines

Montbosq

43rd DIVISION OBJECTIVE

the River Orne and directed on Falaise. On the evening of 27 July, with Cobra progressing well and conscious that the Canadians had suffered heavily during their attack east of Caen, Montgomery changed his plans. Instead of continuing to attack the German strength in the east, he decided that British Second Army would mount a major assault through the bocage south of Caumont and on the boundary between the US and British forces. There were no significant German formations in this sector and he envisaged the attack as operating like a door swinging eastwards so as to ensure that Panzer Group West could not interfere with the American advance. Montgomery's intention was to mount Operation Bluecoat no later than 2 August, but there was a growing feeling, especially in the US media, that the British were leaving the fighting to the Americans. Consequently, he brought Bluecoat forward to 30 July.

At the time, the Caumont sector was held by the British XXX Corps, with just two infantry divisions. General Miles Dempsey's plan was to strengthen XXX Corps with 7th Armoured Division and to deploy VIII Corps with two armoured and one infantry divisions. Gerard Bucknall, the com-

Tigers lying up in a wood to conceal themselves from Allied aircraft.

mander of XXX Corps, objected to the concept of a two-corps attack, pointing out that the shortage of routes in the Caumont area would create congestion and arguing that a single-corps headquarters was better able to react quickly to a sudden German collapse. Dempsey overruled him and laid down that the main attack would be made by Bucknall, with O'Connor's VIII Corps providing flank protection on his right. Bucknall would begin his attack with just his two infantry divisions – 43rd Wessex and 50th Northumbrian supported by an armoured

brigade – with 7th Armoured Division being held in a concentration area north of Caumont until the initial objectives had been seized. Given the closeness of the country, these were ambitious, with 43rd Division being expected to advance over six miles in the first ten hours. Once they had been achieved, 7th Armoured was to pass through and exploit south-east to Mont Pinçon. VIII Corps would attack with 15th Division on the left and 11th Armoured on the right, with the Guards Armoured Division being initially held in reserve. Apart from guarding XXX Corps's left flank it was also to exploit to Pont Aunay, although Montgomery saw Vire as the key objective.

Bluecoat opened at 6am on 30 July, with 50th Division beginning its attack. Two and a half hours later, 43rd Division joined in. Their opponent was the inexperienced 276th Infantry Division, but it had taken advantage of the terrain to create a series of machine-gun nests and had also laid mines on the banks of the numerous streams in the area. These steps were very effective and 43rd Division, hampered by the fact that it was forced to attack on a very narrow frontage, which meant that only one brigade could be used at a time, was soon falling behind schedule.

VIII Corps fared better. The 15th Scottish Division, supported by tanks of the 6th Guards Tank Brigade, whose first action this was, penetrated to a depth of nearly six miles by the end of the day, in contrast to 43rd Division's bare mile and a half. The 11th Armoured Division, once it had broken through the forward German defences, made similar good progress and it seemed as though a breakthrough was possible.

During the night, 11th Armoured Division became entangled with elements of the US V Corps on its right, the reason being that the inter-Allied boundary had not been clearly defined. Even so, it pressed on at first light, with reconnaissance elements securing an intact bridge over the River Souleuvre. In contrast, the 15th Scottish Division was unable to advance further because

(Right) At one point it looked as though 11th Armoured Division had got into the rear of the German defences and was poised to seize the key communications centre of Vire. This, however, was determined to be in the American sector. Also VIII Corps was veering away from XXX Corps which had the main task of closing the door on the movement of Panzer divisions from the east to combat the US break-out.

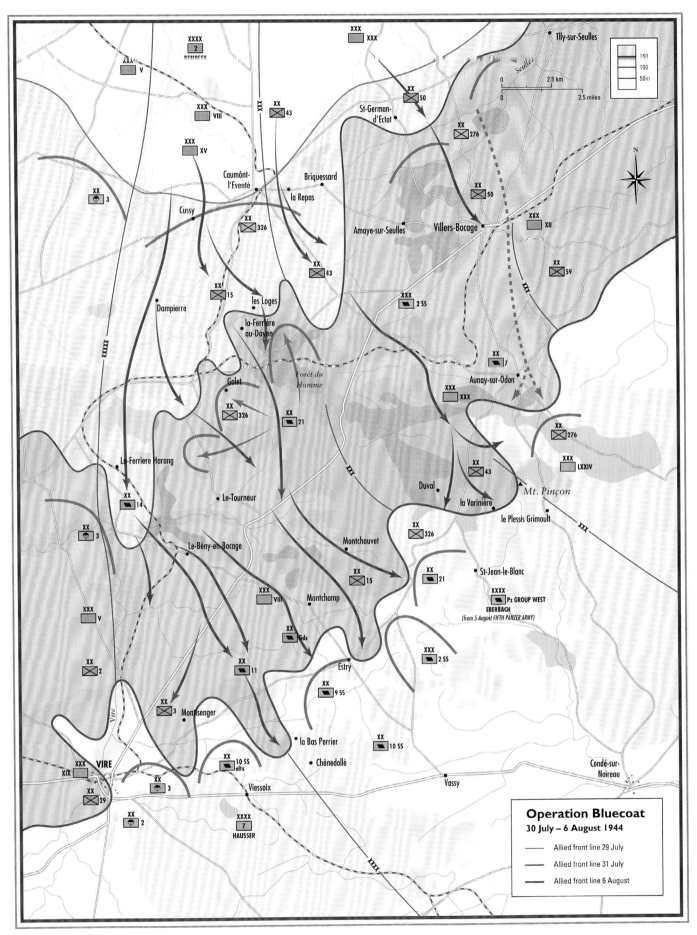

Operation Bluecoat

30 July – 6 August 1944

— Allied front line 29 July

— Allied front line 31 July

— Allied front line 6 August

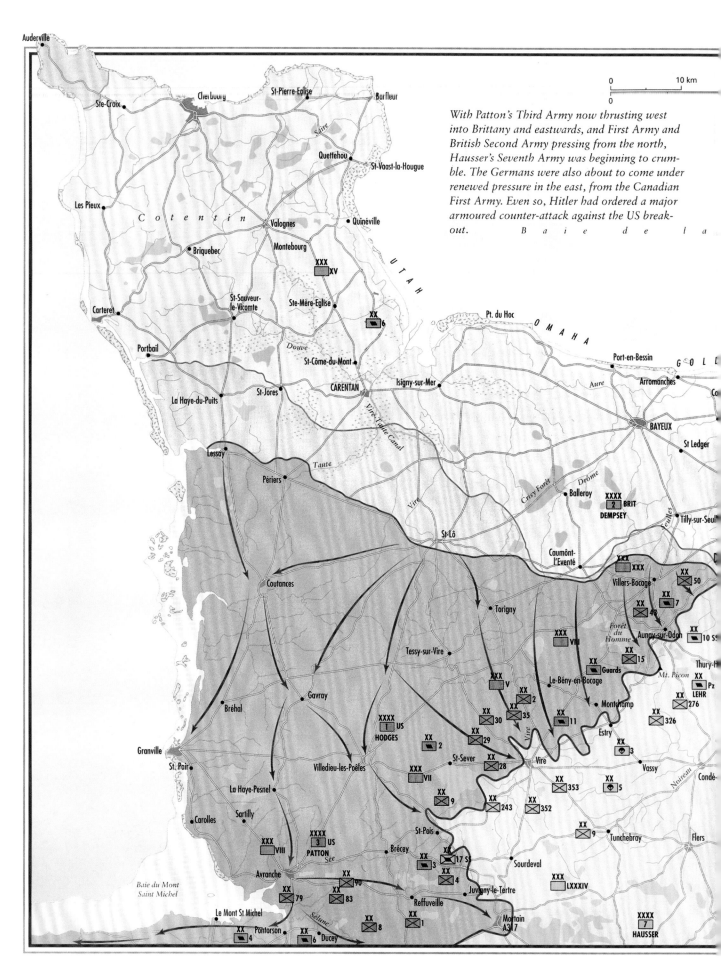

With Patton's Third Army now thrusting west into Brittany and eastwards, and First Army and British Second Army pressing from the north, Hausser's Seventh Army was beginning to crumble. The Germans were also about to come under renewed pressure in the east, from the Canadian First Army. Even so, Hitler had ordered a major armoured counter-attack against the US break-out.

Auderville
Ste-Croix
Cherbourg
St-Pierre-Eglise
Barfleur
Quettehou
St-Vaast-la-Hougue
Les Pieux
C o t e n t i n
Valognes
Quinéville
Briquebec
Montebourg
Carteret
St-Sauveur-le-Vicomte
Ste-Mère-Eglise
UTAH
Portbail
St-Côme-du-Mont
Pt. du Hoc
OMAHA
Port-en-Bessin
GOLD
La Haye-du-Puits
St-Jores
CARENTAN
Isigny-sur-Mer
Aure
Arromanches
BAYEUX
St Ledger
Lessay
Douve
Taute
Périers
Vire
Crisy Forêt
Drôme
Balleroy
Tilly-sur-Seul
St-Lô
Caumont-l'Eventé
Villers-Bocage
Coutances
Torigny
Aunay-sur-Odon
Tessy-sur-Vire
Forêt du Homme
Gavray
Le-Bény-en-Bocage
Montchamp
Thury-H
Bréhal
St-Sever
Vire
Estry
Vassy
Condé-
Granville
St. Pair
Villedieu-les-Poêles
Mt. Picon
La Haye-Pesnel
Tunchebray
Flers
Carolles
Sartilly
St-Pois
Brécey
Sourdeval
Avranche
Reffuveille
Juvigny-le-Tertre
Mortain
Le Mont St Michel
Pontorson
Ducey
Baie du Mont Saint Michel
Sélune
Vire-Taute Canal
Sée

XXX XV
XX 6
XXXX 2 BRIT DEMPSEY
XXX XXX
XX 50
XX 7
XX 43
XX 10 SS
XXX VIII
XX 15
XX Guards
XX Pz LEHR
XX 276
XXX V
XX 2
XX 35
XX 30
XX 11
XX 326
XXXX 1 US HODGES
XX 2
XX 29
XX 3
XX 28
XXX VII
XX 353
XX 5
XX 9
XX 243
XX 352
XX 9
XXXX 3 US PATTON
XXX VIII
XX 17 S
XX 3
XXX LXXXIV
XX 79
XX 83
XX 90
XX 4
XXXX 7 HAUSSER
XX 8
XX 1
XX 4
XX 6

Baie de la
Noireau
Seulles
Vire

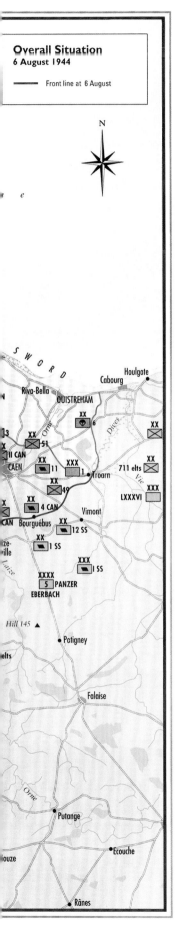

**Overall Situation
6 August 1944**

—— Front line at 6 August

N

SWORD

Houlgate
Cabourg
Riva-Bella
OUISTREHAM
Orne
Dives
6
51
II CAN
XX
CAEN
11
1
711 elts
Troarn
Vie
49
LXXXVI
4 CAN
Vimont
Bourguébus
12 SS
ze-ille
1 SS
II SS
5 PANZER
EBERBACH
Hill 145
Potigney
elts
Falaise
Orne
Putange
Ecouche
ouze
Rânes

the slow progress of XXX Corps had left it with an open left flank. The Guards Armoured Division was also deployed, but traffic congestion in the Caumont area slowed its progress and not until late afternoon was it able to pass through 15th Scottish Division and then almost immediately ran into resistance. In the XXX Corps sector, 43rd Division made slightly better progress, but 50th Division continued to be held up, leaving the former still with an exposed left flank. Bucknall remained keen to deploy 7th Armoured Division and during the night it moved from north of Caumont to a forward assembly area south-east of the town. Congestion was bad and became even worse the following morning when it began to advance through the area captured by 43rd Division. There was only one road running south in this sector, that from Caumont to Breuil via Cahagnes. Worse, because of the open flank, it was under German artillery fire from the east. The congestion was aggravated because a brigade of 50th Division was also using the road with a view to launching an attack eastwards into the German salient facing 50th Division. Consequently, by nightfall on 1 August 7th Armoured's head was some three and a half miles south of Cahagnes while its tail was still north of Caumont.

Two of the leading lights of 12th SS Panzer Division. Fritz Witt (left) commanded the division until killed on 14 June, while Max Wünsche commanded its Panzer regiment. He was captured on 24 August.

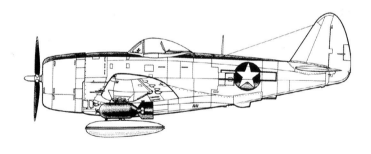

The American Republic P-47 Thunderbolt fighter-bomber, which could carry up to 2,500lbs of bombs or ten rockets.

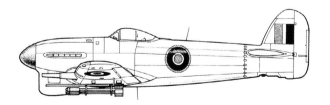

The British equivalent was the Hawker Typhoon, which made a particular contribution to frustrating the German counter-attack at Mortain.

These delays enabled Panzer Group West to deploy blocking forces. First to make an appearance was 21st Panzer Division, which was able to slow the progress of the Guards Armoured Division, although 11th Armoured continued to move south towards Vire, with only poor roads acting as a brake on progress. Then, II SS Panzer Corps began to arrive. The leading battle group of 10th SS Panzer Division had considerable difficulty in negotiating its way through Aunay-sur-Odon because of bomb damage, but by first light on 2 August the Division was in position covering the approaches to Aunay and Ondefontaine, which were now XXX Corps's next objectives.

If Bluecoat was not going to plan, at least as far as XXX Corps was concerned, it was preventing Panzer Group West from deploying armour to halt the American break-out. On 1 August, Patton's Third Army, which was to carry out the exploitation phase, officially came into being and Bradley was now an army group commander, command of the US First Army being given to Courtney H. Hodges, who had been Bradley's deputy. Eisenhower, who had never appointed Montgomery as the Allied land commander, decided that, although Bradley, as commander 12th US Army Group, was now equal in status to Montgomery and his 21st Army Group, he hesitated to take direct control of the land battle himself and was content to allow Montgomery to continue to have de facto control of the ground campaign. However, he never made this clear publicly and this was to cause further rifts.

As it was, Bradley's attention was now focussed on clearing Brittany and this was to be Patton's first priority. Troy H.

Middleton's VIII Corps was given the task. Within the peninsula itself was the equivalent of some four German divisions, but their movements were hampered by the presence of some 50,000 members of the FFI, whose operations were co-ordinated by the Jedburgh teams which the Allies had inserted. On the afternoon of 1 August, General John S. Wood's 4th Armored Division passed through Pontaubault and entered Brittany, closing on its principal city, Rennes, before the end of the day. Wood himself was in favour of advancing south to Angers, where he would be in a position to turn the entire German left flank, but Middleton ordered him to stick to the original plan. Bypassing Rennes, which was left to 8th Infantry Division to occupy, Wood made for the port of Lorient on the Brittany south coast, while 6th Armored Division cleared the northern part of Brittany and reached Brest. Hitler declared both ports Festungen and hopes that the Allies could quickly turn them to their own use were dashed. Brest did not fall until 19 September, while Lorient, together with St-Nazaire further south on the Atlantic coast, held out until the end of the war. John S. Wood himself remained bitter at what he viewed as an unnecessary diversion, which had tied up one third of Patton's army at a time when it could have been employed much more decisively elsewhere.

The remainder of the Third US Army was initially hampered by the fact it was reliant on a single road, that running from Avranches to Pontaubault. The Germans were well aware of this and mounted a number of air attacks on the critical bridge carrying it over the River Sée at Avranches, albeit without damaging it. Thanks, however, to Patton's own determination and drive, he succeeded in passing no fewer than seven divisions down the road in just seventy-two hours, after which they began to fan out eastwards.

Meanwhile, in the British sector Bluecoat continued. Late at night on 1 August 11th Armoured Division was ordered to continue its advance south, with Vire and Tinchebray as its objectives, while the Guards Armoured advanced to Vassy and 15th Scottish protected the Guards' left flank. By the end of the day, 11th Armoured had reached the Vire–Vassy road, with its reconnaissance elements actually being engaged by German troops in Vire itself. The Guards Armoured, on the other hand, was blocked by elements of II SS Panzer Corps at Estry. Vire could

A US M8 105mm self-propelled howitzer mounted on a Sherman tank chassis, known as Priest by the British. Some had their guns removed to convert them to armoured personnel carriers.

(Right) Unlike previous major attacks in the east, Totalize was launched at night, aided by carpet bombing. Initial progress was good, but momentum slowed because of the inexperience of the armoured divisions, which had recently arrived in Normandy, and the bitter resistance offered by 12th SS Panzer Division.

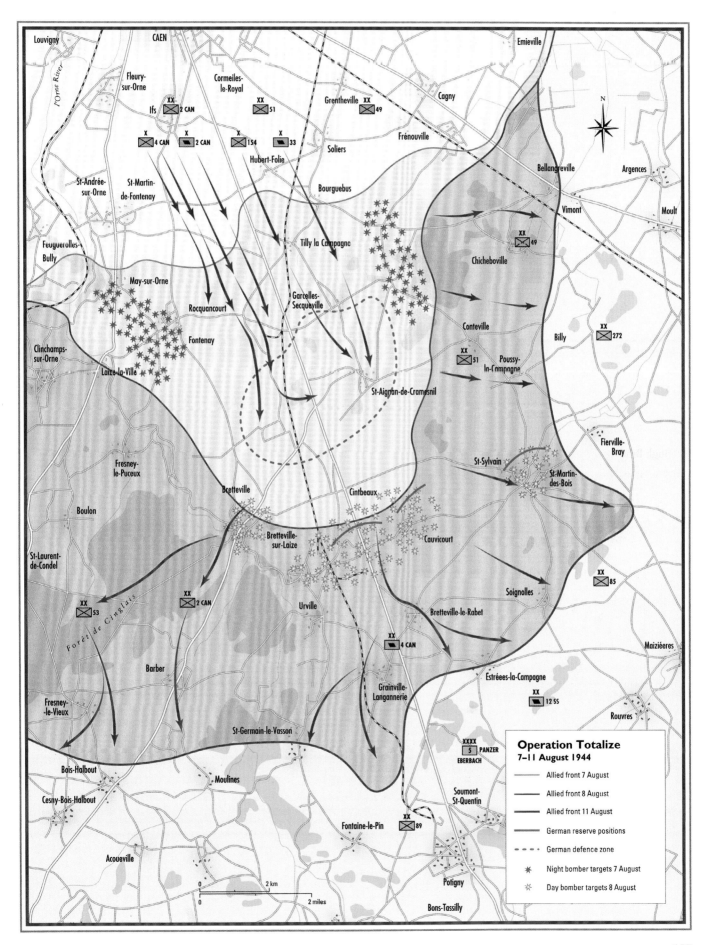

Operation Totalize
7–11 August 1944

Allied front 7 August
Allied front 8 August
Allied front 11 August
German reserve positions
German defence zone
Night bomber targets 7 August
Day bomber targets 8 August

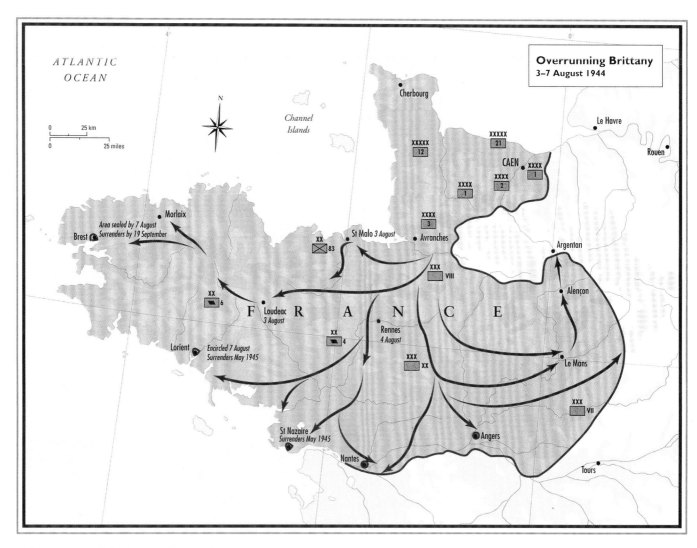

Overrunning Brittany
3–7 August 1944

The remnants of the German forces in Brittany were soon over-run, thanks to a lightning advance by the US 4th Armored Division, followed by 6th Armored. But they could not achieve the garrisons of Brest and St Nazaire, which were under Hitler's orders not to submit. When Brest did finally fall, giving the Allies another port, it was too late to affect the supply crisis which had by then brought their thrust eastwards to a virtual halt.

still be taken, but on the evening of the 2nd Pip Roberts, commanding 11th Armoured, was ordered to halt. There were two reasons for this. First, it was decided that Vire was in the American sector, but also the direction of advance of the British VIII Corps was beginning to diverge from that of XXX Corps. This itself was still making little progress. The 10th SS Panzer Division was able to use infiltration tactics to block 43rd Division's advance on Ondefontaine and that of 7th Armoured on Aunay. Indeed, so frustrated did the army commander, Miles Dempsey become, that he sacked Bucknall, the corps commander, and the Desert Rats commander, Erskine, for lack of drive. He also ordered VIII Corps to turn to the south-east to conform with XXX Corps.

On the German side, an emissary from Hitler arrived at von Kluge's headquarters late on 2 August. He brought instructions that the front was to be restored at all costs. Von Kluge protested, stating that now the Americans had entered Mortain and the British were containing II SS Panzer Corps, there was no way of dealing with the yawning gap in the Avranches area. Rather, he argued, the only sensible course was to withdraw to the River Seine, using the Panzer divisions to delay the Americans while this happened. On 4 August Hitler rejected this out of hand. Von Kluge was to use all his armour to slice the break-out in the neck between Mortain and Avranches. It was not an order that the C-in-C West felt that he could disobey and, aware that Patton's armour was already approaching Le Mans, he decided that he must strike as soon as possible if Hausser's Seventh Army was not to be totally cut off. He therefore agreed with Hausser that the attack was to be mounted on the night of 6/7 August. But instead of the eight Panzer divisions that Hitler expected him to use, von Kluge was only able to deploy four – 1st SS, 2nd SS, 2nd and 116th. The British pressure made it impossible to release any others.

Allied air reconnaissance and Ultra gave indicators of what was afoot and Bradley was able to take precautions. He deployed five infantry divisions, supported by tanks, to cover the sector from Vire to Mortain and held back three of Patton's divisions west of Mortain. In addition, he attacked Vire itself. Recognizing its importance as a communications centre, the Germans used part of the force earmarked for the armoured counterstroke to counter-attack at Vire, but it was no avail and the town was in US hands by the end of 6 August. Worse for the Germans was that much of the armoured force was not in a position to cross the start line for the attack at the scheduled time, which was just after midnight. Von Kluge insisted there be no delay and those divisions which were ready did attack on time. The 2nd Panzer Division used the cover of darkness to advance seven miles towards Avranches, while the SS to their south regained Mortain. Early-morning fog was another welcome ally, but when it lifted the picture changed dramatically. US P-47 Thunderbolt and RAF Typhoon fighter-bombers were quickly in action, launching unceasing attacks on the German armour. Hitler had promised the support of 1,000 planes, but none were to be seen in the air, such was the continuing Allied mastery of it, and the attack

A rough and ready means of cleaning the barrel of a British 25pdr gun after intense firing.

quickly ground to a halt, with many crews simply abandoning their tanks, fearful of being struck by the rocket-firing Typhoons. Simultaneously, Bradley began to apply pressure to the flanks of the German penetration, threatening to cut it off.

This marked the last significant clash between the Canadians and their now long-time adversary 12th SS Panzer Division, which held on to the ridge to the north of Falaise until the threat from 2nd Canadian Division from the west forced it to withdraw. Meanwhile, the Americans were advancing from the south, threatening to create a huge pocket to trap the bulk of the German forces in Normandy.

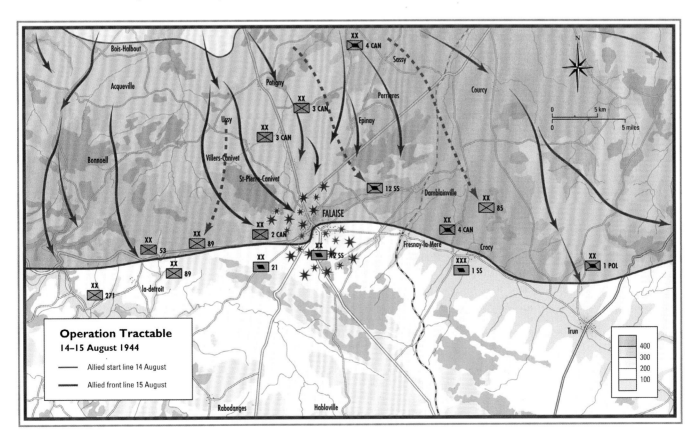

Break-Out

On the 21st Army Group front, the British had not been idle. XXX Corps maintained its pressure and by 6 August Aunay-sur-Odon was finally in its hands. The 43rd Division was also now tackling Mont Pinçon, which, after a grim battle, it secured on the same day. Further to the east, the Canadians launched Operation Totalize on the night of 7/8 August. The object was to break through the defences south and south-east of Caen and advance towards Falaise so as to block the retreat of the forces facing Second Army. At 11pm on the 7th, over 1,000 RAF heavy bombers attacked the defences on the flanks of the attack. 2nd Canadian and 51st Highland Divisions, each supported by an armoured brigade, then advanced. They quickly broke through, but some villages held out, which began to slow the advance. The Canadians' old opponents, 12th SS Panzer Division, then began to counter-attack. Nevertheless, General Guy Simonds, commanding Canadian II Corps, was determined to press on. The next phase was the release of his armoured divisions – 4th Canadian and 1st Polish,

both in action for the first time. As they moved forward, 680 B-17s of the US Eighth Air Force attacked the villages to their front. Unfortunately, some of the bombs fell short, inflicting some 150 casualties on the Allied troops. Even so, the armour advanced and made progress. Simonds wanted to push on, but it halted for

With the Canadians temporarily halted short of Falaise, Patton's Third Army was beginning to advance north from the Argentan area to trap the German Seventh Army and much of Fifth Panzer Army. The Germans, however, managed to occupy Argentan and for the time being deny it to the newly arrived French 2nd Armoured Division.

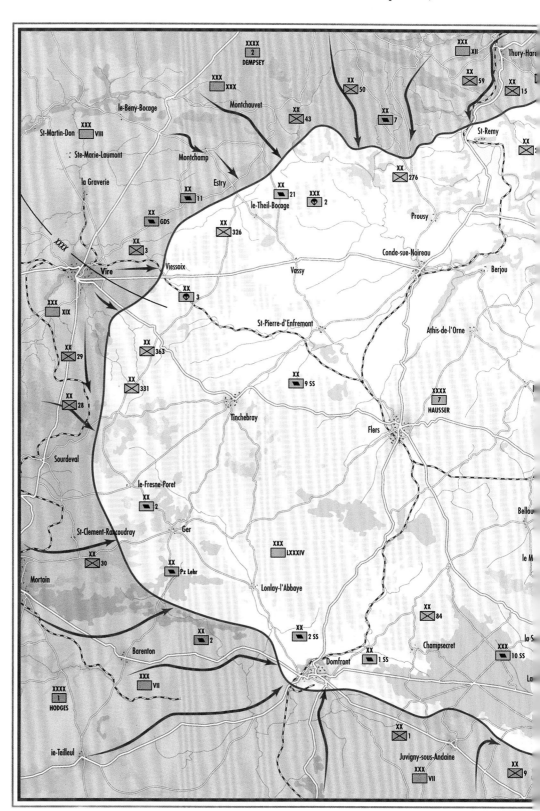

the night, allowing the Germans a breathing space. They began to construct a new defence line on the River Laison and gradually fell back on this, covered by the Hitler Youth Division, which continued to fight tenaciously. As a result, the Canadian attack lost momentum and eventually came to a halt, short of the Laison, on 11 August.

What Totalize did achieve, however, was to dispel any further thoughts that von Kluge had of transferring divisions from 5th Panzer Army, as Panzer Group West had become on 5 August. This was in spite of further demands to do so from Hitler so that

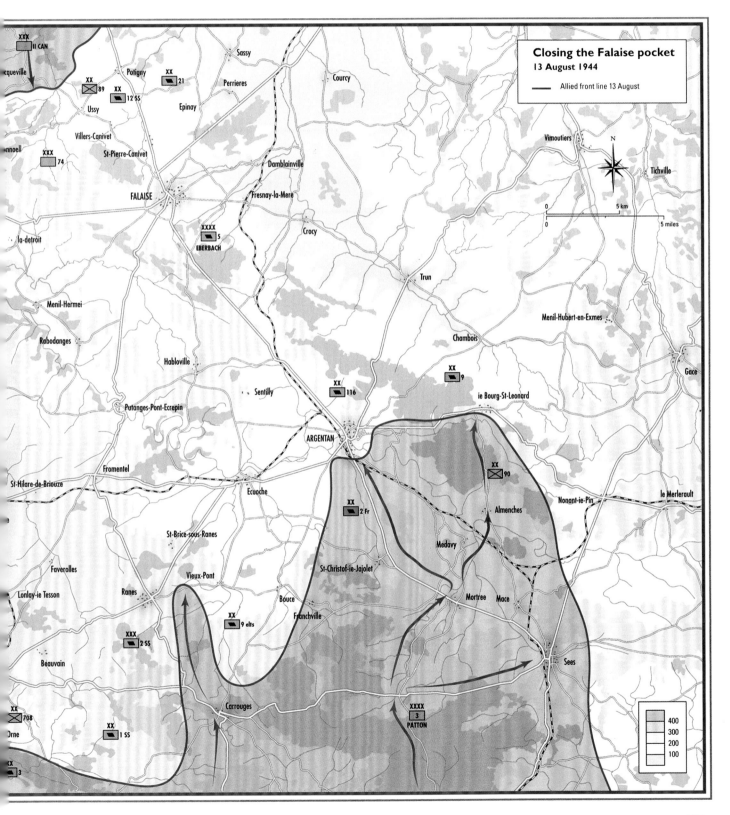

Closing the Falaise pocket
13 August 1944

—— Allied front line 13 August

the American break-out could be halted. Von Kluge, though, was still fearful of disobeying the Führer, especially since there was a witch hunt on to arrest anyone that could have been involved in the 20 July attempt on his life. His only other available Panzer Division was the 9th, which had recently arrived from southern France and had been deployed to block Patton's deep thrust, which had reached the River Loire and turned east. In spite of Hausser's objections that this would enable the Allies to envelop both Seventh and Fifth Panzer Armies, von Kluge ordered it to move from Le Mans to Avranches. Hitler kept up his demands for

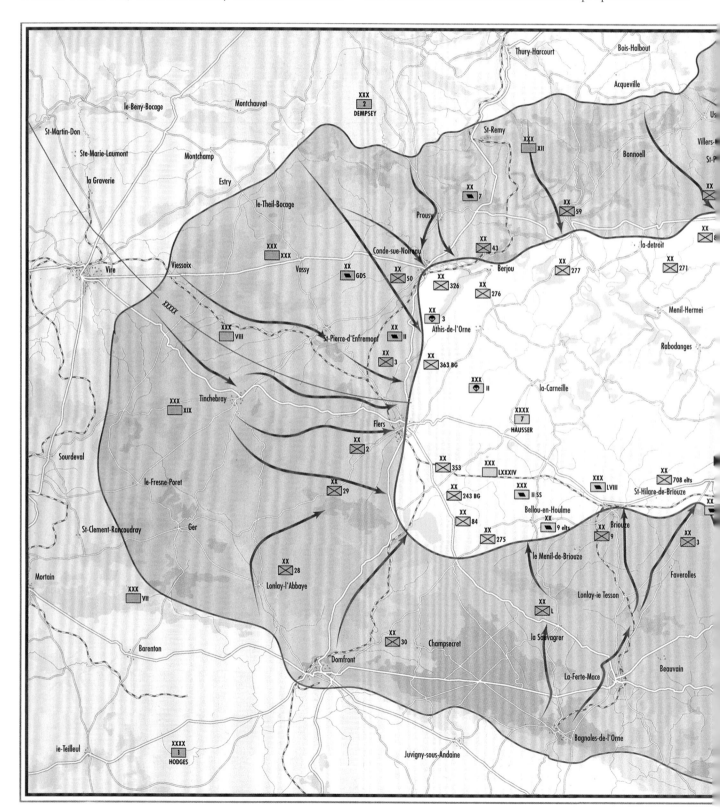

another attack westwards into the American flank, laying down that six Panzer divisions were to be used and that Fifth Panzer Army's commander, Heinrich Eberbach, was to command it. He reported to von Kluge on 9 August, but just after he arrived a report came through that Patton's armour was striking north

from Le Mans and threatening Alençon, the main supply base for Seventh Army, and there were few troops available to defend it. Von Kluge knew that if Alençon fell, Seventh Army's fate would be sealed. He asked Hitler's permission to transfer Eberbach's armour to deal with this new threat, but received no positive answer, apart from a stream of signals questioning his motives. This prevarication played further into the hands of the Allies.

As the picture unfolded, Montgomery began to realize that there was an opportunity to trap and destroy the German armies west of the Seine rather than follow his original plan of advancing eastwards, north and south of Paris. This was reinforced by an Ultra intercept revealing the German intention to strike again, south of Mortain. He therefore issued fresh orders on 11 August. The Canadians were to press on to Falaise and then Argentan, while the British advanced to the Flers–Argentan road. Simultaneously, the Americans were to pass through Alençon and take up a line running from Carrouges east to Sées, which lies to the south-east of Argentan. This would trap the

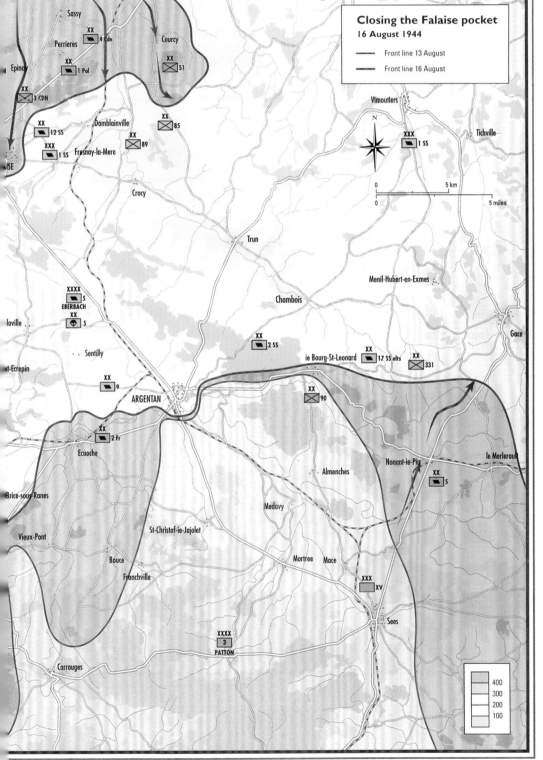

Closing the Falaise pocket
16 August 1944

—— Front line 13 August
—— Front line 16 August

Bradley had decided that Patton should move no further north from Argentan for fear of clashing with the Canadians, who had now entered Falaise and would advance south to close the pocket. On the German side, Hitler had still not given permission for Hausser's Seventh Army, now being pounded from the air, to withdraw from the pocket.

German Seventh Army and the bulk of Fifth Panzer in a pocket, with no roads to provide escape routes to the east. But in case the Germans did manage to extricate sizeable forces from the pocket, Montgomery instructed Bradley to continue to plan for an airborne operation in the Chartres area, which he had previously ordered him to do to accelerate the advance towards Paris. Bradley was also to hold three divisions in the Le Mans area to link up with the airborne element at Chartres. In this way Montgomery hoped to prevent the Germans from creating a fresh defence line on the River Seine.

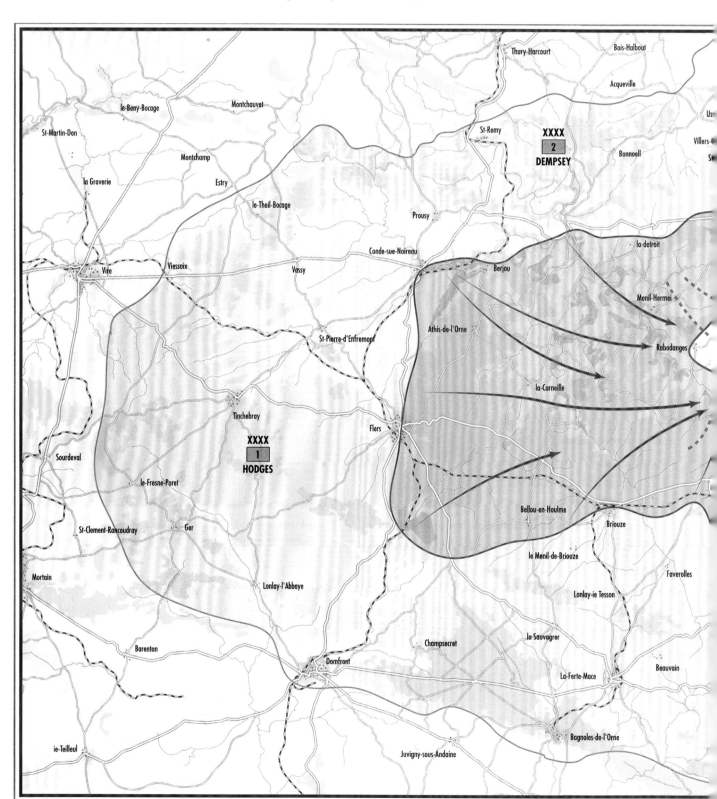

The Allied airborne forces themselves had experienced a frustrating time since D-Day. The US 82nd and 101st Airborne Divisions remained in the line until 18 July, when they had been moved back to Britain to re-equip. The British 6th Airborne Division had no such respite and was continuing to hold the

Allied eastern flank. Back in Britain itself were the British 1st Airborne Division and the Polish Parachute Brigade, which had been alerted for a number of possible operations which had then been cancelled, either because the weather was unsuitable or they had been overtaken by events. On 2 August, with the two US divisions now back in Britain and ready for further combat, the First Allied Airborne Army was formed under the command of General Lewis H. Brereton, who had been in charge of the US Ninth Air Force. Planning for the Chartres operation began, but like those that had preceded it, the air assault never took place.

On 12 August, Patton's men, in the form of the 2nd French Armoured Division, entered Alençon. The division had landed in France a fortnight earlier and was commanded by General Philippe Leclerc (a pseudonym adopted by Viscount Philippe de Hautecloque to protect his family in Occupied France) who had joined de Gaulle in summer 1940. He had begun by rallying French Equatorial Africa to the Free French cause and

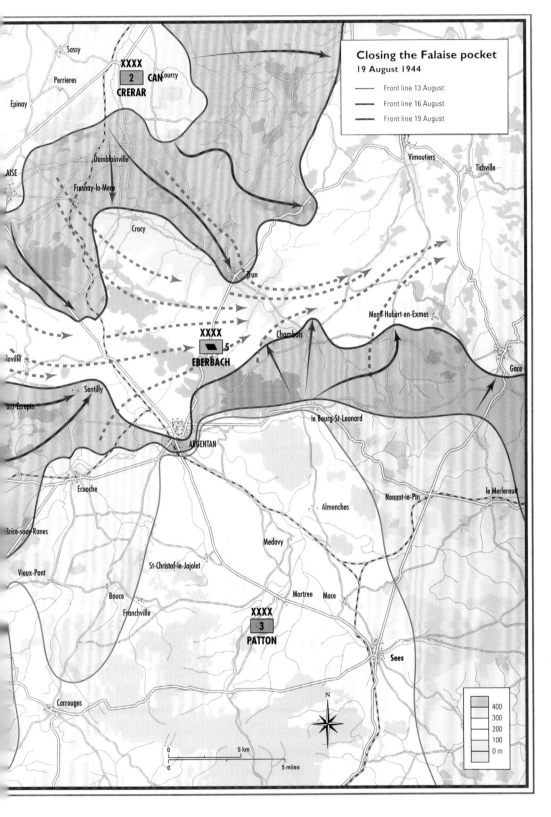

With Model having superseded von Kluge as CinC West, Hausser was finally given leave to extricate the German Seventh Army as best he could. It became a race against time as the neck of the pocket shrank. It was finally sealed by the end of 19 August, although II SS Panzer Corps did launch a counter-attack early the following day, temporarily opening an escape route.

The Falaise pocket at the end of the battle.

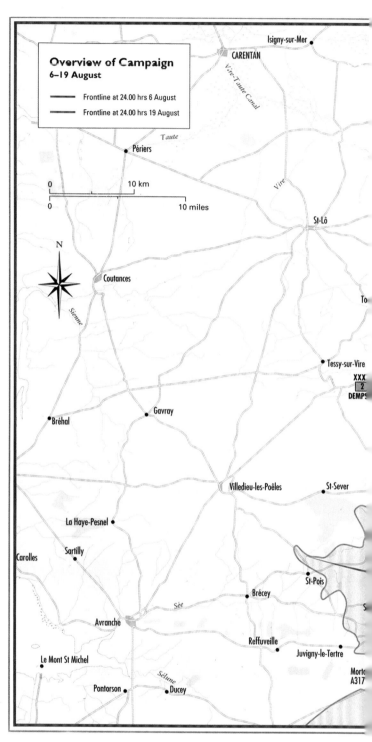

then had led a small force from Chad across the Libyan desert to join the British Eighth Army for the campaign in Tunisia. Simultaneously, the 5th Armored Division captured Sées. General Wade Hampton Haislip, the XV Corps commander, now ordered both divisions to make for Argentan. By this time Eberbach had been given permission to switch his Panzer forces from Mortain, and managed to deploy elements of 116th Panzer Division to Argentan just before Haislip's tanks arrived. The latter now took up position on both sides of the town. Patton himself wanted Haislip to press on to Falaise, but this order was countermanded by Bradley, who feared a clash with the Canadians. He was also aware that Eberbach was moving more armour from the Mortain area, threatening the left flank of XV Corps. To guard against this, Patton ordered his XX Corps to move up from the Mayenne–Le Mans area to Carrouges. Even so, he was furious over the halt order, believing that Haislip could have advanced quickly to Falaise and sealed the pocket. Though the decision had been Bradley's alone, Patton was convinced that the order came from Montgomery 'either due to jealousy of the Americans or utter ignorance of the situation or to a combination of the two', as he noted in his diary.

The Canadians renewed their offensive on 14 August. This time they planned to attack by day, using smoke to cover the assault. RAF Bomber Command despatched 411 Lancasters and 352 Halifaxes to attack the German positions astride the River Laison. The bombing was generally accurate, but one Canadian artillery battalion did suffer casualties, when some bombers mis-

took the yellow flares its men were firing for those used for marking the targets. The Canadian 3rd Division, many of its men mounted on US-made Priest 105mm self-propelled guns, with armament removed and known as Kangaroos or Unfrocked Priests, and 4th Armoured Division, together with the 2nd Armoured Brigade, advanced through the smoke in blocks, rather than columns, using the sun to guide them. They closed quickly to the river and crossed it in the afternoon. By nightfall they were just three miles from Falaise. Unfortunately, that night

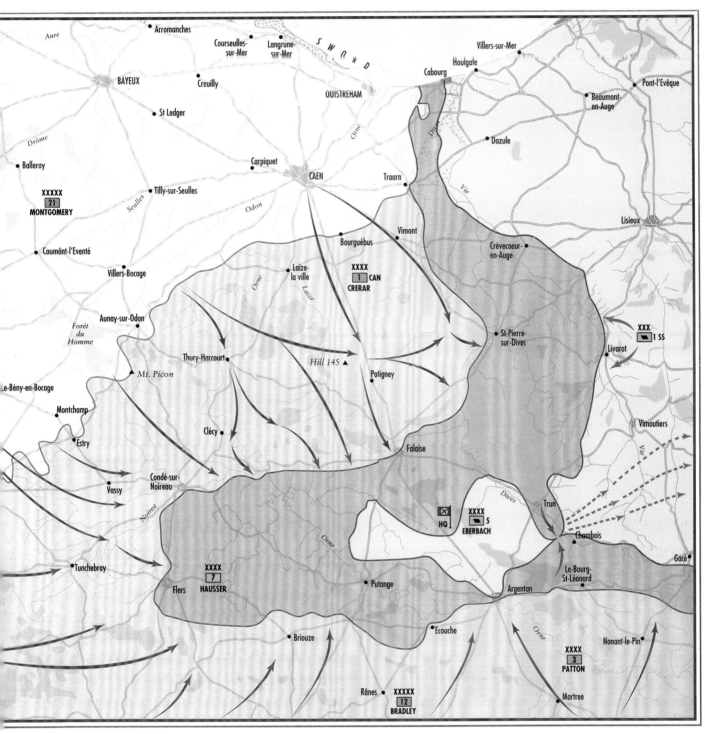

the Germans captured an officer who was carrying the attack plan. Consequently, next morning the Canadians once more found themselves up against the 12th SS Panzer Division, which had quickly taken up position on the last ridge before Falaise. Throughout 15 August, although now reduced to some 500 men and fifteen tanks, with a few 88mm guns in support, it resisted all efforts to dislodge it. Only when the 2nd Canadian Division was sent round and threatened Falaise from the west on the following day did the 12th SS relinquish its hold on the ridge. By the

Falaise marked the final phase of the Normandy campaign. Hitler's refusal to countenance an earlier withdrawal condemned much of Army Group B to death or captivity.

end of the 17th, almost the whole of the town was in Canadian hands and the gap between them and Patton's men around Argentan was reduced to a mere twelve miles.

As late as 16 August, when the Canadians began to enter Falaise, von Kluge had still issued no order for Hausser's Seventh Army to withdraw from the pocket that had now been

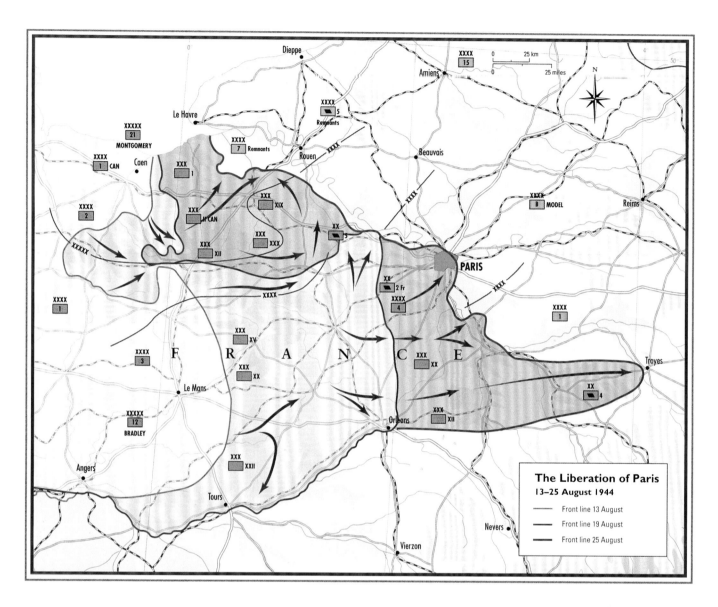

The Liberation of Paris
13–25 August 1944

Front line 13 August
Front line 19 August
Front line 25 August

An advance direct on Paris was not part of Eisenhower's plan, but developments within the city caused a change of heart. For diplomatic reasons, it was important that the French be seen to liberate their own city. Meanwhile, Bradley's 12th US Army Group had secured crossings over the Seine to the west and south-east and the German First Army, withdrawing from southern France, was beginning to come into play.

created, apart from logistic elements. He had been hesitant to do this while Hitler continued to demand further counter-attacks south of Mortain. The situation was aggravated by what happened to the C-in-C West himself on 15 August. He had set out from HQ Army Group B to visit the pocket, when he came under an artillery bombardment and fighter-bomber attack. His radio car was knocked out and he himself spent much of the day in a ditch, totally out of communications with anyone. Hitler quickly became aware of this and was convinced that von Kluge was in negotiation with the Allies through an unnamed captured German general. He decided

there and then that he must be replaced. He immediately summoned Walther Model from the Eastern Front, where he had succeeded in saving the muchbattered Army Group Centre through a vigorous counter-attack, which helped to bring the Russian offensive to a halt. When von Kluge was finally in radio contact once more that night, he was instructed to leave the pocket and place himself at HQ Fifth Panzer Army. From here he telephoned Jodl at OKW and asked permission to withdraw Seventh Army. Hitler's eventual reply was that it should merely withdraw to the east bank of the River Orne and establish a new defence line there. But that was totally unrealistic, since it would mean that it would have the Canadians at its back.

Model arrived in France on 17 August. The wretched von Kluge was ordered back to Germany. Certain that he would be arrested, he committed suicide while en route. Model realized that the situation was desperate, with Allied air-power remorselessly pounding the troops within the pocket. Without seeking Hitler's permission, he ordered Hausser to extract what he could from the now shrinking pocket and establish a new front based on the River Dives. But even this was likely to be very difficult. On that same day, the First Canadian Army launched another attack, this time across the River Dives itself. By the evening of the 18th, Polish tanks were overlooking Chambois. Simultaneously, the Americans had closed up to Le Bourg St-Leonard. Between these two places there was a void of some six miles through which the remnants of Fifth Panzer and Seventh Armies were pouring. Hausser sent II SS Panzer Corps to dislodge the Poles so that the gap could be widened, but to no avail. Twenty-four hours later, the US 90th Division and Leclerc's tanks linked up with the Poles at Chambois and the Falaise pocket was finally sealed. In desperation Hausser's remaining armour launched an attack against the Canadians on the River Dives at dawn on 20 August. It managed to open a narrow corridor north of the village of St-Lambert, which itself was subjected to repeated attacks. Although under constant artillery fire, more men managed to escape the cauldron that the pocket had now become, but by evening the pocket was once more sealed. The following day, II SS Panzer Corps made another attempt against the Poles, but again in vain. It, too, now joined the other remnants streaming back towards the River Seine. They left behind 10,000 dead and 50,000 prisoners in the pocket. The battle for Normandy was finally over.

Model now had to try to re-form his shattered armies and establish a new defence line. But he was also faced by another threat. On 15 August 1944, General Alexander Patch's US Seventh Army landed on the French Riviera. The original intention had been to mount Anvil, as it was originally codenamed, simultaneously with the Normandy landings, but there was insufficient amphibious shipping to make this possible. The British had never liked the concept and, with the Allies finally entering Rome in early June and advancing into northern Italy, they continued to argue for its cancellation, especially since the troops earmarked for Anvil were to come from Italy. They believed that a much more effective strategy was to threaten the Third Reich from the South, as well as the West and East. Eisenhower was insistent that the landings went ahead, since he wanted to open up Marseilles as a supply port. He was supported by the US Joint Chiefs of Staff, who had never attached much importance to Italy, and by President Roosevelt. Consequently, the British were forced to

An American 75mm howitzer in action.

relent and Dragoon, as it was renamed, went ahead.

The southern part of France was the responsibility of General Johannes Blaskowitz and his Army Group G, which consisted of ten divisions, but only three of them were near the beaches. This fact, combined with overwhelming Allied air supremacy and a powerful naval bombardment force, made Dragoon a more straightforward operation than Overlord and the landing force quickly began to press inland and westwards along the coast towards Marseilles. Behind the Seventh Army came Jean-Marie de Lattre de Tassigny's Armée B, soon to become the First French Army. Marseilles would fall on 28 August, while the two armies began to advance rapidly northwards up the Rhône valley, much assisted by the FFI, which was at its strongest and most organized in this region. Model recognized that sooner or later this new thrust would reach the Franco-German border, but, given the ever more desperate situation in northern France, there was little that he could do about it.

Any hopes that Model had of forming a defence line on the River Seine had already been dashed by the time the Falaise pocket was finally sealed. Patton may have been deeply frustrated by Bradley's refusal to allow him to close the pocket more quickly than he did, but he was compensated by Bradley allowing him to use the bulk of his army to advance rapidly eastwards. It was not quite what Montgomery had in mind, since he

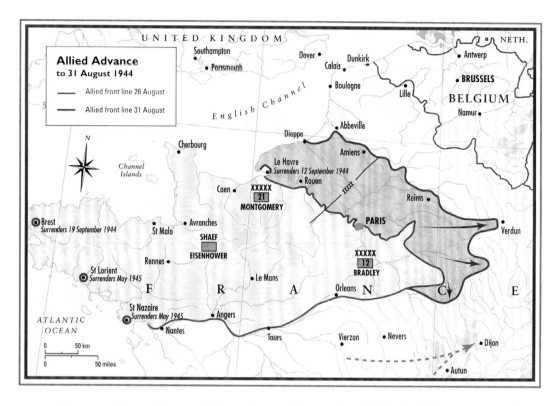

Events were now begin-ning to move increasingly rapidly as the German forces in northern France struggled desperately to extricate themselves. On the Allied side, however, the supply lines, still largely reliant on the port of Cherbourg, were becoming stretched.

ing back to consult with Bradley, who gave the green light, and at dawn on the following day two of Wyche's battalions crossed. By that evening he had established a firm bridgehead. Encouraged by this, Bradley ordered Patton to secure another

wanted Patton to close to Dreux and then swing north towards Le Havre to act as a backstop for the envelopment of Fifth Panzer and Seventh Armies. Patton had removed the bulk of XV Corps from the Argentan area and duly sent it to Dreux, which it reached on 16 August. Simultaneously, his other two corps had advanced to Chartres, thus negating the airborne assault in this area, and Orléans. Bradley now halted Third Army for two days, fearing that it would become over-extended, but allowed it to resume its advance on the 18th. Next day, General Ira T. Wyche's 79th Division found an intact foot bridge over the Seine at Mantes-Gassicourt, to the west of Paris. Patton hesitated, fly-

The break-out over the Seine. A British truck crosses the river on a pontoon bridge.

bridgehead, this time at Melun to the south-east of the French capital. This was achieved on 23 August. It meant that the River Seine was no longer a position from which the Germans could draw breath and reorganize.

As for Paris itself, the original Allied intention had been to encircle the city through double envelopment and then hope that the German garrison would surrender without a fight. They feared that, if they entered it directly, there could be heavy fight-ing, which would cause civilian casualties and damage to its his-toric buildings and monuments. But events within the capital itself forced a change of plan. Sensing that liberation was close, a series of strikes by public-service workers had begun on 10 August. There was, however, a split in the Resistance movement. The Gaullist elements wanted to adopt a 'wait-and-see' strategy, especially since an envoy had informed them that the Allies were not planning to liberate it until mid-September. The Communists, who had majorities on most of the local commit-tees, were for an immediate uprising. The Gaullists feared that if this happened, the Communists might well seize the machinery of government. Consequently, on 19 August, their leader, who was de Gaulle's delegate-general, initiated an insurrection, just as the Communists were about to launch their own. The Germans in and around the city numbered some 20,000 men under General von Choltitz, the former LXXXIV Corps com-

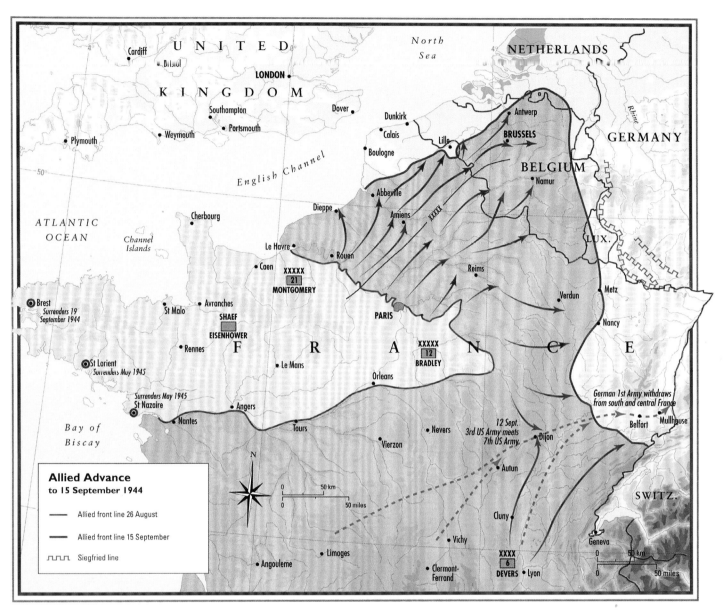

Allied Advance
to 15 September 1944

—— Allied front line 26 August

—— Allied front line 15 September

⊓⊔⊓⊔ Siegfried line

mander and who had been involved in the destruction of Rotterdam in May 1940 and Sevastopol, the Russian Black Sea port, in 1942. There were fears that he would use the same methods to crush the poorly armed Resistance groups. There was also awareness that the Poles had risen in Warsaw in expectation of being liberated by the Red Army, which had halted on the other side of the River Vistula at the conclusion of its Bagration offensive against Army Group Centre, and that the Germans were destroying much of the Polish capital.

Thanks to the Swedish Consul-General in Paris, von Choltitz was persuaded not to adopt the same brutal methods and a temporary truce was even arranged, although it was soon broken. This was in spite of an order from Hitler for him to defend Paris to the last round. The skirmishing continued, with more and more Parisians taking part. It was not, however, until 23 August

The Allied advance had now come to almost a complete halt. Almost the whole of France, apart from the easternmost region and much of Belgium had been liberated, but prospects for ending the war before 1945 had faded.

that Eisenhower relented and Leclerc's 2nd Armoured Division was detached from the US Third Army to make a dash for the capital. Leclerc initially made slow progress and the US 4th Infantry Division was deployed to give him support. It then became almost a race between the French and Americans as to who would get to the centre first. Leclerc won, sending an armoured combat group through back streets and side roads on the evening of the 24th. This prompted von Choltitz to order his troops to withdraw east of the Seine. Next day, he himself surrendered to Leclerc, but small groups of German soldiers continued to fight on. That evening, Charles de Gaulle entered Paris and on the following day made a triumphal walk up the Champs Elysées, with snipers still active. This ensured that he, and not the Communists, would now control France.

To the Allied high command, Paris was merely a diversion. With the Germans withdrawing rapidly eastwards in disarray, firm decisions were now needed to develop operations to take best advantage of this. On 21 August, Eisenhower had held a meeting at his Advanced HQ in Normandy. He stated that, with effect from 1 September, he would take personal charge of 12th and 21st Army Groups and that the former was to advance to the Franco-German border. Montgomery objected to this, arguing that the Allies should remain concentrated and advance to the

The high price of liberation. French inhabitants return to their shattered town after the fighting has passed on.

Ruhr via Antwerp. This was the beginning of the Broad-versus Narrow-Front debate, which dogged the high command for much of the remaining part of the war. While Eisenhower agreed that 21st Army Group should clear the Pas-de-Calais and secure Antwerp, he was not prepared to switch Bradley's forces to the north, except to help Montgomery if he got into trouble. The two men met face-to-face on 23 August, the same day that Eisenhower had relented over Paris. Montgomery pressed the single-thrust strategy once more, proposing that, while he seized Antwerp, Bradley should advance on his right flank on an axis Brussels-Aachen-Cologne. He also told Eisenhower that he could not combine the jobs of supreme commander and ground force commander. The latter should either be Montgomery or Bradley. Convinced that US public opinion would not stand for a British general to be formally in command of US troops for any longer, Eisenhower resisted Montgomery's demands. The

most that he would concede was that 21st Army Group's advance to Antwerp would be given priority. He also accepted it was not strong enough on its own to advance to the Ruhr. Montgomery would therefore be allowed to co-ordinate US divisions operating on his right flank, although they would not be placed under his command.

By 29 August the Allies had closed up to the River Seine. Simultaneously, Model was desperately trying to organize another defence line on the Rivers Somme and Marne. This proved impossible. After the withdrawal across the Seine he had been left with a mere 120 tanks and many of his divisions had been reduced to virtual skeletons, with only the infantry divisions of Fifteenth Army, which had not been fighting in Normandy, still reasonably intact. In addition, Patton, never one to stand inactivity, had already launched Third Army across the Seine and reached the Marne, brushing aside what German resistance there was. The van of his army was now approaching Reims. His rapid advance was, however, bringing into focus a growing problem, that of resupply. While Cherbourg was now functioning to full capacity, the further east the Allies advanced, the more stretched their supply lines became. Patton himself had already outrun his forward depots and was reliant on air resupply, as well as captured German fuel stocks. On 28 August, however, the aircraft bringing him fuel had to be diverted in preparation for an airborne operation in the Pas-de-Calais, which, like so many others before it, did not actually take place. For this reason, Bradley wanted Patton to halt until the advance of First Army on his left was well underway. Only with difficulty did Patton persuade his superior to allow him to push on to the River Meuse.

Model's reaction to Patton's lightning advance was to order what mobile elements he had to concentrate in the area Châlons-Reims-Soissons in order to block Third Army. As for the defence of the Somme, this was quickly compromised by Lawton Collins's US VII Corps, which had passed through the bridgehead across the Seine at Melun and was advancing to Soissons, thus outflanking the Somme.

In the 21st Army Group sector, Montgomery ordered First Canadian Army to advance up the coast and secure the Channel ports. The British Second Army was to advance out of the bridge-

(Right) While stalemate appeared to be developing in the West, elsewhere the pressure on German forces was being maintained by a series of ongoing offensives, especially on the Eastern Front, where the German hold on the Balkans was about to crumble.

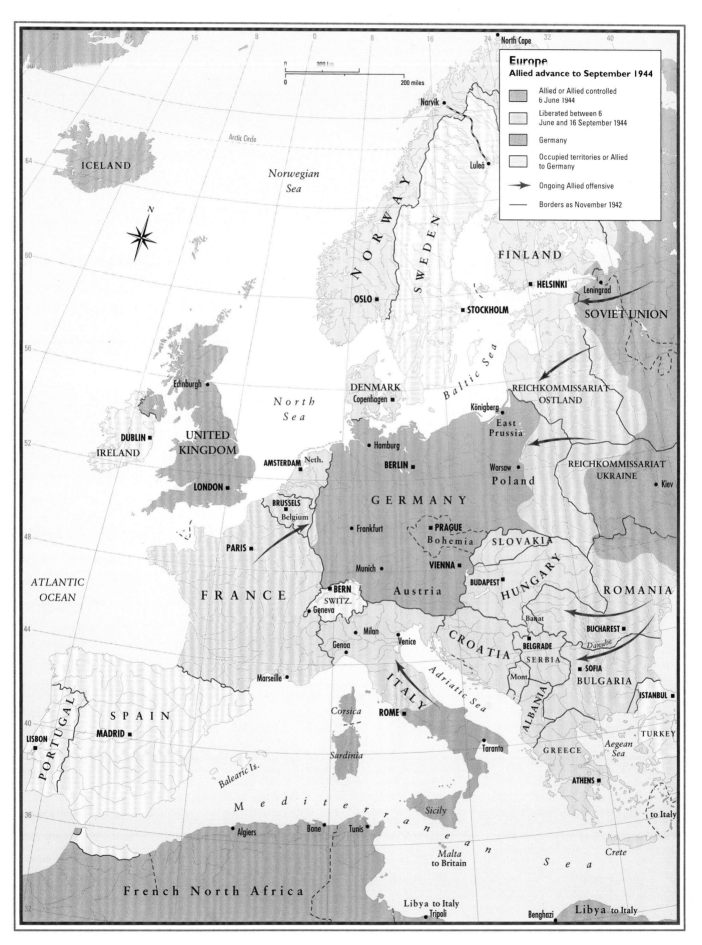

Europe
Allied advance to September 1944

Allied or Allied controlled 6 June 1944

Liberated between 6 June and 16 September 1944

Germany

Occupied territories or Allied to Germany

Ongoing Allied offensive

Borders as November 1942

head that it had established at Vernon and make a 'swift and relentless' advance northwards. It was to be spearheaded by XXX Corps, now commanded by Brian Horrocks, who had proved an able corps commander in North Africa until being badly wounded in a German air attack in Tunisia. He unleashed the now veteran 11th Armoured Division. By midday on 30 August, Roberts's tanks were some forty miles from Amiens, having encountered only light opposition. Horrocks ordered to him drive on through the night to secure the city and its bridges over the Somme. Roberts achieved this before dawn on the following day. This finally put paid to Model's plans for holding the Somme. He also suffered another blow. Sepp Dietrich, who had been commanding Seventh Army for the past two weeks, was in the process of handing over command to Heinrich Eberbach. The headquarters was, however, very close to 11th Armoured Division's axis of advance. Dietrich left in time, but Eberbach and most of his staff were captured while eating breakfast. The US XIX and VII Corps were coming up on Horrocks's flank and by 2 September all three corps had crossed the Belgian frontier. With Patton still rampaging towards the Franco-German border, it seemed as though the German forces in the West were facing imminent collapse.

The Allied fuel crisis was growing, however, by the day. The extensive damage done to the French railways meant that they could not be used, and air resupply could only carry a very limited amount, especially since part of it had to be diverted to bring foodstuffs to the population of Paris and many of the

British Sappers heaving a section of a Bailey bridge into position.

transport aircraft remained tied to the Allied Airborne Army, now preparing for a projected drop to seize crossings over the River Scheldt in Belgium. The bulk therefore had to be transported by road. On 25 August, every available truck was pressed into service to bring the fuel to forward depots south-west of Paris and by the 29th they were delivering over 12,000 tons per day. But the Red Ball Express, from the US railroad slang for fast freight, was itself consuming a daily 300,000 gallons of precious fuel. The rapidity of the advance further aggravated matters. Hopes that Channel ports might be speedily opened were also dashed. As he had done with the Atlantic ports, Hitler declared them Festungen, which were to be defended to the last. Thus, the Canadians quickly closed on Le Havre, but they had to place it under siege and it would not fall until 12 September, too late to affect the outcome. They did quickly capture Dieppe, thus revenging in part the disaster than had befallen them in August 1942, but it took a week to open the port and its capacity was limited. While 21st Army Group was beginning to feel the shortage and was only maintaining its advance by reducing the Canadian allocation so as to maintain the advance into Belgium, 12th Army Group was in serious trouble because of its very much longer supply lines.

On 1 September, Eisenhower duly assumed direct command of the Allied ground forces and considered the fuel crisis, especially that pertaining to 12th Army Group. His priority was still on capturing Antwerp and so he allocated 5,000 tons per day to Courtney Hodges' First Army, the bulk of which was advancing on Montgomery's left flank, and a mere 2,000 tons to Third Army, which was now halted on the Meuse for want of fuel, although its forward elements had got as far as Métz and the River Moselle. This inevitably was not to Patton's liking, especially since he now had his sights set on the main German defence belt covering its western border with France, the Siegfried Line.

He managed to persuade Eisenhower to allow him to press on, once the ports in the Pas de Calais had been secured, and in the meantime was allowed to secure crossings over the Moselle. This decision meant that the Allied forces were diverging north and east still further. Worse, Model was succeeding in gathering troops to bar Patton's way.

In the meantime, the advance of the British XXX Corps continued. On the late afternoon of 3 September, the Guards Armoured Division entered Brussels. At the same time, 11th Armoured made a dash for Antwerp, reaching it on the following day and catching the German garrison by surprise, so much so that its massive docks were still almost completely intact. Furthermore, the German Fifteenth Army, which was facing the Canadians advancing up the French coast, could now be trapped. With the Seventh Army virtually destroyed, the route to the Ruhr now lay open. To Montgomery and Churchill it seemed as though the war could be ended well before the end of the year, that is if the Allied effort was concentrated in this direction. Montgomery tried to persuade the Americans once more to adopt this plan, but Bradley was more interested in Patton's advance to the Saar, and so was Eisenhower. Montgomery was therefore left to do what he could on his own, but his fixation on the Ruhr caused him to ignore the situation around Antwerp. For, unless the estuary of the Scheldt was secured, Antwerp could not be used as a port and Fifteenth Army had an escape route across into Holland. The Canadians, too, had not been able to move quickly. They had been hampered by problems over bridging the numerous rivers which they had to cross and much of their strength was tied up in besieging and opening the Channel ports. In consequence, the fuel problem remained and Fifteenth Army stayed in being and continued to block the seaward approaches to Antwerp.

On the German side, Hitler once more recalled Gerd von Rundstedt to active duty as C-in-C West. Model had been finding it increasingly difficult to combine the task of rescuing Army Group B with that of C-in-C West. Indeed, by the beginning of September the two headquarters were sixty miles apart and he had to leave Günther Blumentritt, his chief of staff, to look after HQ C-in-C West. He was therefore relieved when Hitler proposed bringing back von Rundstedt, who arrived at the HQ, now

The bizarre resting place of this PzKwIV is likely to have been the result of an Allied air attack.

near Koblenz, on 5 September. Hitler had instructed him to prevent the Allies from opening up Antwerp, which Fifteenth Army was already beginning to do, create a strong base in Holland, and protect the Ruhr and Saar. He was fortunate that the Allied fuel problem had now reached crisis proportions. Thus, the British Second Army's progress began to slow after the capture of Brussels. Worse, it began to meet opposition of the German First Parachute Army, which was forming in Holland, and contained fresh troops of better quality than had been met for some time. The terrain around the canals north of Brussels also favoured the defence. Hodges' US First Army was also suffering, with some of its armoured formations immobilized through lack of fuel. True, patrols did cross the German border close to Luxembourg on 11 September, but there was no fuel available to exploit this. Likewise, Patton had resumed his offensive towards the Saar on 5 September, but could do no more than establish bridgeheads across the Moselle in the face of the force that Model had built up here and the lack of the necessary fuel and ammunition to punch a hole in the defences.

Thus, by mid-September 1944, the Allied advance, which had held out so much promise just two weeks earlier, had ground to almost a complete halt, enabling the Germans to restore some cohesion to their defence. The odds on ending the war in autumn 1944 had lengthened considerably and the spectre of a grim winter campaign grew ever larger.

Epilogue

The Allies did have one more opportunity to break the deadlock on the Western Front. On 10 September 1944, Eisenhower approved a plan drawn up by Montgomery for an operation to outflank Germany's main natural defence barrier in the west, the River Rhine. This would be done from the air, with US and British paratroops seizing a series of bridges over waterways in southern Holland, the furthest of which and the key to the whole operation was that over the lower Rhine at Arnhem. Operation Market-Garden was mounted a week later. The US 82nd and 101st Airborne Divisions succeeded in securing their bridges and the ground force, the British XXX Corps, did eventually link up with them. That at Arnhem, which was the objective of the British 1st Airborne Division and Polish

American and Russian troops meet at Torgau on the River Elbe, 25 April 1945.

Parachute Brigade, proved a bridge too far. There were numerous reasons for this. One was poor intelligence, which failed to recognize the significance of II SS Panzer Corps refitting in the Arnhem area after the battle for Normandy. Another was that the XXX Corps axis of advance was too narrow, in some places restricted to a single road, which made it very vulnerable to attack from the flanks.

With the failure of Market-Garden, the Allies were committed to a winter campaign, one which saw the Germans recover to such an extent that they were able to mount a major counter-offensive in the Ardennes in mid-December. The port of Antwerp was eventually opened at the end of November, after amphibious landings on the island of Walcheren, which guards the mouth of the Scheldt, and the clearance of both sides of the river. Once the Ardennes counter-offensive had been beaten back, Eisenhower's Broad-Front strategy remained in force, as the Allies closed up to the Rhine, crossed it in late March 1945 and then began to advance into Germany. The Narrow-Front option then surfaced again, with Montgomery's advocacy of a single thrust to Berlin, but Eisenhower rejected it. The German capital would be left to the Russians, while the Western Allies advanced to the Rivers Elbe and Mulde, as well as entering Austria. By then, the D-Day landings and subsequent campaign in the Normandy bocage appeared a distant memory.

Overlord was a long time in preparation, its origins stretching back to the evacuation from Dunkirk, when it was realized that the Third Reich was unlikely to be defeated unless Allied ground forces returned to the Continent of Europe. Some have since argued that it should have been mounted in 1943,

rather than pursuing the Mediterranean strategy agreed at the Casablanca conference of January of that year. Certainly, this is what the Americans wanted. Yet, the landings had to succeed the first time. If the Allies were thrown back into the sea it would be months or even years before they could try again. In 1943, they still had much to learn about amphibious operations and the shipping available was limited. COSSAC's plan of that summer envisaged an initial landing by only three divisions, because of the limited shipping likely to be available, and the smaller the landing area, the easier it would have been for the Germans to concentrate against it, a point that Eisenhower and Montgomery were well aware of when they reviewed the COSSAC plan and expanded the landing beaches. Another factor is that because the Tunisian campaign lasted much longer than the Allies had expected, there would have been little time to bring back the now-combat-experienced formations, essential to the success of Overlord, from the Mediterranean and prepare them for an invasion which had to take place before the uncertainties of the autumn weather in the English Channel intervened.

While the German forces deployed to the Atlantic Wall were comparatively weak until the end of 1943, there is no doubt that Hitler would have strengthened them in time, since it was impossible to conceal the preparations for the landings. Furthermore, the numerical strength of the German Armed Forces peaked in 1943. True, there had been the disaster at Stalingrad at the beginning of the year, but threatened with a cross-Channel invasion in summer 1943, it is unlikely that Hitler would have mounted the subsequently failed counter-offensive at Kursk that July, which incurred some 200,000 casualties, as well as significant losses in armour and aircraft. In addition, the German forces that were allocated to Italy, as a result of the Allied Mediterranean strategy, would also have been available. It is therefore arguable that the Allies might well have encountered significantly stronger German forces if they had come ashore in summer 1943 and would have been operating from a much narrower beachhead than was ultimately the case.

As it was, the planning and preparation for Overlord were meticulous in their detail. No factor was left unconsidered in ensuring the success of the initial landings. In particular, tribute must be paid to those who conceived and executed Operation Bodyguard, the elaborate deception plan. While parts of it were unsuccessful, the two critical aspects of it – the threats to Norway and the Pas-de-Calais – were very effective. Hitler did not remove a single man from Norway and the retention of sizeable German forces north of the Seine until long after D-Day bear this out. The planners also took to heart the many lessons learned from previous and on-going landing operations. Examples of this were the development of specialized armour and the Mulberry harbours. These measures also called for a high degree of technical innovation. That Overlord did succeed is due in no small part to the legions of often faceless scientists, engineers, and others in and out of uniform, the 'boffins' or 'backroom boys', as they were called at the time.

No one on the Allied side ever believed that the actual

Another liberation and a stark contrast to the grim fighting that these American troops had recently experienced.

mounting of Overlord would be easy. Indeed, some of the decisions that had to be made were knife-edge. The most critical of all was Eisenhower's decision to postpone D-Day by twenty-four hours, because of the weather, and then to confirm it for 6 June. Only he could take that decision and, if wrong, he knew that the responsibility for failure was his alone. It was a perfect example of the loneliness of high command. As it turned out, the weather did create some problems during the landings, notably at Omaha, but the Allies got ashore with significantly fewer casualties than they feared. Part of the reason for this was that the adverse weather had convinced the Germans that the landings were not imminent, thus creating additional surprise. Another was the thorough training that the assaulting troops had received, enabling them to quickly overcome the shock of landing under fire and get on with tackling their various tasks for getting off the beaches. It was, however, congestion on these that was the main reason why the D-Day objectives were seldom reached, although some might say that they were unduly optimistic.

Once ashore, it was a matter of who could reinforce the quickest, the Allies or the Germans. The latter suffered from grave disadvantages. First was the deployment of the armour, with Hitler retaining control of part, and other Panzer divisions kept north of the Seine in the belief that the Normandy landings were a diversion. The Allied air campaign against transportation, ably aided by the efforts of the French Resistance, created physical difficulties in moving formations to Normandy, as did the overwhelming Allied air supremacy over the battlefield and beyond. The Germans had one Panzer and six infantry divisions in Normandy on the eve of D-Day and by D+24 this had risen to eight Panzer, seventeen infantry and one airborne division. By this date the Allies had built up their forces from nothing to five armoured, eighteen infantry, and three airborne divisions, reflecting a higher rate of reinforcement. This continued until by the time of Cobra the Allies enjoyed a significant superiority in strength. The rate of replacement of casualties was considerably higher. During the period 6–30 June the Allies suffered some 61,700 casualties, but received 79,000 individual reinforcements to replace

them. In contrast, the Germans received only a tenth of the number killed, wounded or captured.

Montgomery's overall strategy for the Normandy campaign, to use the British and Canadians to tie down and wear down the German armour so that the Americans could break out, was realistic and sound. It was assisted by the fact that most of the Panzer divisions found themselves committed to line-holding and could not be concentrated into a powerful enough force to mount a really effective counter-attack. True, in terms of duration, the campaign did not proceed as quickly as Montgomery had envisaged. Cherbourg should have fallen on D+8, but did not do so until D+22, Caen, a D-Day objective, was not secured until D+33, while Falaise should have been seized on D+17, but was not reached until D+71. Part of the reason for this was the tenacity with which the Germans fought, in spite of their disadvantages. The Allies, too, took some time to adjust to the claustrophobic nature of the bocage and it was a major omission in their training that they were not prepared for it.

The break-out itself developed very much more quickly than planned, with the Allies liberating the area between Normandy and the Seine in a mere thirty days, when it was expected to take seventy. Much of this can be put down to Patton's drive and initiative, and operations might have progressed at an even faster rate if he had not been ordered to send one of his corps into Brittany. This was part of the original plan, designed to secure more ports, but Hitler's order that these had to be defended to the end meant that two of Patton's armoured divisions found themselves conducting sieges, when they would have been better employed elsewhere.

Hitler's Festungen policy was the one strategy that he got right. It did deny the Allies ports for a considerable time, with some, like Dunkirk, holding out until the end of the war. It was this, and the unexpectedly rapid advance to the Seine and beyond, which stretched the Allied supply lines to such an extent that they eventually snapped. Otherwise, Hitler's refusal to allow voluntary withdrawals played into the hands of the Allies, enabling them to maintain their attritional strategy. Hitler's insistence on mounting counterstrokes into the flank of the break-out when it was too late to affect the outcome, also proved disastrous, leading as it did to the Falaise pocket. In summary, his refusal to allow his commanders on the ground any freedom of action proved fatal to the defence of Normandy and, indeed, the whole of France.

On the other side is Eisenhower's insistence that he would be both Allied supreme commander and ground force commander. By the time that he formally took over command of the latter on 1 September 1944, the Americans were providing the largest proportion of ground troops and it was therefore logical that an American should be in charge. Furthermore, although there were good arguments for Montgomery to be properly appointed to the post, which he had to all intents and purposes held until then, there were two negative factors. First, many of the American commanders found his cocksure manner abrasive. In addition, it was clear that US public opinion would not stand for a Briton occupying this position. To give him his due, Montgomery did tell Eisenhower that he would be happy to serve under Bradley when he was urging him to appoint a separate ground force commander. Eisenhower did not accept this and perhaps he was right to retain command in his own hands, for, once the Allies were ashore in Normandy, it was what was happening on the ground which largely dictated their strategy. Even if Montgomery or Bradley had been placed in charge, Eisenhower's Broad-Front approach would still have prevailed, because he was the supreme commander. As such, he had a much wider understanding of the political issues involved than did his subordinates and it was these issues which ultimately drove the military strategy. If Montgomery's Narrow-Front concept had been politically acceptable, it is still questionable whether it would have worked and that the Allies would have reached the Ruhr before winter set in. The German powers of recovery should not be underestimated and, with Antwerp still closed as a port, there would still have been a supply problem.

Yet, in spite of the controversies surrounding the Normandy campaign, once the Allies were safely ashore the fate of the Third Reich was ultimately sealed. But the significance of their achievement cannot be regarded in isolation. It has to be remembered that ever since June 1941 the bulk of the German war effort had concentrated against the Soviet Union. It was the Russians who bore the brunt for so long and, when the tide began to turn at Stalingrad, inflicted the greatest damage to the German Armed Forces. They also played their part, albeit indirectly, in the success of the liberation of France. Their massive summer offensive against Army Group Centre meant that the supply of German reinforcements to France was always going to be limited. This, however, cannot take away from the fact that Overlord represents the largest amphibious operation in history. Launched against a defender who knew that it was coming, it was remarkably successful. That it was so is thanks to the efforts of many men and women on both sides of the Atlantic, and in German-Occupied Europe. They were all working towards one end, the defeat of a malevolent dictatorship which was bent on creating a new Dark Age.

Rest in Peace.

Codewords
Connected with D-Day

ABC-1   American-British-Canadian talks held in early 1941 to agree strategy in the event of the USA entering the war.

AJAX   British autumn 1941 plan for an attack on Trondheim, Norway.

ANVIL   Allied landings in the south of France (later DRAGOON).

ARABIAN   1942 British study on capturing Brittany (later LETHAL)

ARCADIA   Anglo-US strategic conference held in Washington DC, December 1941–January 1942.

ARGONAUT   Anglo-US strategic conference held in Washington DC, June 1942.

AVALANCHE   Allied landings at Salerno, Italy, September 1943.

BIGOT   Highest security classification relating to the planning of OVERLORD.

BLACK   1941 US plan for securing French North-West Africa by landing at Dakar.

BODYGUARD   Overall Allied plan for deception to support operations in Europe in 1944.

BOLERO   Build-up of US forces in Britain.

BOMBARDON   Floating breakwater used to protect the MULBERRY harbours.

BUTTRESS   Allied landings on toe of Italy, September 1943.

CALIPH   Proposal by Churchill to land 5,000 Commandos at Bordeaux during D+20 to D+30 to support French Resistance.

CHASTITY   Establishment of a port in Quiberon Bay on the French Atlantic coast.

COCKADE   Deception scheme aimed at keeping the German forces tied down in the West during 1943 by making them believe that the Allies were preparing a large-scale assault. It had three elements – STARKEY, TINDALL, WADHAM.

CORNCOB   MULBERRY blockship.

CORNELIUS   Naval concentration phase of NEPTUNE.

CROSSBOW   Allied countermeasures against V-weapons.

CRUIKSHANK   Plan to gain a lodgement in the Low Countries prior to advancing to the Ruhr.

DRAGOON   Allied landings in southern France, August 1944. Originally ANVIL.

ECLIPSE   Allied operations in Europe after a German surrender, largely involving the occupation of the country.

EUREKA   Allied strategic conference held at Tehran, Persia, November–December 1943.

FABIUS   Final amphibious exercises prior to D-Day.

FERDINAND   See ZEPPELIN.

FESTIVAL   1942 landing of troops direct from USA at French North-West African ports after they had been seized by Allied forces sailing from Britain.

FORETOP   1942 plan for large-scale raid on French Atlantic coast U-boat bases.

FORFAR   Series of small-scale Commando raids on French Channel coast in 1943.

FORTITUDE NORTH   Deception plan to convince the Germans that the Allies were preparing to invade Norway. Part of BODYGUARD.

FORTITUDE SOUTH   Deception plan to convince the Germans that invasion the main Allied landings would be in the Pas-de-Calais and that those in Normandy were a diversion. Part of BODYGUARD.

FOYNES   Deception plan designed to conceal the transfer of Allied divisions from Italy to Britain for OVERLORD.

GABRIEL   1942 plan for a major raid on the Cotentin Peninsula.

GAMBIT   Operations by X-craft (midget submarines) to guide the Normandy fleet to the correct beaches.

GLIMMER   Airborne deception operation mounted on night of 5/6 June 1944 to simulate an invasion fleet off Boulogne.

GOOSEBERRY   MULBERRY breakwater created from CORNCOBs.

GRAFFHAM   Parallel deception plan to FORTITUDE NORTH proposing an approach to Sweden for active co-operation in Anglo-Soviet operations in northern Norway.

GREENBACK   Used in 1942 to denote 1943 invasion of the Continent should German morale appear to be cracking. Later RANKIN.

GYMNAST   British plan for the invasion of French North-West Africa in 1942. Became SUPER GYMNAST once the Americans became involved. Later TORCH.

HADRIAN   Plan to seize and hold the Cotentin Peninsula in 1943.

HALCYON   Y-Day, when all naval preparations for OVERLORD were to be complete.

HARDBOILED   1941 deception plan for a notional attack on the Norwegian coast.

HARLEQUIN   September 1943 loading exercise, which was part of COCKADE.

HUSKY   Invasion of Sicily, July 1943.

IMPERATOR   Plan for a large-scale raid on the Continent in 1942.

IRONSIDE   Adjunct to FORTITUDE SOUTH designed to create an Allied threat to the French Biscay coast.

JANTZEN   Summer 1943 exercise to practise concentration and marshalling of troops for a cross-Channel invasion.

JAEL   Overall deception plan for Allied operations in Europe.

JEDBURGH   Allied 3-man teams dropped into France from D-Day onwards to co-ordinate French Resistance operations.

JUBILEE   See RUTTER.

JUPITER   Plan to invade Norway should conditions for OVERLORD not be realized.

LETHAL   See ARABIAN.

LINNET   Possible airborne operation in northern France post-D-Day.

MAGNET   Deployment of US troops to Northern Ireland in early 1942.

MAPLE   Allied minelaying operations during NEPTUNE.

MENACE   Attempted Anglo-Free French landing at Dakar in September 1940.

MESPOT   Original codename for FORTITUDE.

MODICUM   US Presidential mission to Britain in April 1942 to present ROUND-UP and SLEDGEHAMMER plans.

MOHICAN   Original codename for TORCH.

MULBERRY   Artificial harbours deployed to support the Allied forces in Normandy. MULBERRY A supported the Americans and MULBERRY B the British.

NEPTUNE   The amphibious landing element within OVERLORD.

OVERLORD   The overall Allied cross-Channel invasion of France and subsequent operations.

OVERTHROW   Deception plan designed to tie down the maximum German Forces in the west during TORCH. It simulated the seizing of a notional beachhead in Pas-de-Calais.

PHOENIX   Reinforced concrete caisson which acted as a sunken breakwater for the MULBERRY harbours.

PLUTO   Pipeline under the Ocean.

POINTBLANK   Allied strategic air offensive against Germany, 1943-44.

PREMIUM   Adjunct to FORTITUDE designed to reinforce the Allied threat to the Pas-de-Calais, Low Countries and Norway.

QUADRANT   Allied strategic conference held at Quebec, Canada, August 1943.

QUICKSILVER   Deception operation simulating large forces in South-east England threatening the Pas-de-Calais.

RANKIN   Formerly GREENBACK. RANKIN covered a weakening of German forces and morale in the West so as to make invasion possible. RANKIN B reflected a German withdrawal from Occupied Western Europe and RANKIN C an unconditional German surrender.

ROUNDHAMMER   Codename for 1944 cross-Channel invasion used at the TRIDENT conference. Changed to OVERLORD at the end of the conference.

ROUND-UP   Large-scale Allied assault on the Continent in 1943.

ROYAL FLUSH   Deception operations in Sweden and Spain designed to tie down German troops in Norway and southern France.

RUTTER   1942 raid on Dieppe. Later changed to JUBILEE.

SESAME (1)   Major raid somewhere on the coasts of Occupied Europe planned for spring 1942.

SESAME (2)   Secret D-Day orders not to be opened until at sea.

SEXTANT   Allied strategic conference held at Cairo, Egypt, November, December 1942.

SHARPENER   See TUXEDO.

SHINGLE   January 1944 landings at Anzio, Italy.

SICKLE   Move of US air forces to Britain as part of BOLERO.

SKYSCRAPER   Cross-Channel attack plan developed by the Combined Commanders in spring 1943.

SKYE   Creation of fictitious British Fourth Army in Scotland as part of FORTITUDE NORTH.

SLEDGEHAMMER   Allied landing on the Continent in 1942.

SOLO ONE   Deception plan for TORCH directed at Norway.

SOLO TWO   Deception plan for troops taking part in TORCH designed to make them believe that they were bound for the Middle East and would be landing at Dakar en route.

TARBRUSH   Commando reconnaissances of French beaches in May 1944.

TAXABLE   Airborne deception operation to simulate an invasion fleet approaching Calais on the night of 5/6 June 1944.

TIGER   Force U landing exercise.

TINDALL   Part of COCKADE and designed to keep German forces tied down in Norway.

TINDER   Plan for a hasty Allied return to the Continent in the event of a sudden German collapse in 1942.

TITANIC   Use of dummy parachutists on the night of 5/6 June 1944 to support the Allied airborne landings.

TOMBOLA   Supply of fuel from tankers off Normandy to the shore.

TORCH   Anglo-US landings in French North-West Africa in November 1942. Formerly GYMNAST.

TORRENT   Plan for using Special Forces and French Resistance as part of the OVERLORD deception measures.

TUXEDO SHAEF   Advanced Command Post at Portsmouth for D-Day. Changed to SHARPENER.

TRIDENT   Allied strategic conference at Washington DC, May 1943.

VENDETTA   Creation of a threat to the south of France as part of BODYGUARD.

WADHAM   Threat to the Bay of Biscay. Part of COCKADE.

WETBOB   Plan to secure a lodgement in the Contentin peninsula in autumn 1942.

WHALE   Floating pier forming part of MULBERRY.

WIDEWING   Main HQ SHAEF at Bushey Park, near Kingston-upon-Thames.

ZEPPELIN   Mediterranean portion of BODYGUARD. Created threats against Bulgaria, Albania and Istria. Changed to FERDINAND in July 1944.

High Command Diagrams

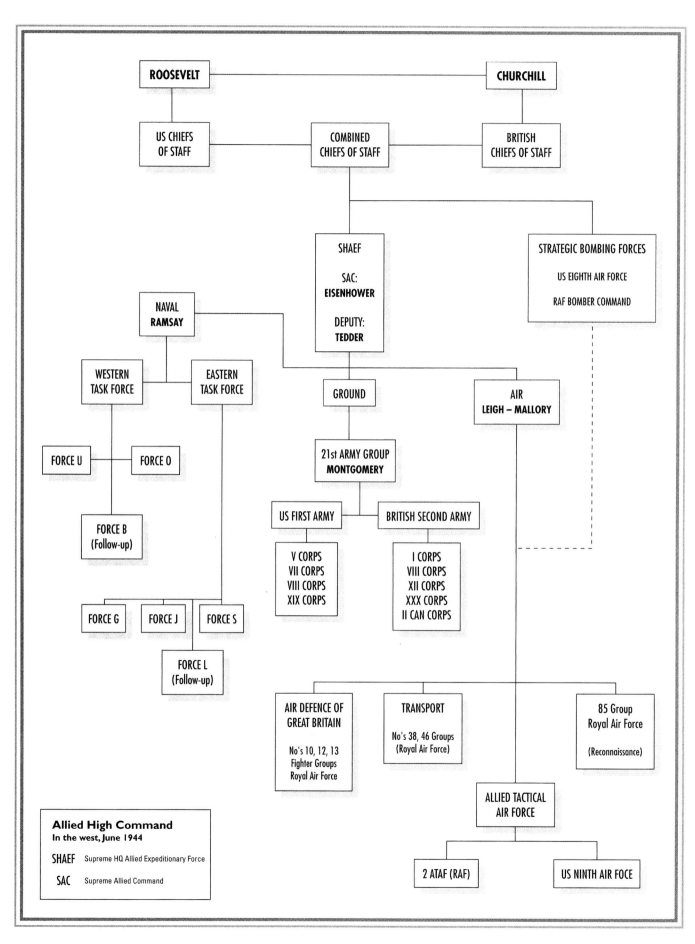

ROOSEVELT — **CHURCHILL**

US CHIEFS OF STAFF — COMBINED CHIEFS OF STAFF — BRITISH CHIEFS OF STAFF

SHAEF
SAC: **EISENHOWER**
DEPUTY: **TEDDER**

STRATEGIC BOMBING FORCES
US EIGHTH AIR FORCE
RAF BOMBER COMMAND

NAVAL **RAMSAY**

WESTERN TASK FORCE

EASTERN TASK FORCE

GROUND

AIR **LEIGH – MALLORY**

FORCE U

FORCE O

21st ARMY GROUP **MONTGOMERY**

FORCE B (Follow-up)

US FIRST ARMY

BRITISH SECOND ARMY

FORCE G

FORCE J

FORCE S

V CORPS
VII CORPS
VIII CORPS
XIX CORPS

I CORPS
VIII CORPS
XII CORPS
XXX CORPS
II CAN CORPS

FORCE L (Follow-up)

AIR DEFENCE OF GREAT BRITAIN
No's 10, 12, 13 Fighter Groups Royal Air Force

TRANSPORT
No's 38, 46 Groups (Royal Air Force)

85 Group Royal Air Force
(Reconnaissance)

ALLIED TACTICAL AIR FORCE

2 ATAF (RAF)

US NINTH AIR FOCE

Allied High Command
In the west, June 1944

SHAEF   Supreme HQ Allied Expeditionary Force

SAC   Supreme Allied Command

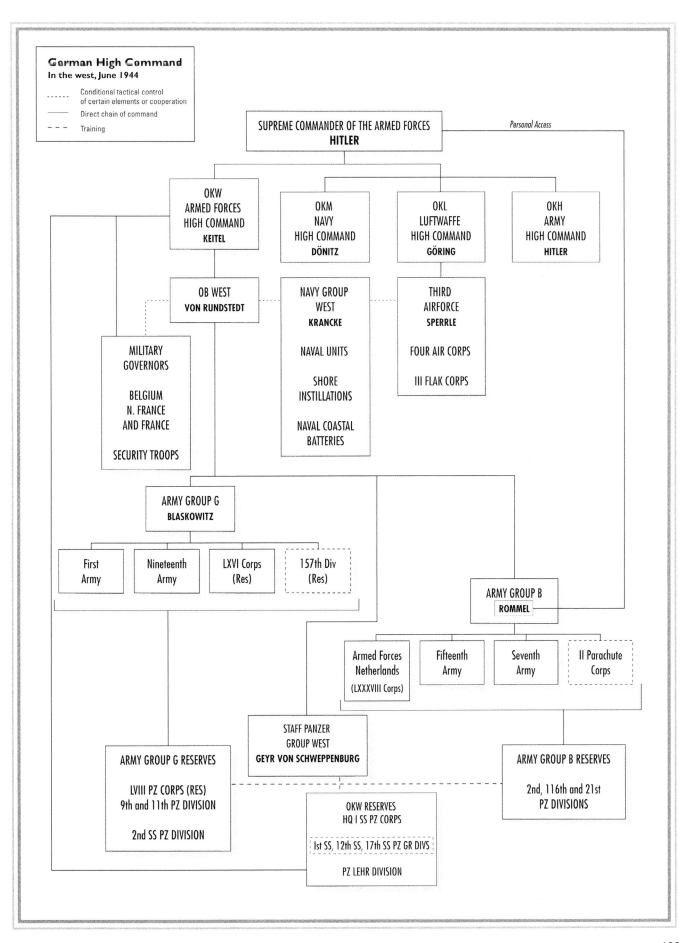

German High Command
In the west, June 1944

- - - - - - Conditional tactical control
of certain elements or cooperation
———— Direct chain of command
– – – Training

SUPREME COMMANDER OF THE ARMED FORCES
HITLER

Personal Access

OKW
ARMED FORCES
HIGH COMMAND
KEITEL

OKM
NAVY
HIGH COMMAND
DÖNITZ

OKL
LUFTWAFFE
HIGH COMMAND
GÖRING

OKH
ARMY
HIGH COMMAND
HITLER

OB WEST
VON RUNDSTEDT

NAVY GROUP
WEST
KRANCKE

NAVAL UNITS

SHORE
INSTILLATIONS

NAVAL COASTAL
BATTERIES

THIRD
AIRFORCE
SPERRLE

FOUR AIR CORPS

III FLAK CORPS

MILITARY
GOVERNORS

BELGIUM
N. FRANCE
AND FRANCE

SECURITY TROOPS

ARMY GROUP G
BLASKOWITZ

First
Army

Nineteenth
Army

LXVI Corps
(Res)

157th Div
(Res)

ARMY GROUP B
ROMMEL

Armed Forces
Netherlands

(LXXXVIII Corps)

Fifteenth
Army

Seventh
Army

II Parachute
Corps

STAFF PANZER
GROUP WEST
GEYR VON SCHWEPPENBURG

ARMY GROUP G RESERVES

LVIII PZ CORPS (RES)
9th and 11th PZ DIVISION

2nd SS PZ DIVISION

OKW RESERVES
HQ I SS PZ CORPS

1st SS, 12th SS, 17th SS PZ GR DIVS

PZ LEHR DIVISION

ARMY GROUP B RESERVES

2nd, 116th and 21st
PZ DIVISIONS

Divisions
Which Fought in Normandy

AMERICAN

1st Infantry 'The Big Red One' was a Regular division which arrived in Britain in August 1942. It landed at Oran during Torch and then went on to fight in Tunisia and Sicily. It returned to Britain in October 1943 and landed on Omaha on D-Day. It formed part of V Corps.

2nd Armored 'Hell on Wheels' was activated in July 1940. Elements of it landed at Casablanca during Torch and fought in Tunisia, but the division as a whole did not come together until the Sicily landings. It went to Britain in autumn 1943 and landed on Omaha on D+3, becoming part of V Corps.

2nd Infantry A Regular division, which arrived in Britain in October 1943. It landed on Omaha during D+1 to D+3 and joined V Corps.

3rd Armored Activated in July 1940 and crossed to Britain in September 1943. It landed in Normandy on 24 June and served in XIX and then VII Corps.

4th Armored Activated in April 1941 and crossed to Britain in December 1943. It landed in Normandy on 11 July and joined VIII Corps.

4th Infantry Activated in June 1940 and crossed to Britain in January 1944. It landed on Utah Beach on D-Day as part of VII Corps, with which it served for the whole campaign, apart from a brief spell with VIII Corps.

5th Armored Activated in October 1941 and crossed to Britain in February 1944. Arrived in Normandy on 24 July and served in XV Corps.

5th Infantry Activated in October 1939 and went to Britain in April 1942. It landed in Normandy on 9 July and joined V Corps.

6th Armored Activated in February 1942 and crossed to Britain in February 1944. It landed in Normandy on 18 July and joined VIII Corps.

7th Armored Activated in March 1942 and arrived in Britain in January 1944. It landed in Normandy on 13–14 August and joined XX Corps.

8th Infantry Activated in July 1940 and went to Britain in December 1943. It landed in Normandy on 4 July and joined VIII Corps.

9th Infantry Activated in August 1940, it took part in Torch, landing at Algiers before going on to fight in Tunisia and Sicily. It sailed to Britain in November 1943 and landed at Utah on D+4, joining VII Corps.

28th Infantry A National Guard division activated in February 1941, it arrived in Britain in October 1943. The Division landed in Normandy on 22 July and joined XIX Corps.

29th Infantry A National Guard division, which was called up for active duty in February 1941 and was known as the 'Blue and Gray' because its components had fought on both sides in the US Civil War. It arrived in Britain in October 1942 and landed at Omaha on D-Day as part of V Corps, but then joined XIX Corps.

30th Infantry A National Guard division, which was activated in September 1940. It crossed to Britain in February 1944, landing on Omaha on D+9. Apart from a very brief spell with VII Corps, it served in XIX Corps.

35th Infantry A National Guard division activated in September 1940, it did not arrive in Britain until May 1944. It landed in Normandy during 5–7 July and served in XIX and then V Corps.

79th Infantry Activated in June 1942, it crossed to Britain in April 1944. It landed on Utah during D+6–D+8, joining VII Corps and then VIII Corps.

80th Infantry Activated in July 1942, it crossed to Europe in July 1944 and landed in Normandy on 3 August, joining XV and then XX Corps.

82nd Airborne Activated in March 1942, it became an Airborne division that August. It arrived in Morocco in May 1943 and then dropped into Sicily. Elements also dropped at Salerno in September 1943. The Division left Italy for Britain in November 1943. It dropped on D-Day and served under VII and then VIII Corps before returning to Britain in mid-July.

83rd Infantry Activated in August 1942 and arrived in Britain in April 1944, it landed at Omaha on D+12 and served successively with VII, VIII, and XV Corps.

90th Infantry Activated in March 1942, crossing to Britain in April 1944. Elements landed at Utah on D-Day and the Division was complete in Normandy by D+4. It served successively in VII, VIII and XV Corps.

101st Airborne Activated in August 1943, it arrived in Britain in December 1943. It dropped on D-Day and served under VII and VIII Corps before returning to Britain in mid-July.

BRITISH

Guards Armoured Formed in June 1941 from Foot Guards battalions, it arrived in Normandy at the end of June 1944 and fought under VIII Corps.

3rd Infantry Known as the Iron Division, a name given to it by Wellington, it was a pre-war Regular division, which was commanded by Montgomery in France in 1940 and landed on Sword Beach on D-Day. Thereafter it served mainly under I Corps.

6th Airborne Formed in May 1943, it landed in Normandy on D-Day and held the eastern flank of the Allied lodgement throughout the campaign.

7th Armoured Formed in 1938 as the Mobile Division, Egypt, it became 7th Armoured in April 1940. It fought throughout the Desert Campaign, gaining its nickname the Desert Rats, and thereafter in Tunisia. It took part in the early months of the Italian campaign and returned to Britain at the end of 1943. It landed on D+1 and served mainly in VIII and XXX Corps.

11th Armoured Formed in Britain in March 1941, it landed on D+7–D+8 and fought mainly under VIII Corps.

15th (Scottish) A second-line Territorial Army division, which was reformed in May 1939. It landed in Normandy on D+8 and served under XXX and VIII Corps.

43rd (Wessex) A pre-war first-line Territorial division, which was complete in Normandy on 24 June and fought under XII Corps.

49th (West Riding) A pre-war first-line Territorial division, it took part in the April 1940 Norwegian campaign. It was then sent to garrison Iceland, returning to Britain in 1943. It was complete in Normandy by D+7 and fought mainly under XXX Corps.

50th (Northumbrian) A pre-war first-line Territorial division, which took part in the 1940 French campaign. It was subsequently sent to the Middle East, fighting from late 1941 onwards in North Africa and Tunisia. It participated in the landings on Sicily and returned to Britain in late 1943. It landed on Gold Beach on D-Day and fought mainly under XXX Corps.

51st (Highland) A pre-war first-line Territorial division, the bulk of it was forced to surrender in France in June 1940. The division was reconstituted and sent to the Middle East in 1942, taking part in the fighting from el Alamein to the end of the Tunisian campaign. It also fought in Sicily and Italy, before returning to Britain, and landed in Normandy on D+2. It served under the Canadians and I Corps.

53rd (Welsh) A pre-war first-line Territorial division, which spent 1940–42 in Northern Ireland before returning to the mainland. It landed in Normandy on 27 June, serving under XII Corps.

59th (Staffordshire) A second-line Territorial division, which landed in Normandy at the end of June and served in XII Corps.

79th Armoured Formed as an ordinary Armoured division in September 1942, its role changed in spring 1943, when it became responsible for the development and operational control of specialized armour ('the funnies'). Although its units spearheaded the landings on 6 June, it never fought as a division.

CANADIAN

2nd Infantry Re-formed at the outbreak of war, the division crossed to Britain in late August 1940, apart from one brigade, which spent the autumn in Iceland before rejoining at the end of the year. It took part in the disastrous Dieppe Raid in August 1942. The division arrived in Normandy on 7 July.

3rd Infantry Mobilized in May 1940, the division crossed to Britain in July 1941. It landed on Juno Beach on D-Day.

4th Armoured Created in Britain in January 1942 from the 4th Canadian Infantry Division, it arrived in Normandy at the end of July 1944.

FRENCH

2nd Armoured Formed in May 1943 from General Leclerc's Free French L Force, which had crossed the Libyan Desert and fought in Tunisia, it was originally called 2nd Free French Division, but was converted to an armoured division in July 1943. It then moved from North Africa to Britain and arrived in Normandy at the end of July, serving in Third US Army.

POLISH

1st Armoured Raised in February 1942 from Free Polish forces which had escaped from France in 1940. It arrived in Normandy at the end of July 1944 and fought under First Canadian Army.

GERMAN

Panzer Lehr Formed in November 1943 from Panzer demonstration units at training schools, it deployed to eastern France in February 1944. It was sent to Hungary that April, returning to France in May and deploying to the Le Mans area. It began to move to Normandy on D-Day and was complete on D+3, serving under I SS Panzer Corps.

1st SS Panzer Adolf Hitler Originally formed in 1924 as Hitler's personal bodyguard, it fought in Poland as a motorized regiment and in France 1940 as a division. It served on the Eastern Front from 1941, but was transferred to northern Italy in summer 1943, where it was converted to a Panzer division. It returned to the Eastern Front winter 1943–44 and was then sent to Belgium to be reconstituted. It was finally complete in Normandy on 6 July, having begun its move from Belgium on 17 June. Served in I SS Panzer Corps.

2nd Division Formed in 1935, it took part in the Polish and French campaigns, followed by that in the Balkans in April 1941. It took part in the invasion of Russia and remained on the Eastern Front until January 1944 when it deployed to Amiens, France to refit. It arrived in Normandy in late June and was part of XLVII Panzer Corps.

2nd Parachute Formed in spring 1943 from the nucleus of 2nd Parachute Brigade, which fought in North Africa. It was posted to Brittany, but then transferred, in August 1943, to Italy. From here it went to the Eastern Front, where it fought until May 1944, when it returned to Germany to refit. It then deployed to Brittany and remained there.

2nd SS Panzer Das Reich Formed during winter 1940–1 and first saw action in the April 1941 Balkans campaign. It served on the Eastern Front 1941–42, but was sent to refit in France in summer 1942, taking part in the occupation of Vichy France that November. It then returned to the Eastern Front, but was withdrawn again to France to refit in February 1944, being sent to the Toulouse area. It began its move to Normandy on D+1, but was not complete until about D+14.

3rd Parachute Formed in the Reims area of France in late 1943, it was posted to Brittany in January 1944. On D+1 it was ordered to the Avranches area and then to St-Lô, but was not complete until D+12. It came under II Parachute Corps.

5th Parachute Formed in March 1944 at Reims, it was deployed to Rennes in May as Seventh Army reserve. On D-Day it was still not combat-ready, but one regiment was attached to 17th Panzer Grenadier Division. The remainder of the division came under LXXXIV Corps and then II Parachute Corps.

9th Panzer Formed as 4th Light Division in 1938, it fought in Poland and was then converted to a Panzer division. It took part in the May 1940 invasion of the West and the Balkans campaign the following spring. It served in Russia from the outset until January 1944, when it moved to southern France to refit. In June 1944 it was north-west of Marseilles. It was rushed to Normandy in early August, joining II SS Panzer Corps.

9th SS Panzer Hohenstaufen Organized in France in early 1943, it was sent to the Eastern Front in March 1944. It was hastily sent back to France, together with 10th SS Panzer, after D-Day and arrived in Normandy on 25 June. It was part of II SS Panzer Corps.

10th SS Panzer Frundsberg Its history was identical to 9th SS Panzer Division.

12th SS Panzer Hitlerjugend Recruited primarily from members of the Hitler Youth, it was activated as a Panzer Grenadier division in June 1943, carrying out its training in Belgium. It was converted to a Panzer division that October and moved to the Normandy area in April 1944. It formed part of I SS Panzer Corps.

16th Luftwaffe Field Formed in winter 1942–43 and sent to Holland. In late June 1944 it was sent to Normandy, joining LXXXIV Corps.

17th Luftwaffe Field Formed in 1943 as a Static division, it was initially deployed to the French Atlantic coast. In spring 1944 it was deployed east of Le Havre and joined Fifth Panzer Army in mid-August.

17th SS Panzer Grenadier Götz von Berlichingen Named after a German Middle Ages robber baron, it formed in western France in October 1943 and included not just Germans, but Belgian and Roumanian Nationalist elements as well. In June 1944 it was in the Tours area and arrived in Normandy on D+4. It served successively in II Parachute and LXXXIV Corps.

21st Division This bore no relation to its predecessor which had fought under Rommel in North Africa, although it did include some Afrika Korps veterans. It was formed in France in mid-1943 and was the only mobile division deployed close to the beaches on D-Day. It served in I SS Panzer Corps.

48th Infantry Formed in February 1944 in Belgium from 171st Reserve Division, it joined XLVII Panzer Corps in mid-August.

77th Infantry Formed in Poland in winter 1943–44 from the remnants of other formations, it moved to France in early 1944 and was stationed between the Cotentin and Brittany peninsulas as part of LXXXIV Corps.

84th Infantry Formed in Poland in February 1944 from the remains of other divisions, it was sent to the Rouen area of France in May. It joined LXXXIV Corps in early August.

85th Infantry Formed in the rear area of Fifteenth Army in France from various disbanded and newly formed units in February 1944, it joined LXXXI Corps (Fifth Panzer Army) in early August.

89th Infantry Formed in Norway in February 1944, it was posted to Le Havre on the French Channel coast in June. It moved to Normandy at the end of July, joining II Parachute Corps.

91st Airlanding Raised in early 1944 from Reserve Army personnel, it was trained in the anti-airborne role and was deployed to the base of the Cotentin peninsula in May 1944. It was part of LXXXIV Corps.

116th Panzer Formed as 16th Motorized (later Panzer Grenadier) Division in late summer 1940, it fought in the Balkans in April 1941 and then served on the Eastern Front. In early 1944 the remnants were withdrawn to France and, absorbing 173rd Reserve Panzer Division, became 116th Panzer Division. It was deployed to the Pas-de-Calais and was sent to Normandy on 20 July, joining XLVII Panzer Corps.

243rd Infantry Formed in August 1943, using remnants of 387th Infantry Division, it was originally designated a Static division. It was sent to Normandy that October and was given a degree of mobility. It defended the Carentan-Montebourg-Bricquebec-Lessay sector and was part of LXXXIV Corps.

265th Infantry Formed in July 1943 and was a Static division, which was sent to Brittany the following month, where it joined XXV Corps. Apart from one battle group, which joined LXXXIV Corps in July, it remained in Brittany.

266th Infantry Also formed in July 1943 as a Static division and, like 265th Infantry Division, sent to Brittany that August. It included a sizeable number of Russians and other Ostlander and remained in the peninsula, although one battle group at St-Malo came under II Parachute Corps in July 1944.

271st Infantry Initially formed in France in summer 1940 as a Static division, it was disbanded that autumn. It reformed in December 1943, drawing from the disbanded 137th Division, and deployed to Holland. It moved to Montpellier in southern France in March 1944 and joined II SS Panzer Corps in Normandy that July. It subsequently served in LXXIV Corps.

272nd Infantry Like the 271st, it had a brief pre-existence in 1940 and was re-formed in December 1943 in Belgium. In April 1944 it was sent to the Franco-Spanish border and arrived in Normandy on 13 July, joining I SS Panzer Corps. It subsequently transferred to LXXXIV Corps.

275th Infantry Formed as a cadre in western France in January 1944, it deployed to Brittany the following month, where it received Reserve units from Poland and southern France. It was partially motorized in spring 1944 and organized as battle groups. One of these was deployed to Normandy on D-Day, but was not complete under the command of 17th Panzer Grenadier Division until D+7. The remainder moved to Normandy during the middle part of July, coming under LXXXIV Corps.

276th Infantry Briefly in existence in 1940, it was re-formed in December 1943 and sent to Dax, south-western France, the following month to complete its training. It was sent to Normandy in mid-June, joining XLVII Panzer Corps and, later, II Parachute Corps.

277th Infantry It had a brief pre-existence in summer 1940 and was reformed as a cadre in 1942. Having been brought up to strength, it went to Croatia in December 1943 and to Narbonne in southern France in February 1944. It arrived in Normandy in mid-June, joining II SS Panzer Corps. Later it served under II Parachute Corps.

326th Infantry Formed at Narbonne, France, in December 1942, it became part of Fifteenth Army reserve in Febuary 1944. It joined II Parachute Corps in Normandy on 21 July.

331st Infantry Formed in Austria in late 1941, it was sent to the Eastern Front in February 1942. It returned to Germany to refit in February 1944 and was posted to the Pas-de-Calais that May. It joined LXXIV Corps (Fifth Panzer Army) in August 1944.

343rd Infantry Formed as a Static division in October 1942, it went to France the following spring. It was located in the Brest area, where it remained.

344th Infantry Formed as a Static division in the Bordeaux area of France in October 1942, and guarded a sector in the Bay of Biscay. It joined LXXIV Corps (Fifth Panzer Army) in August 1944.

346th Infantry Formed in France in October 1942, it was stationed in Brittany until February 1944, when it was transferred to the Le Havre sector. It joined LXXXIV Corps in early July.

352nd Infantry Formed from elements of 268th and 321st Infantry Divisions in October 1943, it was posted to the eastern part of the Cotentin peninsula in January 1944. It covered the Omaha-Gold sector and came under II Parachute Corps.

353rd Infantry Formed from cadres of 328th Division in October 1943, it was sent to Brittany the following month. It was ordered to Normandy on D+4, arriving by D+12 and joining II Parachute Corps.

363rd Infantry Formed from elements of 339th Division in Poland in October 1943, it deployed to Denmark in April 1944. That June it transferred to Belgium and then joined LXXXIV Corps in Normandy in July.

708th Infantry Formed in May 1941, it was sent to the Bordeaux area of France the following month. It joined II Parachute Corps in Normandy at the end of July 1944.

709th Infantry Formed in May 1941 as a Static division and sent to Brittany the following month. In December 1942 it was moved to Cherbourg and on D-Day covered the east coast of the Cotentin peninsula down to Carentan as part of LXXXIV Corps.

711th Infantry Formed as a Static division in April 1941, it was sent to north-eastern France that August. In December 1941 it moved to Rouen and then, in spring 1944, to the Deauville sector. It joined LXXXVI Corps in Normandy in early July.

716th Infantry Formed in May 1941 as a Static division, it was sent to Normandy the following month. In February 1942 it was transferred to Belgium, but returned to Normandy that June, deploying to the Caen area under LXXXIV Corps. It was still there on D-Day and came under command of I SS Panzer Corps.

Further Reading

There have been literally millions of words written on D-Day and the subsequent campaign. The works cited below represent some of the more worthwhile studies.

Ambrose, Stephen E. *The Supreme Commander: The War Years of General Dwight D. Eisenhower.* Doubleday, New York, 1969

Barnett, Correlli. *Engage the Enemy More Closely: The Royal Navy in the Second World War,* Hodder & Stoughton, London, and Norton, New York, 1991

Bennett, Ralph. *Ultra in the West: The Normandy Campaign 1944-1945,* Hutchinson, London, 1979 and Scribner, New York, 1980

Blumenson, Martin. *The Patton Papers 1940-1945,* Houghton Mifflin, Boston, 1974

Blumenson, Martin. *Breakout and Pursuit* Office of the Chief of Military History, US Army, Government Printing Office, Washington DC, 1961

Buffetaut, Yves. *D-Day Ships: The Allied Invasion Fleet, June 1944,* Conway Maritime Press, London, 1994

Chandler, David G. & Collins, James Lawton Jr. *The D-Day Encyclopedia,* Helicon, Oxford, and Simon & Schuster, New York, 1994

D'Este, Carlo *Decision in Normandy* Collins, London and Dutton, New York, 1983

Ellis, L. F. *Victory in the West: The Battle of Normandy,* HMSO, London, 1962

Fraser, David. *Knight's Cross: A Life of Field Marshal Erwin Rommel* HarperCollins, London and New York, 1993

Hamilton, Nigel. *Monty: Master of the Battlefield 1942-1944* Hamish Hamilton, London, and McGraw Hill, New York, 1983

Harrison, Gordon A. *Cross-Channel Attack* Office of the Chief of Military History, US Army, Government Printing Office, Washington DC, 1951

Hastings, Max. *Overlord: D-Day and the Battle for Normandy,* Michael Joseph, London, and Simon & Schuster, New York, 1984

Keegan, John. *Six Armies in Normandy,* Jonathan Cape, London, and Viking, New York, 1982

Lacey-Johnson, Lionel. *Pointblank and Beyond,* Airlife, Shrewsbury, 1991

Messenger, Charles. *The Last Prussian: A Biography of Field Marshal Gerd von Rundstedt 1875-1953,* Brassey's (UK), London, 1991

Morgan, Frederick E. *Overture to Overlord,* Doubleday, London and New York, 1950

Morison, Samuel Eliot. *History of United States Naval Operations in World War II: The Invasion of France and Germany, 1944-January 1945* Vol 11, Oxford University Press and Little, Brown, Boston, 1957

Reynolds, Michael. *Steel Inferno: I SS Panzer Corps in Normandy,* Spellmount, Staplehurst, Kent, 1997

Stacey, C. P. *Official History of the Canadian Army in World War II: The Victory Campaign: The Operations in North-West Europe, 1944-1945* Vol 3, Queen's Printer, Ottawa, 1960

Weigley, Russell F. *Eisenhower's Lieutenants: The Campaigns of France and Germany, 1944-1945,* Sidgwick & Jackson, London, and Indiana University Press, Bloomington, 1981

Wilmot, Chester. *The Struggle for Europe,* Collins, London, 1953 and Harper, New York, 1952

Wynn, Humphrey & Young, Susan. *Prelude to Overlord,* Airlife, London, 1983

Index

Index

Acknowledgments

Pictures are reproduced by permission of, or have been provided by the following:

Bundesarchive: p. 6, 48, 121, 138, 141

Charles Messenger: p. 21, 69, 94, 152

Corbis: p. 40, 73, 106

Hulton Getty: p. 2, 6, 8, 10, 22, 24, 29, 34, 35, 43, 44, 50, 53, 54, 74, 77, 78, 79, 87, 98, 100,
        103, 104, 105, 108, 114, 118, 122, 124, 126, 128, 129, 132, 134, 145, 155, 156, 158, 160,
        161, 162, 163, 165

Popperphoto: p. 6, 42, 67, 108, 112

Private sources: p. 13, 16, 18, 39, 46, 65, 75, 91, 116, 142

Nederlands Instituut voor Oorlogsdocumentatie: p. 85, 111, 134

Illustrations: Peter A. B. Smith

Design: Malcolm Swanston

Typesetting: Francesca Bridges, Jeanne Radford

Cartography: Peter Gamble, Isabelle Lewis, Jeanne Radford, Malcolm Swanston,
        Jonathan Young

Picture research: Peter Phillips, Michèle Sabèse

Editor: Christine Harris